D0154152

MARKETING
IT
PRODUCTS
AND SERVICES

Jessica Keyes

CRC Press
Taylor & Francis Group
Boca Raton   London   New York

CRC Press is an imprint of the
Taylor & Francis Group, an **informa** business

CRC Press
Taylor & Francis Group
6000 Broken Sound Parkway NW, Suite 300
Boca Raton, FL 33487-2742

© 2010 by Taylor and Francis Group, LLC
CRC Press is an imprint of Taylor & Francis Group, an Informa business

Printed in the United States of America on acid-free paper
10 9 8 7 6 5 4 3 2 1

International Standard Book Number: 978-1-4398-0319-6 (Hardback)

Library of Congress Cataloging-in-Publication Data

Keyes, Jessica, 1950-
   Marketing IT products and services / Jessica Keyes.
      p. cm.
   Includes bibliographical references and index.
   ISBN 978-1-4398-0319-6 (hardcover : alk. paper)
   1. Marketing. 2. Information technology--Management. 3. Industrial management.
   I. Title.

HF5415.K464 2010
004.068'8--dc22   2009026888

Visit the Taylor & Francis Web site at
http://www.taylorandfrancis.com

and the CRC Press Web site at
http://www.crcpress.com

This book is dedicated to my family and friends.

Contents

Marketing IT Products and Services

IT managers are responsible for developing computer systems. There's nothing new here. But what happens when management decides that they want to market the software to external customers? Even if the software isn't ready for prime time, it probably still needs to be marketed across divisional lines. In both cases, the IT manager really does need to know a thing or two about the art and science of marketing.

The purpose of *Marketing IT Products and Services* is to enable IT managers and developers to understand the roles, responsibilities, and management techniques of those who are involved in marketing activities.

Special emphasis is placed on the uniqueness of marketing issues that involve technology, because technology markets are characterized by a high degree of innovation, market uncertainty, abrupt technological shifts, and increasingly shortening product/technology life cycles. An understanding of the unique features of these markets is critical in developing successful marketing strategies.

Topics this book covers include strategic market planning, targeting markets (segmentation and evaluation), the market research process, understanding the competition, developing a market and product strategy, developing and managing products, crafting the distribution and sales strategy, understanding the nuances of global markets and international marketing, developing a marketing budget and determining price, and implementation.

Marketing IT Products and Services also comes with a plethora of appendices so you can get up and running right away. Aside from a complete marketing glossary, which provides one-stop shopping for all concepts and terms related to marketing, there are two complete marketing plans—one for a hardware product, and one for a software product. These marketing plans map nicely to what's being discussed in the book. Using these as templates will enable you bypass the "scut" work of developing a marketing plan so that you can focus on the creative aspects of marketing. Since the marketing plan is closely aligned with the organization's business and strategic plans, this book provides you with templates for both of these as well as a template for that all-important business plan executive summary. These appendices are included on the book's CD-ROM.

The CD-ROM also features numerous fill-in templates that are real time-savers. Figure out whether or not your market is loyal to a particular brand using the brand loyalty survey. Assess the competition using the competitor analysis survey, competition matrix, and competitive analysis worksheet. Churn out those press releases using the sample press release. Craft a sales pitch using the sample sales letter. Safely contract with outside services using the sample reseller agreement, non-disclosure agreement, and general letter of agreement. Figure out your market using the demographic comparison worksheet, demographic analysis worksheet, and target market worksheet. Plan your marketing campaign using the market research cost analysis, market planning checklist, industry analysis checklist, general market survey, market position and strategy matrix, and cost benefit study forms.

If you've got a need, this book has a template for you. Happy marketing!

Acknowledgments

I would especially like to thank those who assisted me in putting this book together. My students at the University of Liverpool did some great research on marketing forms and marketing math. Selvaraj Viagappan and Shubham Gupta assisted me by researching various marketing concepts and creating content outlines.

As always, my editor, John Wyzalek, was instrumental in getting my project approved and providing great encouragement. We also had some great seafood lunches!!

About the Author

Jessica Keyes is president of New Art Technologies, Inc., a high-technology and management consultancy and development firm started in New York in 1989.

Keyes has given seminars for such prestigious universities as Carnegie Mellon, Boston University, University of Illinois, James Madison University, and San Francisco State University. She is a frequent keynote speaker on the topics of competitive strategy and productivity and quality. She is a former advisor for DataPro, McGraw-Hill's computer research arm, as well as a member of the Sprint Business Council. Keyes is also a founding board of director member of the New York Software Industry Association. She completed a two-year term on the Mayor of New York City's Small Business Advisory Council. She currently facilitates doctoral and other courses for the University of Phoenix. She has been the editor for WGL's *Handbook of eBusiness* and CRC Press's *Systems Development Management* and *Information Management*.

Prior to founding New Art, Keyes was managing director of R&D for the New York Stock Exchange and has been an officer with Swiss Bank Co. and Banker's Trust, both in New York City. She holds a master's of business administration from New York University, and a doctorate in management.

A noted columnist and correspondent with over 200 articles published, Keyes is the author of the following books:

The New Intelligence: AI in Financial Services, HarperBusiness, 1990
The Handbook of Expert Systems in Manufacturing, McGraw-Hill, 1991
Infotrends: The Competitive Use of Information, McGraw-Hill, 1992
The Software Engineering Productivity Handbook, McGraw-Hill, 1993
The Handbook of Multimedia, McGraw-Hill, 1994
The Productivity Paradox, McGraw-Hill, 1994
Technology Trendlines, Van Nostrand Reinhold, 1995
How to Be a Successful Internet Consultant, McGraw-Hill, 1997
Webcasting, McGraw-Hill, 1997
Datacasting, McGraw-Hill, 1997
The Handbook of Technology in Financial Services, Auerbach, 1998

The Handbook of Internet Management, Auerbach, 1999
The Handbook of eBusiness, Warren, Gorham & Lamont, 2000
The Ultimate Internet Sourcebook, Amacom, 2001
How to Be a Successful Internet Consultant, 2nd ed., Amacom, 2002
Software Engineering Handbook, Auerbach, 2002
Real World Configuration Management, Auerbach, 2003
Balanced Scorecard, Auerbach, 2005
Knowledge Management, Business Intelligence, and Content Management: The IT Practitioner's Guide, Auerbach, 2006
X Internet: The Executable and Extendable Internet, Auerbach, 2007
Leading IT Projects: The IT Manager's Guide, Auerbach, 2008

Chapter 1

Introduction to Strategic Marketing Management

When you think of marketing, what comes to your mind? Do you think of an advertising campaign? Perhaps you remember some automobile commercials from the last comedy show you watched. Or do you think about the yearly sale at your favorite clothing store? Maybe what you first think of is the annoying telephone call during dinner last night from someone trying to sell you a newspaper subscription.

These are all examples of marketing elements we face each day. Marketing is an integral part of our society, and we are all familiar with its basic purpose: to sell a product or service. In our case, we are going to focus on selling technology products and services. However, no matter what you are pitching, the fundamentals of marketing remain the same.

One way to look at marketing is to consider it as a cycle that includes a range of activities (Figure 1.1), which are explained in the following text:

Research: The process of marketing should begin with research. Research includes tasks such as collecting information about the organization's target markets, including customer demographics, psychographics, and competitive intelligence. Some say that a market can be created. Others insist that marketing is purely a response to an identified market need. In other words, pioneers create the "need," while followers try to jump on the bandwagon. Research assists in distinguishing between these two viewpoints.

Strategy and planning: Data collected during the research activity are inputted into the strategic planning process. A strategic marketing plan will be created. A series of tactical plans (e.g., promotional, advertising) will be derived

1

Figure 1.1 The marketing cycle.

from the strategic plan. The strategic marketing plan includes elements of the other activities in this list.

Branding: Building a brand involves marketers' examining the market positioning of the product (or firm) in the marketplace and establishing how they would like the product to be perceived by consumers. For example, Donald Trump has become a billionaire essentially by branding himself in the United States. Sony has branded itself as a global leader in consumer electronics.

Product development: Product development is usually initiated after research has been conducted. For example, an automobile company's market research finds that there is an untapped opportunity for hybrid sport-utility vehicles (SUVs). The product development initiative involves research and development, and careful attention to innovation management within the company.

Pricing: Determining price is not easy, but it is the easiest factor to adjust. Price communicates to the market the company's intended value positioning of its product or brand. Think Mercedes Benz versus Ford and Rolex versus Timex.

Sales: After the product or service has been established and before it goes to the market, the marketing team will train the sales force to understand the product or service, answer questions, support the customer, and close sales.

Point-of-purchase (POP) materials are those items that a sales force might need to help sell a product. Examples include sale signs on top of sales racks in clothing stores, brochures next to cosmetics at the cosmetics counter, and blank DVDs in a technology store.

Public relations (PR), media relations, public affairs, and investor relations: The softer side of marketing involves communication with various target publics. Public relations enables the company to make the public aware of its products (e.g., press releases that wind up as articles in newspapers). Media relations deals specifically with the press and often involves courting one or more members of the press for favorable coverage of the product or service. Public affairs, also known as governmental affairs, deals with various governmental entities that impact the organization. Firms whose stock is traded publicly will have investor relations departments that act as the intermediary between the investing public and the firm.

Marketing communications: PR and media relations are often subsumed into marketing communications, which provides the literature that supports the sale of the product or service. If you've recently gone to a trade show, you have probably brought back a shopping bag (with the logo of a company that hopes to sell you something) filled with product literature. In today's digital society, marketing communications might also encompass a company's Web site, Internet promotions and advertising, e-mail marketing, and even social networking efforts.

Distribution: Building a product is only half the equation. Getting it to the consumer is the other half. The distribution strategy consists of packaging, use of channels and affiliates, retailing, wholesaling, and even e-commerce.

Customer service: Good marketers want to know about their customers' experience, including complaints and questions. This enables the company to determine if there are any product issues. On the basis of these issues, research is performed, and the entire marketing cycle starts again. Customer relationship management (CRM) systems are often the basis for connectivity to customers (as well as potential customers). Use of CRM extends beyond customer service throughout the organization (i.e., sales, marketing, management).

Essentially, marketing can be defined as the process by which companies create value for customers and build strong customer relationships to capture value from customers in return. The process of marketing uses all the just-described activities to create and communicate that value to customers.

The Micro-Marketing Level

Marketing concepts can be used in both for-profit and nonprofit organizations; they can be used by individuals or governments. The modern micro-marketing perspective considers customer needs first, rather than focusing on what the organization can easily produce. It also goes beyond just persuading a customer to buy, and reflects a need to build a relationship with the customer. Finally, it is important to remember that effective marketing at the micro level depends on collaboration among a number of managerial functions and requires an understanding of the macro-marketing system.

The Macro-Marketing Level

Different countries, states, communities, and even neighborhoods present different circumstances and combinations of customers, needs, and wants. These factors determine which macro-marketing system a given community is in. It is important to identify the general macro-marketing system, as well as the stage of a community's economic development, in order to use micro-marketing effectively and to help develop the systems to create greater utility.

For example, say a company is interested in expanding its television sales. Televisions require electricity and a broadcast signal, and use different transmission systems in different countries (e.g., Pal, NTSC). The company will accept only monetary currency for its televisions. If this company does not consider macro-marketing systems and a macro level of economic development, it might decide to try to sell its televisions to a nomadic tribe. The nomads do not have electricity and only occasionally trade their excess sheep for clothes that other tribes offer them in exchange. The company in this example would clearly be making a big mistake. While this example is absurd, organizations do make mistakes when they do not understand a society's macro-marketing system and stage of economic development.

Business Plan versus Strategic Plan versus Marketing Plan

Like IT, marketing is a single component of an organization's strategic plan. Organizational strategic planning suggests strategies to identify and move toward desired future states. It consists of the process of developing and implementing plans to reach goals and objectives. Strategic planning operates on a grand scale and takes in "the big picture" as opposed to tactical planning, which by definition has to focus more on individual, detailed activities.

A good strategy will have the capability to obtain the desired objective; fit well both with the external environment and with an organization's resources and core competencies; appear feasible and appropriate; be able to provide an organization with a sustainable competitive advantage, ideally through uniqueness and sustainability; and prove to be dynamic, flexible, and adaptable to changing situations.

A business plan is a summary of how a business intends to organize an endeavor and implement activities necessary and sufficient for the venture to succeed. It is a written explanation of the company's business model. A business plan can be seen as a collection of subplans, including a financial plan, production plan, technology plan, and marketing plan.

Strategic marketing planning is complex, but it is guided by basic principles. Among these is the marketing concept that emphasizes the concentration of all the activities of a firm into meeting the needs of its target markets—at a profit. Ideally, the strategy should take advantage of trends in the external market, not buck them or try to radically alter them.

Ideally, the ingredients of a good marketing mix flow logically from the relevant dimensions of the target market. Information gaps, competition, and the changing marketing environment make developing a good mix very difficult. Successful strategies are based on sound marketing planning processes.

Strengths, Weaknesses, Opportunities, Threats (Trends) (SWOT[T])

It is important to leverage the distinctive capabilities of an organization as a key component in developing a market-driven strategy. This means that an organization must know itself and where it is going. A SWOT (strengths, weaknesses, opportunities, and threats) analysis is extremely effective, but to be useful it must be based on facts and objective opinions. A biased or flawed analysis can hurt your marketing plans. It is only after this analysis that a competitive strategy can take shape. The next step is to understand where you and your competitors stand in the market. It is equally important that the strategic direction chosen be aligned with the organization's capabilities and differentiators. A sample SWOT for a fictional animal greeting card Web site can be found at http://www.wilsonweb.com/wmt5/plan-swot.htm.

Most industries have a firm that has the largest market share and leads competitors in price changes, distribution coverage, and promotional intensity. Intel is one of these firms; it has to work hard to stay at the top. See "Only the Paranoid Survive" (Andrew Grove, Intel site: http://www.intel.com/pressroom/kits/bios/grove/paranoid.htm). This company knows that if it does not outdo itself in the microprocessor business, some other company will. Along with microprocessor competitors, Intel faces rivals in a variety of market niches. Intel combats competitors not just by designing chips with more features, but also by pushing the limits of its manufacturing technology. Indeed, this is the company's chief strategic means of product leadership.

However, strategy involves much more than internal analysis. Companies must also analyze which markets look attractive—now and into the future. This is why the SWOT model has been extended to including trend analysis, SWOT(T), as shown in Figure 1.2.

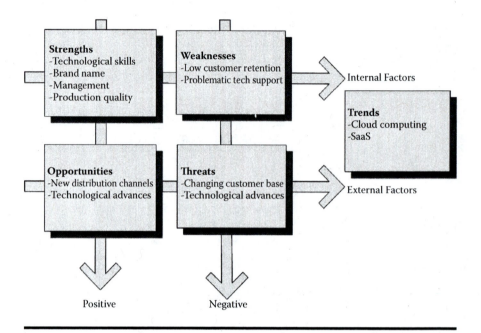

Figure 1.2 Strengths, weaknesses, opportunities, threats (trends) (SWOT[T]).

A strength is something a firm does well. It may be a process, a patent, some other product-related activity, great customer service, delivery, or channel support. Well-developed strengths can lead to a distinct competitive advantage.

Weaknesses are areas in which the firm performs less well than competitive firms. These are areas in which the firm needs to improve, or at least not compete head-to-head with better-performing organizations.

Opportunities are events, conditions, or situations in the external environment that are particularly well suited or attractive to the way a firm does business or is planning to do business. The firm tries to match its strengths to opportunities that emerge, are emerging, or will emerge within the planning period.

Threats are events, or conditions, in the external environment that are not well suited or attractive to the way a firm does business or is planning to do business. Companies try to avoid threats or minimize their impact.

Trends are external factors in the business or the environment that may impact the company positively or negatively. Forecasting and trend analysis, both being techniques used in market research, are used to determine future trends.

A SWOT(T) analysis can assist your company if it is considering a strategy that focuses on a target market that is already being served by several strong competitors. These competitors are usually successful because of a competitive advantage. A competitive advantage might be based on a better marketing mix, which may include improved distribution, effective promotion, or lower prices. Offering a marketing mix that is identical to that of competitors will not provide superior value or create a competitive advantage for your firm. Your firm needs to position or differentiate its marketing mix as better for customers.

4Ps: The Marketing Mix

The marketing mix is what most marketing people call the "4Ps": product, price, place, and promotion, as shown in Figure 1.3. So, what do these things mean?

- Product: A product is the need-satisfying offering of a firm, including physical goods or services (e.g., a new car). The product also includes the features, benefits, quality level, accessories, installation, instructions, warranty, product line extensions, packaging, and branding of the product. All aspects of the product area (e.g., benefits, quality, service dimensions) must match customer needs. Demographic dimensions of the target market determine where customers are located. Where customers shop helps to define channel alternatives. Whether, and how, customers search for information helps to define the promotion blend.
- Price: The price is the amount of money charged for the product or service (i.e., a thing of value). In determining price, a firm must consider factors such as cost of producing the product, return on investment, competitive pressures, discounts, and allowances.
- Place: This involves making goods and services available in the right quantities at the right locations. In determining the place, a firm must consider such factors as objectives, channel type, distribution, kinds or locations of stores, transportation, storage, and managing or coordinating sales channels.

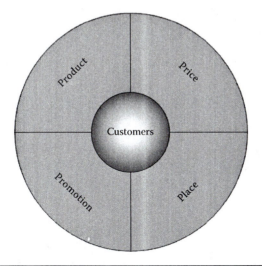

Figure 1.3   The 4Ps or marketing mix.

■ Promotion: Promotion is the communication of information between a seller and a potential buyer. It involves objectives, promotional blend, salespeople, advertising, and publicity.

Individual decisions made for each of the 4Ps are guided by the need to develop logical and coherent strategies, plans, and programs. Each P describes a separate function that requires managerial decision making. However, those decisions are not made in isolation: They affect and are affected by the decisions made for every other P. For example, a can of soda might cost one amount in a vending machine at a local business but may cost double that amount in a vending machine on a college campus. As the place changes, the price of the can of soda might also change.

The 4Ps must be creatively blended because marketing planning is more than making decisions about each area of the marketing mix and then assembling the parts. The job of integrating the four Ps belongs to the marketing manager.

Marketing Planning

Marketing planning involves finding a competitive advantage in meeting the needs of some target markets that it can satisfy very well. Once the manager has selected the target market, decided on the marketing mix, and developed estimates of the costs and revenue for that strategy, the marketing plan provides a blueprint for implementation.

The marketing plan spells out the timing of the strategy. As part of the blueprint for implementation, it should include the time frame for the elements of the plan, along with expected estimates of sales and profit, so that the plan can be compared to actual performance in the future.

A complete plan spells out the reasons for decisions about the marketing mix by including information about customers, competitors, the environment, the company's objectives, and its resources. The plan should be routinely checked and updated. As some elements of the plan or the marketing environment change, the whole plan may need a fresh approach. Most companies implement more than one marketing plan at the same time. The specification of a target market and a related marketing mix form a marketing strategy. A marketing plan is created by adding time-related details to the marketing strategy. Several plans make a marketing program, as shown in Figure 1.4. The marketing program blends all the firm's plans into one big plan.

Marketing Ethics

Ethics is a set of values of acceptable behavior that outlines the decisions individuals or organizations make. The conscious application of principles of moral rights and

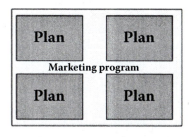

Figure 1.4 The marketing program is composed of one or more marketing plans.

wrongs and fairness in marketing decision making, practice, and behavior in the organization is what practicing ethics in marketing means.

There has been an increasing focus on adhering to ethical values. This is because customers develop a better attitude toward an organization and its products or services when a firm behaves ethically. Unethical practices generally lead to lack of trust, bad publicity, dissatisfied customers, or, sometimes, legal action.

The Federal Trade Commission (FTC) and various local and state government agencies are responsible for creating policies and enforcing laws to prevent unethical marketing practices. Marketing associations also play a role in this. One such example is the American Marketing Association, which has specified a code of ethics that is available on its Web site: www.ama.org.

There are a wide variety of practices that are considered unethical. These include the following:

1. Misleading pricing: This can be done in the form of giving discounts valid only when other products are also bought, omitting significant conditions of the sale, providing deceptively suggestive selling prices, or making false price comparisons.
2. Misleading promotion practices: Deliberately misstating how a product performs or is constructed; making false or highly exaggerated claims; and intentionally mislabeling the contents, weight, size, or other critical information are examples of this practice. Using a bait-and-switch selling method (a method in which a product or service is sold, often at a lesser price, to catch the fancy of customers who are then encouraged to buy a more costly product); selling defective or hazardous products without disclosing their dangers; not honoring warranty obligations; failing to reveal information concerning pyramid sales (a sales method in which people are recruited for a plan that generates revenue only by recruiting others), etc., are other unethical practices in this category.

Ethical issues may also come up during the distribution process. For the most part, sales personnel are evaluated on the basis of their sales performance. Performance pressures may lead to ethical dilemmas.

Example

Pushing products that generate better commissions and pressuring retailers to purchase more than they need are temptations. Influencing the retailers to trim down display space for competitors' products, or paying retailers to sell their product and not that of competitors should also be considered unethical.

Direct marketing is also coming under the radar of unethical marketing. Distasteful practices range from trivial irritants, such as the bad timing and unnecessarily high frequency of commercials or sales letters, to some offensive or even illegal practices. Annoying telemarketing calls, persistent and high-pressure selling, sales appeals disguised as contests, use and exchange of mailing lists leading to junk mailing, television (TV) commercials that are too lengthy or run too recurrently, etc., are some examples of practices that pose ethical dilemmas.

Subliminal Advertising

Subliminal advertising messages are embedded in another medium. Such messages are not recognized by the conscious mind but are processed by the subconscious mind. This has the potential to affect future actions, behaviors, attitudes, thoughts, beliefs, and value systems.

A certain amount of subliminal persuasion happens regularly despite the fact that such hidden messaging is considered to be deceptive by the FTC. Some subliminal techniques used include the following:

1. Some hardware products are unnecessarily stuffed with completely useless wads of aluminum just to make them heavy. The general perception among customers is that the heavier the product, the more sturdy and substantial it is. As a result, they end up paying higher prices.
2. Stress makes people unconsciously adhere to comforting and familiar rituals, a fact that is very well exploited by marketers.
3. The fact that slow music with a tempo lower than the human heartbeat causes shoppers to shop slowly, and hence buy more, is put to good use by shopkeepers.
4. A product's place of origin also has the potential to subliminally influence what customers buy. Fancy, high-tech, metropolitan cities' names on a product have a cachet that seems to appeal to the self-esteem of most people.

Murketing

Murketing, a term coined by Rob Walker (http://www.murketing.com), is a vague advertising method used to promote a brand in ways that are extremely nontraditional. The term murketing is a combination of "murky" and "marketing," emphasizing the fact that this is a type of marketing that is murky and sometimes confusing, in which the advertisements do not really relate to the product or service. Murketing creates a buzz around a product by the creation of a blurred brand identity with a lot of scope for manipulation in the future. Such marketing focuses on new media, infiltrating chat rooms, distributing viral videos, and establishing promotional blogs or mysterious treasure hunts across the Web. The aim is a slow and thorough market penetration by creating an image around the product instead of focusing on mere brand recognition. While murketing is not considered unethical at this time, the practice can stretch the limits of acceptable practice.

Conclusion

Analysis of marketing opportunities requires an understanding of the marketing environment at both the macro and micro levels. Strategic planning must then follow and be supported by effective organization, implementation, and controls of the organization.

In the early 1700s, a Dutch inventor, trying to simulate ice skating during the summer months, created the first pair of roller skates by attaching spools to his shoes. His "in-line" arrangement was the standard design until 1863, when the first skates with rollers set as two pairs appeared. The two-pair design became the new standard, and in-line skates virtually disappeared from the market.

In 1980, two hockey-playing brothers found an old pair of in-line skates while browsing through a sporting goods store. They modified the design of the skate by adding hard plastic wheels, a boot, and a toe brake. They sold their product as the "Rollerblade Skate." During the 1980s, Rollerblade focused on marketing its skates to hockey players and skiers as a training skate. However, after they performed some market research, they discovered that there was a bigger market for their product. People thought that in-line skating was great fun as well as a wonderful aerobic workout. By 1997, after repositioning the product, there were more than 27 million users of in-line skates in the United States alone (Kerin et al., 2006).

The next time you go to the grocery store, look at all the different products that you encounter. Do different brands appeal to different segments of people? Try describing these target markets. What type of market research do you think the marketers of these products performed before positioning their brands? What do you think they put into their marketing plans? And, above all, what do you think their strategy was?

References

Kerin, R., Hartley, S., Berkowitz, E., and Rudelius, W. (2006). *Marketing*. New York: McGraw-Hill.

Chapter 2

Strategy and Implementation

You just heard through the company grapevine that your biggest competitor is about to launch the Web site to end all Web sites. From what you hear, this Web site is not only going to enable the competitor's customers to order online, but they'll also be able to check order status and even communicate in real time with sales staff. If this is not bad enough, your competitor will simultaneously be launching an internal Web site that will enable it to buy all of its supplies and parts online and even control and monitor its supply chain. Just how will you approach this challenge? What issues will you look at? Whom will you interview? What will you study?

Don't think this doesn't happen. The success of Amazon.com came as a big surprise to Barnes & Noble (B&N). Who would have thought that a no-name virtual start-up would soon outpace and outsell the biggest bookseller in the world? B&N started life as a sleepy bookseller chain. In the late 1980s, it morphed itself into the largest chain of superstore bookstores in the United States. When the Internet appeared on the scene in the early 1990s, B&N joined a host of other companies that took a "wait and see" approach to the newfangled concept of e-business. It waited and watched as tiny Amazon.com, a company no one had ever heard of, opened its e-doors in 1995. Unfortunately, it continued to wait and watch as Amazon.com became the world's largest bookstore, leaving B&N far behind.

B&N found out the hard way that it was impossible to compete without jumping on the e-business bandwagon. And jump it did, by launching barnesandnoble.com with German-based megamedia firm Bertlesmann in 1997. B&N's stated strategy is to be an e-commerce leader in the sale of books, music, and digital video discs (DVD)/video. While Amazon had the luxury of building its e-business from the ground up,

13

B&N was a well-established company. E-business, therefore, had to be retrofitted to existing business processes and functions. While they geared up quickly, they still find themselves a very distant second to über-bookstore Amazon.com.

Trying to replicate the profitable moves of the market leader, however, is fraught with danger in the online world. B&N found this out the hard way. In December of 1999 (Fry, 2000), the U.S. District Court for the Western District of Washington issued a preliminary injunction to bar B&N from infringing on Amazon's patented "1-Click" shopping feature. Amazon went on to e-patent a whole host of other e-commerce processes, including its associates concept. U.S. Patent 6,029,141 is entitled "Internet-Based Customer Referral System" and discusses a method of selling items through associate Web sites. Small Web site providers often want to sell products without the bother and cost of dealing with ordering and fulfillment. The Amazon associates program enables these small businesses to earn commissions for purchases of products on Amazon's Web site if the consumer links to Amazon from the associates' Web sites via virtue of a special code. Multiple million members strong (http://www.amazon.com/gp/browse.html/ref=gw_bt_as/002-2514903-9765660?node=3435371), this program makes Amazon a formidable, perhaps even unbeatable, competitor.

Competing with a first mover, particularly one as creative and dynamic as Amazon.com, is no mean feat. Over the years, Amazon has morphed from, as the media so succinctly put it, the Earth's biggest bookstore to the Earth's biggest anything store. B&N is in the process of morphing as well. It has begun to go beyond books and CDs and is now selling calendars and providing free courses. Can electronics and clothing be far behind?

The goal, then, is to create a viable strategic plan that will, if not make you a first mover, at least let you effectively compete with first movers. In the world of high tech, this is often a make-or-break scenario.

Strategic Planning

It is said that "failing to plan is planning to fail." Strategic management can be defined as the art and science of formulating, implementing, and evaluating cross-functional decisions that enable an organization to achieve its objectives. Put simply, strategic management is planning for an organization's future. The plan becomes a road map to achieving the goals of the organization, with marketing as the centerpiece of this plan. Similar to the person taking a trip to another city, the road map serves as a guide for management to reach the desired destination. Without such a map, an organization can easily flounder.

The value of strategic planning for any business is that it can be proactive in taking advantage of opportunities while minimizing the threats from the external environment. The planning process itself can be useful to rally the troops toward common goals and create buy-in to the final action plan. It is important to keep

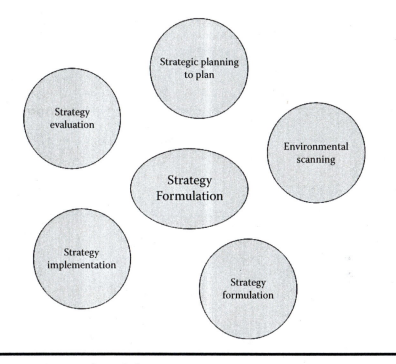

Figure 2.1   Strategy formulation.

in mind that planning is a process, not a one-shot deal. The strategy formulation process, which is shown in Figure 2.1, includes the following steps:

1. Strategic planning to plan (assigning tasks, time, etc.)
2. Environmental scanning (identifying strengths and weaknesses in the internal environment, and opportunities and threats in the external environment)
3. Strategy formulation (identifying alternatives and selecting appropriate alternatives)
4. Strategy implementation (determining roles, responsibilities, and time frames)
5. Strategy evaluation (establishing specific benchmarks and control procedures, revisiting plan at regular intervals to update plan, etc.)

Business tactics must be consistent with a company's competitive strategy. A company's ability to successfully pursue a competitive strategy depends on its capabilities (internal analysis) and how these capabilities are translated into sources of competitive advantage (matched with external environment analysis). The basic generic strategies a company can pursue are shown in Figure 2.2:

a. Cost leadership
   1. Lower prices
   2. Lower costs

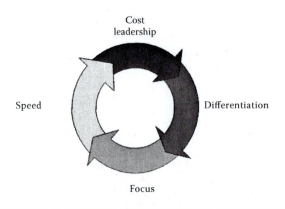

Figure 2.2   Basic competitive strategies.

    3. Experience curve
    4. "One size fits all"
    5. Large volume
    6. Conformance quality
    7. Example: Cheapest car wash in town (self-serve)
  b. Differentiation
    1. Higher prices
    2. Product innovation
    3. Higher value added
    4. A product for each market
    5. High relative perceived quality
    6. Example: "Touch-free" car wash (drive through)
  c. Focus
    1. Specific customers
    2. Specific market segment
    3. Either focused cost leadership or focused differentiation
    4. Target cost leadership or differentiation strategy to specific segments of the market
    5. Example: Car wash catering to high-end vehicles, hand detail, polish, wax specifically designed for Mercedes, Lexus, etc.
  d. Speed
    1. Speed of new product innovation and product introduction
    2. Example: Applies mainly to software and biotech products

In all strategy formulations, it is vital for the company to align the strategy's tactics with its overall source of competitive advantage. For example, many small companies make the mistake of thinking that product giveaways are the best way to promote their business or add sales. In fact, the opposite effect may happen if there is a misalignment between price (lowest cost) and value (focus).

Michael Porter's (Harvard Business School) Five Forces model gives another perspective on an industry's profitability. This model helps strategists develop an understanding of the general external market opportunities and threats facing an industry, which gives context to specific strategy options.

Specific strategies that a company can pursue should be aligned with the overall generic strategy selected. Alternative strategies include forward integration, backward integration, horizontal integration, market penetration, market development, product development, concentric diversification, conglomerate diversification, horizontal diversification, joint venture, retrenchment, divestiture, liquidation, and a combined strategy. Each alternative strategy has many variations. For example, product development could include research and development pursuits, product improvement, etc. Strategy selection will depend on management's assessment of the company strengths, weaknesses, opportunities, and threats (SWOT), taking into consideration strategic "fit." This refers to how well the selected strategy helps the company achieve its vision and mission.

Strategy Implementation

A 1999 study found that nearly 70% of strategic plans and strategies are never successfully implemented (Corboy and O'Corrbui, 1999). Strategies frequently fail because the market conditions they were intended to exploit change before the strategy takes effect. An example is the failure of many telecoms that were born based on projected pent-up demand for fiber-optic capacity fueled by the growth of the Internet. Before much of the fiber could even be laid, new technologies were introduced that permitted a dramatic increase of capacity on the existing infrastructure. Virtually overnight, the market for fiber collapsed (Sterling, 2003).

Over a three-year period, Downes (2001) studied strategy execution mistakes and concluded that execution obstacles are of two varieties: problems generated by forces external to the company, as our telecom example demonstrates; and problems internal to the company. According to Downes, internal issues test the flexibility of companies to launch initiatives that represent significant departures from long-standing assumptions about who they are and what they do. Can they develop new marketing techniques appropriate to new channels without destroying existing brand equity? Can they integrate new software into their infrastructure? Can they align their human resources?

What could these companies have done to ensure that their programs and initiatives were implemented successfully? Did they follow best practices? Were they aware of the initiative's critical success factors? Was there sufficient senior-level involvement? Was planning thorough and all-encompassing? Were their strategic goals aligned throughout the organization? And most importantly, were their implementation plans able to react to continual change?

Although planning is an essential ingredient for success, implementing a strategy requires more than just careful initiative planning. Allocating resources, scheduling, and monitoring are indeed important, but it is often the intangible or unknown that gets in the way of ultimate success. The ability of the organization to adapt to the dynamics of fast-paced change as well as the desire of executive management to support this challenge is what really separates the successes from the failures.

TiVo was presented with a challenge when it opted to, as its CEO puts it, "forever change the way the world watches TV." The company pioneered the digital video recorder (DVR), which enables viewers to pause live TV and watch it on their own schedules. There are millions of self-described "rabid" users of the TiVo service. In a company survey, over 40% said they'd sooner disconnect their cell service than unplug their TiVo.

TiVo is considered disruptive technology because it forever changes the way the public does something. According to Forbes.com's Sam Whitmore (2004), no other $141 million company has even come close to transforming government policy, audience measurement, direct response and TV advertising, content distribution, and society itself.

But TiVo started off on shaky footing and continues to face challenges, which it must address to survive. Therefore, TiVo is an excellent example of continual adaptive strategic implementation and is worthy of study.

Back in the late 1990s, Michael Ramsey and James Barton, two forward thinkers, came up with the idea that would ultimately turn into TiVo. They quickly assembled a team of marketers and engineers to bring their product to market and unveiled their product at the National Consumer Electronics show in 1999. TiVo hit the shelves a short four months later. Ramsey and Barton, founders and C-level executives, were actively involved in every step of the way—a key for successful strategic implementations.

Hailed as the "latest, greatest, must-have product," TiVo was still facing considerable problems. The first was consumer adoption rates. It takes years before any new technology is widely adopted by the public at large. To stay in business, TiVo needed a way to jump-start its customer base. On top of that, the firm was bleeding money, so it had to find a way to staunch the flow of funds out of the company.

Their original implementation plan did not include solutions to these problems. But the firm reacted quickly to its situation by jumping into a series of joint ventures and partnerships that would help it penetrate the market and increase profitability. An early partnership with Philips Electronics provided it with funding to complete its product development. Deals with DirecTV, Comcast Interactive, and other satellite and cable companies gave TiVo the market penetration it needed to be successful. The force behind this adaptive implementation strategy was Ramsey and Barton, TiVo's executive management team. Since implementations often engender a high degree of risk, the executive team must be at the ready should there be a need to fall back on "Plan B." Ramsey and Barton's willingness to jump into the fray to find suitable partnerships enabled TiVo to stay the course—and stay in business.

But success is often fleeting, which is why performance monitoring and continual modification of both the strategic plan and the resulting implementation plan are so very important. Here again, the presence of executive oversight must loom large. Executive management must review progress on an almost daily basis for important strategic implementations. While many executives might be content just to speak to their direct reports, an actively engaged leader will always involve others lower on the chain of command. This approach has many benefits, including reinforcing the importance of the initiative throughout the ranks and making subordinate staff feel that they are an important part of the process. The importance of employee buy-in to strategic initiatives cannot be underestimated in terms of impact on the success of the ultimate implementation. Involved, excited, and engaged employees lead to success. Unhappy, fearful, and disengaged employees do not.

TiVo competes in the immense and highly competitive consumer electronics industry, where being a first mover (Porter, 1980) isn't always a competitive advantage. Competition comes in fast and hard. ReplayTV and EchoStar, the owner of the DISH network, with over 7 million subscribers, are direct competitors. It's the indirect competitors, however, that TiVo needs to watch out for. Although Microsoft phased out its UltimateTV product, the company still looms large by integrating some extensions into its Windows XP operating system that provide similar DVR functionality. TiVo's main indirect competitors (Pearce and Robinson, 2005), however, are digital cable's pay-per-view and video-on-demand services. The question becomes, will the DVR be relegated to the technological trash heap of history, where it can keep company with the likes of Betamax and eight-track tapes? Again, this is where executive leadership is a must if implementation is to be successful. Leaders must continually assess the environment and make adjustments to the organization's strategic plan and resulting implementation plans. They must provide their staff with the flexibility and resources to quickly adapt to changes that might result from this reassessment.

In spite of all its partnerships, the massive market for TiVo has yet to materialize. In the United Kingdom, TiVo stopped selling its DVRs in 2003, giving credence to the "flop theory." Part of the reason is that despite its rabid customer base and multiple partnerships, widespread adoption of the technology continues to be slow. There are several reasons for this. One is the perceived lack of privacy. Since the device is truly personal, it is quite possible to track viewing habits precisely. There have been at least two humorous TV movies on attempts by some men to outfox their machines by recording lots of macho war movies, causing their TiVos to gather incorrect preference data ("UK company: Heave ho, TiVo!," 2003). TiVo responded to this problem by informing its customers of its privacy and opt-out policies with renewed vigor. TiVo is combating consumer lethargy through a combination of consumer education, benefits-focused advertising, and clever product placement on popular TV.

An even bigger challenge is the changing face of TiVo's partnerships. In 2005, DirecTV sold off all but the company's core satellite TV operations. Among the assets sold was its TiVo equity partnership. Given this particular challenge, it's not too surprising that TiVo has begun to search for new paths for its technology—essentially, continually updating its implementation plan as conditions change. It continues to seek partnerships with content providers, consumer electronics manufacturers, and technology providers to focus on the development of interactive video services. One of its more controversial ideas was the promotion of "advertainment." These are special-format commercials that TiVo downloads onto its customers' devices to help advertisers establish what TiVo calls "far deeper communications" with consumers.

TiVo continues to try to dominate the technology side of the DVR market by constant research and development (R&D). It currently has 70 granted patents and 106 patents pending ("TiVo granted eight new domestic and foreign patents," 2005). Even if TiVo—the product—goes under, TiVo's intellectual property will provide a continuing strategic asset.

Heraclitus, a Greek philosopher living in the sixth century B.C. said, "Nothing endures but change." That TiVo has survived up to this point is a testament to its willingness to adapt to continual change. That it managed to do this when so many others have failed demonstrates a wide variety of strategic planning and implementation skill sets. It has an organizational structure that is able to quickly adapt to whatever change is necessary. Although a small company, its goals are carefully aligned throughout the organization, at the organizational, divisional, as well as employee levels. Everyone at TiVo has bought into the plan and is willing to do what it takes to be successful. It has active support from the management team, a critical success factor for all strategic initiatives. Most importantly, it is skillful at performance management. It is acutely aware of all environmental variables (i.e., competition, global economies, consumer trends, employee desires, industry trends, etc.) that might affect its outcomes and shows incredible resourcefulness and resiliency in its ability to reinvent itself.

Pearce and Robinson (2005) assert that "the strategy and the firm must become one." In doing so, the firm's managers must direct and control actions and outcomes and, most critically, adjust to change. Executive leadership can do this not only by being actively engaged themselves but also by making sure all employees involved in the implementation are on the same page. How is this done? There are several techniques, including the ones already mentioned. Executive leadership should frequently review the progress of the implementation and jump into the fray when required. This might translate to finding partnerships, as was the case with TiVo, or simply quickly signing off on additional resources or funding. More importantly, executive leadership must be an advocate—cheerleader—for the implementation with an eye toward rallying the troops behind the program. Savvy leaders can accomplish this through frequent communications with subordinate employees. Inviting lower-level managers to meetings, so that they become advocates within their own departments, is a wonderful method of cascading strategic goals throughout the organization. E-mail communications, speeches, and newsletters are other ways of getting the message across.

Executive leadership should also be mindful that the structure of the organization can have a dramatic impact on the success of the implementation, as Pearce and Robinson discuss. The authors dissect the 21st-century organizational structure that includes the following characteristics: bottom up, inspirational, employees and free agents, flexible, change, and "no compromise," to name a few. Merge all of this with a fair rewards system and compensation plan, and you have all the ingredients for a successful implementation. As you can see, organizational structure, leadership, and culture are the key drivers for success.

Implementation Problems

Microsoft was successful in gaining control of people's living rooms through the Trojan horse strategy of deploying the now ubiquitous Xbox. Hewlett-Packard (HP) was not so successful in raising its profile and cash flow by acquiring rival computer maker Compaq—to the detriment of its CEO, who was ultimately ousted. Segway, the gyroscope-powered human transport brainchild of the brilliant Dean Kamen, received a lukewarm reception from the public. Touted as "the next great thing" by the technology press, the company had to reengineer its implementation plan to reorient its target customer base from the general consumer to specific categories of consumers, such as golfers, cross-country bikers, and businesses.

Successful implementation is essentially a framework that relies on the relationship between the following variables: strategy development, environmental uncertainty, organizational structure, organizational culture, leadership, operational planning, resource allocation, communication, people, control, and outcome (Okumus, 2003). One major reason why so many implementations fail is that there are no practical, yet theoretically sound, models to guide the implementation process. Without an adequate model, organizations try to implement strategies without a good understanding of the multiple variables that must be simultaneously addressed to make implementation work (Alexander, 1991).

In HP's case, one could say that the company failed in its efforts at integrating Compaq because it did not clearly identify the various problems that surfaced as a result of the merger and used a rigorous problem-solving methodology to find solutions to the problems. Segway, on the other hand, framed the right problem (i.e., "the general consumer is disinterested in our novel transport system") and ultimately identified alternatives that could help it realize its goals.

The key is to first recognize that there is a problem. This isn't always easy, as there will be differences of opinions among the various managerial groups as to whether one exists and as to what the problem actually is. In HP's case, the problems started early on, when the strategy to acquire Compaq was first announced.

According to one fund manager who didn't like the company before the merger, the acquisition just doubled the size of its worst business (De Aenlle, 2005). We should also ask about the role of executive leadership in either assisting in the problem determination process or verifying that the right problem has indeed been selected. While HP's Carly Fiorina did a magnificent job of implementing her strategy using what Robinson and Pearce describe as the three key levers (i.e. organizational structure, leadership, and culture), she most certainly dropped the ball by disengaging from the process and either did not recognize that there was a problem within HP or just ignored the problem for other priorities. Elizabeth Bailey (2003), a director on diverse boards including CSX and Honeywell, says that the management team needs to pull together to solve problems. The goal is to help position the company for the future. You're not just dealing with the issues of the day, but you are always looking for the set of issues that is over the next hill. A management team that is working well sees the next hill, and the next hill. It's the highest form of problem solving.

There are many questions that should be asked when an implementation plan appears to go off track. Is it a people problem? Was the strategy flawed in the first place? Is it an infrastructural problem? An environmental problem? Is it a combination of problems? Asking these questions will enable you to gather data that will assist in defining the right problem to be solved. Of course, answering yes to any one or more of these questions is only the start of the problem definition phase of problem solving. You must also drill down into each of these areas to find the root causes of the problem. For example, if you determined that there is a people problem, you then have to identify the specifics of the problem. For example, in a company that has just initiated an offshoring program, employees may feel betrayed, bereft, angry, scared, and overwhelmed. Unless management deals with these emotions at the outset of the offshoring program, employee productivity and efficiency will undoubtedly be negatively impacted.

Radical change to the work environment may also provoke negatively aggressive behavior. When the U.S. Post Office first automated its postal clerk functions, management shared little about what was being automated. The rumor mill took over, and somehow employees got the idea that massive layoffs were in the works. Feeling that they needed to fight back, some postal employees actually sabotaged the new automated equipment. Had management just taken a proactive approach by providing adequate and continuing communications to the employees prior to the automation effort, none of this would have happened.

Sussman (Lynch, 2003) neatly sums up management's role in avoiding people problems through use of what he calls "the new metrics"—Return on Intellect (ROI), Return on Attitude (ROA), and Return on Excitement (ROE). As the title of the Lynch article suggests, it is important that leaders challenge the process, inspire a shared vision, enable others to act, model the way, and encourage the heart.

It is also quite possible to confuse symptoms of a problem with the problem itself. For example, when working with overseas vendors, it is sometimes hard to reach these people due to the difference in time zones. This is particularly true when working with Asian firms, as they are halfway across the globe. Employees working with these external companies might complain of lack of responsiveness when the real problem is that real-time communications with these companies are difficult due to time zone problems. The problem, then, is not lack of responsiveness of these foreign vendors, but lack of an adequate set of technologies that enables employees and vendors to more easily communicate across different time zones, vast distances, and in different languages (i.e., Webcast tools, instant messaging tools, etc., are all being used for these purposes).

Once the problem has been clearly framed, the desired end state and goals need to be identified and some measures created so that it can be determined whether the end state has actually been achieved. Throughout the problem-solving process, relevant data must be collected and the right people must be involved. Nowhere are these two seemingly simple caveats more important than in identifying the end state and the metrics that will be used to determine whether the goals have been achieved.

Strategy implementation usually involves a wide variety of people in many departments. Therefore, there will be many stakeholders who will have an interest in seeing the implementation succeed (or fail). To ensure success, the implementation manager needs to make sure that these stakeholders are aligned, have bought into the strategy, and will do whatever it takes to fix the problems that have been identified. The definition of the end state and associated metrics are best determined in cooperation with these stakeholders, but they must be overseen and approved by management. Once drafted, these must become part of the operational control system.

In recent years, the balanced scorecard approach has been linked to strategy implementation. The scorecard technique aims to provide managers with the key success factors of a business and to facilitate the alignment of business operations with the overall strategy (Kaplan and Norton, 1996). Kaplan and Norton addressed strategy implementation specifically in their approach by identifying four main implementation factors: (1) clarifying and translating the vision and strategy, (2) communication and linking, (3) planning and target setting, and (4) strategic feedback and learning. Each of the four balanced scorecard perspectives, as shown in Figure 2.3, has associated metrics and other indicators that can be used to assess the success of an implementation. If the implementation was properly planned, and performance planning and measurement well integrated into the implementation plan, a variety of metrics and triggers will already be available for review and possible adaptation to the current problem-solving task.

A variety of alternatives will probably be identified by the manager. Again, the quality and quantity of these alternatives will depend on the stakeholders involved in the process. Each alternative will need to be assessed to determine (1) viability, (2) completeness of the solution (i.e., does it solve 100% of the problem, 90%, 50%, etc.), (3) cost of the solution, (4) resources required by the solution, and (5) any risk factors involved in implementing the alternative. In a failed implementation

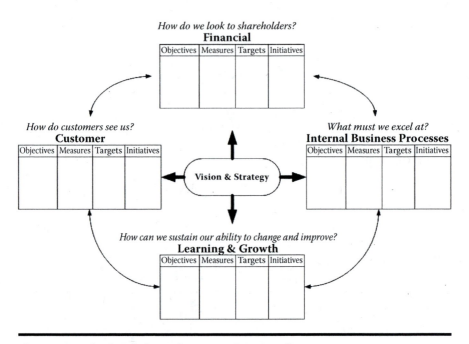

Figure 2.3 The four balanced scorecard perspectives.

situation that resulted from a variety of problems, there might be an overwhelming number of possible alternatives. None of these might be a perfect fit. For example, replacing an overseas vendor gone out of business only solves a piece of the problem and, by itself, is not a complete solution. In certain situations, it is quite possible that a complete solution may not be available. Also, no solution may be workable. In this case, a host of negative alternatives—such as shutting down the effort or selling the product, service, or division—may need to be evaluated.

Once a decision is made regarding the appropriate direction to take, based on the alternative or combination of alternatives selected, a plan must be developed to implement the solution. We can either develop an entirely new implementation plan or fix the one we already have. There are risks and rewards attached to either approach, and the choice made will depend on the extent of the problems identified in the original plan.

Conclusion

Strategic planning is not a one-time event. It is rather a process involving a continuum of ideas, assessment, planning, implementation, evaluation, readjustment, revision, and, most of all, good management. High-tech marketing managers need to make sure that their marketing strategies are carefully aligned with corporate

Figure 2.4   The relationship between the business plan, strategic plan and marketing plan.

and departmental strategic plans, and are consistent with the organizational business plan, as shown in Figure 2.4.

References

Alexander, L. D. (1991). Strategy implementation: Nature of the problem, in Hussey, D., (Ed.), *International Review of Strategic Management* (Vol. 18, pp. 91–97). New York: John Wiley & Sons.

Bailey, E. (2003, June). Interview with Elizabeth Bailey. Retrieved from http://execed. wharton.upenn.edu/ebuzz/0306/thoughtleadersi.html.

Corboy, M., and O'Corrbui, D. (1999, November). The seven deadly sins of strategy. *Management Accounting* 77(10).

De Aenlle, C. (2005, March 13). See you, Carly. Goodbye, Harry. Hello investors. *New York Times*.

Downes, L. (2001, May 14). Strategy can be deadly—Industry trend or event. *Industry Standard*.

Fry, J. P. (2000, July). "Web site development and the business method patent: Are you '1-click' away from an infringement suit?" *Journal of Internet Law*, 10-13. Retrieved from EBSCOhost database.

Kaplan, R. S., and Norton, D. P. (1996). *The Balanced Scorecard—Translating Strategy into Action*. Boston: Harvard Business School Press.

Lynch, K. (2003, April). Leaders challenge the process, inspire a shared vision, enable others to act, model the way, encourage the heart. *Kansas Banker* 93(4).

Okumus, F. (2003). A framework to implement strategies in organizations. *Management Decision* 41(9).

Pearce, H. A., and Robinson, R. B. (2005). *Strategic Management: Formulation, Implementation and Control,* 9th edition. New York: McGraw-Hill/Irwin.

Porter, M. E. (1980). *Competitive Strategy.* New York: Free Press.

Sterling, J. (2003). Translating strategy into effective implementation: Dispelling the myths and highlighting what works. *Strategy and Leadership* 31(3), pp. 27–34.

TiVo granted eight new domestic and foreign patents. (2005, March 1). PR Newswire.

U.K. company: Heave ho, TiVo!. (2003, February 7). EIU ViewsWire.

Whitmore, S. (2004, July 7). What TiVo teaches us. *Forbes*. Retrieved from http://www.forbes.com/2004/07/06/0707whitmore-print.html.

Chapter 3

Understanding the High-Tech Customer

There are thousands of IT products and services out there. You will need to make your mark in such a way that customers are attracted to your product or service above all others amid all the marketing noise. How to do this? The key is differentiation.

Treacy and Wiersema (1997) discuss the three primary sources of product or service differentiation:

1. Product innovation: Create new products and services that keep you ahead of competitors.
2. Customer intimacy: Develop intimate knowledge of customer needs and ways of satisfying them.
3. Operational excellence: Deliver acceptable quality and product characteristics at the lowest possible cost.

These three sources should be kept in mind when dealing with IT end users as well as external customers of the organization.

A customer satisfaction survey done by the Marketing Science Institute (1996) found that customers want their products and services delivered with the following four characteristics:

1. Reliability: Customers want dependability, accuracy, and consistency.
2. Responsiveness: Customers want prompt delivery and continuous communication.

3. Assurance: Customers want to be assured that the project team will deliver projects on time, with quality, within budget, and within scope.
4. Empathy: Customers want the project team to listen to and understand them. The customer really wants to be treated like a team member.

The goal is to select or develop, and then deploy, initiatives that fulfill these four requirements.

The Customer Satisfaction Survey

The easiest and most common way to find out what your customers think about your organization, products or services, and systems is to ask them. This is accomplished with the customer satisfaction survey.

Those doing business on the Internet will find it rather easy to deploy a customer survey. It can be brief, such as the one in Figure 3.1, or a bit more lengthy, such as one on the Port Authority of New York and New Jersey Web site (http://www.panynj.gov/CommutingTravel/airports/html/ken_survey.php), which asks customers for their thoughts on airport customer service.

There are quite a few survey hosting services available on a pay-per-use basis. KeySurvey (keysurvey.com) and Zoomerang (zoomerang.com) are just two.

If a Web-based or e-mail-based survey is not practical, then you can conduct your survey via either traditional mail or phone. Since traditional mail surveys

Figure 3.1   A brief customer satisfaction survey.

suffer from a comparatively low return rate—1%–3%—it is recommended that you utilize the telephone approach.

The steps in a successful customer survey include the following:

1. Assemble the survey team: The makeup of the survey team depends on the type of survey and the target customer base. If you are going to call external customers, then the best people for the job are to be found in the marketing, sales, or customer service departments. If this is an IT-derived survey and the customer base is composed of internal customers, then project leaders would be the best candidates for the job.

2. Develop the survey. Surveys, which are questionnaires, need to be carefully constructed. There are a number of Web sites that provide the ability to create and deploy online surveys. surveymonkey.com/ is one such site. This Web site also provides a great deal of instruction about the process.

3. Collect customer contact data: Name, company name, address, and phone number are the minimum pieces of information you will need for this process. You might also want to capture sales to this client, years as a client, and other relevant data.

4. Select a random sample of customers for the survey: You can't, and shouldn't, survey all your customers unless your customer base is very small. Random sampling is the most popular approach to reducing the number of questionnaires you will be sending out. Alternatively, you can use the systematic sampling approach. In this method, you include every nth customer in your survey population.

5. Mail a postcard alerting customers about the survey: The postcard or letter should take the following form:

   Dear Mr. Smith,

   According to our records, you purchased our training services. We are interested in knowing how helpful our services were and will be calling next week to ask for your comments. Your responses will help us find out what we are doing well and where we need to improve.

   Our questions will take only a few minutes, so please give us a hand. Thank you in advance for your help.

   Cordially,

   Someone in authority

   His or her title

6. Conduct interviewer training for staff.

7. Call customers and complete a Customer Satisfaction Survey instrument for each person.

8. Send the completed surveys and call sheets to the designated survey analysis team: This might be someone in the marketing department or, in the case of an internal IT survey, the manager designated for this task.
9. Summarize survey results and prepare a report: If you are using Web-based or other automated surveying tools, you will be provided with analytical capabilities. If you are doing this manually, then it is advisable to use Excel or some other spreadsheet package for analysis.

Using Force Field Analysis to Listen to Customers

Nelson (2004) talks about a common problem when dealing with customers: haggling about the product's feature list. She recommends using force field analysis to more quickly and effectively brainstorm and prioritize ideas with a group of customers.

The power of this technique, usable in small as well as in large groups, is in uncovering the driving as well as restraining forces for your products or services. Driving forces can be features, services, a Web site—anything that helps propel customers to success. Restraining forces can be quality issues, complex implementation, convoluted processes, lack of support, unclear procedures—anything that prevents your customers from being successful.

The procedure is simple to follow:

1. State the problem, goal, or situation for which you want feedback.
2. Divide your customer feedback group into smaller groups of 8 to 10. Sit them around a table, and elect a scribe. A facilitator should also be appointed for each table.
3. Each discussion should take no longer than 30 min.
4. The table facilitator goes around the table asking each person to contribute one force. The table scribe records each new force.
5. Go around the table one or two more times until everyone is in agreement that his or her top three forces have been listed.
6. Review the list with the group.
7. Each person gets three votes for his or her top three forces.
8. The scribe will tally the votes for each force.
9. A meeting moderator should go around the room soliciting the top three driving forces from each table.
10. A meeting scribe should document the forces in a spreadsheet projected at the front of the room.
11. Each person in the room gets three votes for his or her top three forces.
12. The meeting scribe should enter the number of votes for each driving force.
13. When done, sort the list by votes to rank them.

The process is then repeated for the restraining forces. A sample list follows:

Driving forces:

Integration across modules	50 votes
Excellent tech support	45 votes
Standards-based technology	38 votes

Restraining forces:

Product quality not always consistent	70 votes
Difficult to migrate from release to release	60 votes
User security is inadequate	30 votes

Force field analysis enables you to listen to your customers, which should lead to increased customer satisfaction and, perhaps, an improvement in the quality and competitiveness of your products or services.

The Customer Economy

MacRae (2002) discards the idea of the new economy in favor of what he refers to as the customer economy. In this model, the customer is firmly in control. The key indicator in this economy is ETDBW, or "easy to do business with." In this economy, the customary metrics of profit and loss and return on assets are much less important than customer loyalty. The new customer-friendly manager focuses on the following metrics:

1. Retention
2. Satisfaction
3. Growth
4. Increases in customer spending
5. Rate of defection or predicted rate of defection

MacRae recommends going to the source to maintain customer loyalty. One way to do this is to create a customer advisory council. This is most effective when the leaders of the organization participate as well.

The customer advisory council can be helpful in answering the following questions:

1. What are the customer's needs?
2. How has the customer's behavior toward the enterprise changed since the customer was acquired?
3. How does the customer use these products, and what products could the customer own?
4. Which channels does the customer use most and for what types of transactions?
5. What channels should each customer be using?
6. What kind of Web-based experience does the customer have?
7. How much does it cost to service each customer's transaction?

The Patricia Seybold Group has developed two customer-focused metrics (Aldrich, 2001). The Quality of Experience (QoE) provided by IT services impacts employee productivity and channel revenue, as well as customer satisfaction. The metric assesses the user's experience with IT in terms of responsiveness and availability. Responsiveness is a measure of how long the user is waiting for information to be displayed. This is usually referred to as response time or download time. QoE expands on this definition to address everyone's experiences with IT: customers', employees', partners', etc.

One year after introducing QoE in 2000, Seybold introduced the Quality of Customer Experience (QCE) metric. This is a set of metrics that allows the organization to assess, monitor, and manage the customer experience. The customer experience, according to this definition, is far broader in scope than just accessing the company Web site. It might also include the following:

1. Phone interactions
2. E-mails
3. Visits to your offices
4. Direct-mail marketing
5. Advertising
6. Employee behavior
7. How the product actually performs
8. How the service is performed
9. How the company is perceived by the community; alternatively, how the department is perceived by the rest of the company

Seybold considers the heart of QCE to be customer outcomes and the resulting moments of truth. A customer measures the success of his or her experience in terms of reaching the desired outcome. Moments of truth are those points in the customer's experience where the quality of your company's execution substantially affects his or her loyalty to your company and its products or services. In other words, moments of truth signify key points in the customer's experience where he or she judges the quality of the experience. Therefore, the heart of QCE assessment is measuring the customer's success in executing the steps necessary within your systems to achieve his or her desired outcomes.

For QCE to work properly, these moments of truth (or key success metrics) have to be determined. They can be different for different people, so the best way to tackle this exercise is to develop a case study or scenario and run through it pinpointing the moments of truth for each stakeholder involved in the scenario. Seybold calls this process Customer Scenario Mapping. Consider the scenario of a company that needs a replacement motor—fast. The maintenance engineer needs to get production back up by 6:00 a.m. the next morning. His moments of truth are as follows: (1) the motor is right for the job, (2) he has all the parts and tools he needs, and (3) he finishes before the shift supervisor shows up to bug him. The maintenance engineer

Table 3.1   Representative QCE Metrics

	Navigation	Performance	Operations	Environment
Customers find and purchase in 15 min	Average number of searches per order line item Average number of support calls per order Average elapsed time to select product and place the order	Average elapsed time to search Average elapsed time to select and purchase Number of steps required to select and purchase Average time to answer incoming phone call	Number of seconds average response time experienced by customers Number of seconds average response time experienced by employees who are interacting with customers Percentage availability of customer-facing applications Number of customers on hold waiting for customer service	Internet performance index

must order his motor through his company's purchasing agent. The purchasing agent has his own moments of truth: (1) find and order a motor in 15 min, delivery confirmed; (2) best choice for motor was in the first page of search results; (3) enough information was offered to enable a decision; (4) order department quickly confirmed delivery without making the purchasing agent wait or repeat himself; and (5) invoicing is correct.

Some of the metrics derived from this mapping include the ones given in Table 3.1.

Conclusion

Without a profound understanding of the target customer, the product or service being marketed will miss its mark. Marketers, particularly those targeting IT customers, must continuously attune themselves to customer needs, wants, and desires. The only way to do this is to stay in touch with customers, using techniques such as surveys, implementation of customer advisory councils, and providing a great customer service. All of this must be bookended by metrics measuring both the presales and the postsales customer experience.

References

Aldrich, S. (2001, October 11). Measuring Moments of Truth. Patricia Seybold Group Report.

MacRae, D. (2002, May 10). Welcome to the "Customer Economy." *Business Week Online.*

Marketing Science Institute (1996). Smart Workplace Practices.

Nelson, B. (2004, May/June). Using force field analysis to listen to customers. *productmarketing.com: The Marketing Journal for High-Tech Product Managers.* Vol. 2, Issue 3.

Treacy, M., and Wiersema, F. (1997). *The Discipline of Market Leaders: Choose Your Customers, Narrow Your Focus, Dominate Your Market.* Boulder, CO: Perseus Books Group.

Chapter 4

The Expanding Market

In Chapter 1, we discussed the micro-environment and the macro-environment. As a result of its business environment, an organization will face many challenges and opportunities, which will ultimately affect the way in which it markets its products and services. The marketing environment is dynamic, as it is impacted by modern trends and environmental factors. In a global environment that operates 24/7/365, marketers must keep constant vigil concerning the changes happening in the world. These include the following:

1. **Globalization**: Globalization used to be the purview of only the largest firms, the major power players of industry. Today, even small businesses, with the right expertise, financial stability, and capabilities, are sharing their knowledge and products with the world. Are your competitors going global and growing their profits? Are you?
2. **Technology**: Do you remember life before e-mail? Or when a basic hard-diskless computer was considered high tech? Technology has fueled the demand for rapid change and created entirely new industries, vocabularies, and jobs as a result. Customers are using technology to find new vendors and services. Will they be able to find your organization?
3. **Diversity**: Our workplaces, neighborhoods, and customer bases are becoming more and more diverse; with that, a whole host of new challenges and opportunities result. When these people arrive, they don't simply leave their languages and cultures behind. They bring them along, adding a new dimension of flavor—and complexity—to the marketing landscape. As managers, we must learn not only how to manage in such a culturally diverse environment, but also how to serve customers who are different from ourselves. Of course, ethnic and cultural diversity is just the tip of the iceberg. We also

have to consider diversity among ages, gender, religious/ethnic beliefs, as well as physical abilities. How can we best serve customers who are different from ourselves?

4. **Rapid change and innovation**: Think about how fast everything is changing these days. Fax machines and FedEx used to be the only high-tech ways to exchange information. Advancements in a whole host of areas, ranging from biotechnology to space, have revolutionized our world—and it keeps on changing. How does the rapid pace of change affect your business and your customers?

Some people feel that marketing contributes to the development of monopolies, or, at the very least, monopolistic competition. They contend that marketing leads to higher prices, restricted output, and reductions in national income and employment. However, as firms succeed, success attracts competition and encourages innovation. An example of this enhanced form of innovation is the SmartPad by Seiko. It captures handwritten notes and drawings and puts them into a personal digital assistant (PDA). Seiko was not first on the market with PDAs. They entered the fray long after John Sculley of Apple invented the term PDA to refer to the Apple Newton. Products such as the SmartPad increase consumer choice, attract competition, and help grow the economy.

Advertising is the most often criticized micro-marketing activity. But what about the macro-marketing view of advertising? Is advertising a waste of resources? In relation to the volume of products sold, advertising is an efficient way to communicate product-benefit information. This efficiency contributes to economies of scale in production, distribution, and sales. Does marketing make people buy things they don't need?

Critics say that marketing creates needs for products of little social value. But most consumers are not puppets; people are not as suggestible as this criticism suggests. Competition offers consumers different alternatives, and consumers' needs and wants do indeed change.

If consumers do not want change, they can usually find plenty of need satisfaction from other, older products, but most people want better need satisfaction than they already have. Marketers work to improve the overall quality of life by making products that lead to higher levels of need fulfillment.

The biggest criticism of marketing is the overall perception that most companies will never be truly socially responsible, whatever ethical noises they make, if their prime motive is pushing products (Mitchell, 2003). Mitchell makes a good point, as there is increasing consumer interest in a wide variety of "ethical" issues, such as the environment, human rights, and the potential harmful effects of products (e.g., alcohol, fast food). As if to illustrate this point, in 2002 a major lawsuit was filed against McDonalds, Burger King, KFC, and Wendy's (http://www.foxnews.com/story/0,2933,58652,00.html). The lead plaintiff, an overweight man, contended that the four defendants were irresponsible and deceptive in their advertisements about the nutritional value of their food. The plaintiff, who ate at these fast-food restaurants four or five times a week, blamed them for his myriad problems, including obesity, diabetes, and two heart attacks. His lawyer further claimed that the fast-food giants create an addiction in their consumers, particularly among the poor and young. Ultimately this lawsuit was lost, but not before it generated much adverse publicity for the defendants.

Global Markets and International Marketing

Have you recently visited the Home and Garden department of your neighborhood supercenter? If so, did you notice that nearly all of the patio furniture was imported from China? But if you were to visit China or Taiwan, you would find American-made products such as home appliances, automobiles, televisions, and computers. Today, more than 300 U.S. companies are operating in China. Similarly, companies from Europe, Latin America, Australia, the Middle East, Asia, and Africa are exporting to or importing from China. This interaction is making China the world's fastest-growing economy, and the ideal destination for foreign direct investment (FDI). Scores of companies from around the globe are opening factories in low-wage China and exporting low-priced, high-quality goods to consumers everywhere. This is causing severe, burgeoning, and intractable balance of payments deficits for most of China's trading partners.

This is a growing trend, not only among the United States, China, and Taiwan, but also among nations across the globe. Today, an unprecedented number of countries, both developed and developing, are entering the global trading system and producing goods and services in huge quantities for an ever-increasing consumer base on every continent. This phenomenon is referred to as globalization. One of the by-products of globalization is the concept of "offshoring." This is the movement of jobs (e.g., programming, editing) to lower-cost locations, such as India and China. Information technology has been particularly affected by this trend. Help desk, quality assurance, and lower-end programming jobs have been draining away from the United States, Europe, and Israel for several years. Most recently, companies such as Microsoft and IBM have located research centers in lower-cost locations such as China and the Czech Republic. Therefore, it is just a matter of time before the more engineering-oriented technology jobs are also offshored. The trend toward offshoring has a negative effect on the local economy as well as on the majors students select when attending college, with fewer students opting for technology-related majors (e.g., engineering, computer science). Some critics have forecast a coming scarcity of talent, leading to a decline in scientific competitiveness.

Thanks to recent advances in technology (e.g., computers, Internet, telecommunications), the march toward a single "global marketplace" continues at an accelerated pace. This march is supported and sustained by new, efficient modes of transportation and trade liberalization policies that are espoused by the World

Trade Organization and various regional organizations, as well as the World Bank and the International Monetary Fund. As multinational firms operate in an increasingly borderless environment, they encounter numerous challenges, including cultural differences.

To compete aggressively, effectively, and successfully in today's global marketplace, global companies need CIOs and other tech managers with the requisite skills to work in multicultural environments and manage a diverse workforce. In general, the culture of a society comprises the shared values, behaviors, beliefs, values, goals, and attitudes learned from prior generations, imposed on present generations, and passed on to future generations. Elements of culture include religion, language, social structures, education, political, and economic systems. These elements of culture distinguish one group of people from another. Hence, being aware of and becoming sensitive to these elements enables and empowers global managers to analyze global business trends in order to develop and implement strategic plans. For example, a manager would perform the following: set objectives, quantify goals, formulate strategies, devise tactical plans, create contingency plans, and implement them in ways that will maximize value for the organization's various stakeholders. Furthermore, global managers must be cognizant of and guide against the dangers of ethnocentric behavior, which is defined as the belief in the superiority of one's own ethnicity or culture, usually leading to contempt and disrespect for other cultures. This is a clear recipe for failure.

Ghana is seen by many as the gateway to the resource-rich Economic Community of West African States (ECOWAS), which comprises 16 countries with a combined population of nearly 230 million. The community is endowed with vast quantities of natural resources, including gold, diamonds, iron ore, cocoa, coffee beans, bauxite, uranium, and petroleum. In order to develop these resources, most global companies must interact with Ghana because it has developed a Center for Global Investment with incentives, rules, and regulations that are transparent and enforceable. It has developed an infrastructure that supports global business operations, including Internet services, banking systems, improved transportation services, and dependable and affordable utilities, just to name a few.

In spite of the positive advances, the major challenge was the lack of adequate accommodation to meet the growing demand by foreign investors. As a possible solution, the Ghanaian government contemplated a joint venture with Sweden to build a 350-bed, four-star beachfront hotel in the capital city of Accra. As representatives from both sides negotiated the terms of the joint venture, major cultural differences surfaced that derailed the project. For example, the Swedish partners wanted majority ownership in the venture, which the Ghanaians rejected on the grounds of neocolonialism. The Swedish partners wanted their staffing policies to be ethnocentric, but the Ghanaians viewed this as an insult to their culture. They wanted Ghanaian employees to be trained and promoted to managerial positions within a determined time frame. The Swedish partners wanted nearly all of the menu items to reflect Swedish cuisine, while the Ghanaians wanted to serve and showcase their local/traditional foods to foreign visitors. Compensation, work hours, holidays, training, development, and planned activities at the hotel all became bones of contention that could not be resolved. Thus, the project was abandoned. The failure of this joint venture raises questions. Why didn't the Swedish partners study Ghanaian culture? If they had, they would have found that majority ownership is the preferred approach and that ethnocentrism is a cultural taboo.

Indeed, the process of globalization has heightened expectations regarding the contributions of companies to environmental and social progress (Cattaui, 2000). Global companies, in effect, are held to a higher standard because most consider that they are the prime movers in making globalization happen. Cattaui, the secretary-general of the International Chamber of Commerce, suggests that global companies would do well to do the following:

1. Adhere to and support a broad variety of business guidelines, such as the OECD Guidelines for Multinational Enterprises, the ICU's Rules of Conduct on Extortion and Bribery in International Business Transactions, and the various OCC marketing and advertising codes.
2. Develop and implement business principles that serve to bridge cultural diversity within companies and enhance awareness of societal values and concerns.
3. Develop and implement internal guidelines on ethics and integrity.
4. Tailor business principles to the different countries in which they operate. A "one size fits all" approach does not usually work.

Marshall McLuhan, considered to be the godfather of modern advertising, said that "the medium is the massage," which is a play on the phrase mass age. Most people translate McLuhan's comment to "the medium is the message." This is quite true. However, in the context of globalization, one can also say that the process is also the message.

An important component of the marketing process is to alter the product or message to suit a specific consumer group. It is not uncommon in the United States to offer different products in different geographic regions. For example, the Campbell Soup Company sells hot and spicy soups in the southwestern United States, where these types of foods are big sellers, and not in the northeast. It is even more important to consider international differences. Reasons for product alteration for international markets include the following:

1. **Legal reasons:** Pharmaceuticals and foods are subject to regulations concerning purity, testing, and labeling. Automobiles must conform to safety and pollution standards. These all vary by country. For example, the United States has stricter pollution standards than European countries, but Europe imposes stricter roof-strength standards than the United States. Some countries prohibit certain types of containers; for example, Denmark bans aluminum cans. Marketing managers must also watch for indirect legal

requirements that might affect product content or demand. It is not unusual to have restrictions on the importation of certain materials or components, which forces the company to construct the product using local substitutes, which might alter the final result. Legal requirements, such as high taxes on certain types of automobiles, might also impact a company's product mix in a particular locale.

2. **Cultural reasons:** Religious differences limit the standardization of products on a global basis. For example, fast-food franchises do not sell pork products in Islamic countries and emphasize vegetarian food in India. Toyota was initially unsuccessful in selling pickup trucks in the United States until it redesigned its interior with enough headroom for drivers to wear ten-gallon cowboy hats.

3. **Ethical reasons:** It has been said that half of all four-year-old children do not know their own name, but two thirds of three-year-olds can recognize McDonald's golden arches (Freedland, 2005). McDonald's has been criticized for turning young people into "avaricious consumers." McDonald's has heeded the resulting outcry and has fine-tuned its offerings to healthier fare (along with the less-than-healthy fare).

4. **Economic reasons:** If consumers in foreign countries lack sufficient income, they may not be able to purchase the product the company is selling. Mattel had to design a cheaper version of its popular Barbie doll for just this reason. Income distribution may also play a role. Whirlpool found this out when it had to buy obsolete washing machines from Korea to sell in countries where people had household servants. It seems they were not interested in the labor-saving capabilities of the Whirlpool products (Dawar and Chattopadhyay, 2000).

Price and product are not the only things that might have to be altered when going global. Promotion and brand names also need to be reviewed. General Motors thought that its Nova model could be called the same in Latin America because the name means "star" in Spanish. However, people started pronouncing it as "no va," which is Spanish for "it does not go." Coca-Cola tries to use global branding wherever possible. However, the word *diet* in "Diet Coke" has connotations of illness in Germany and Italy. Diet Coke has been rebranded "Coca-Cola Light" in many countries outside of the United States, although it is also known as "Coca-Cola diet" in the United Kingdom and Israel. The most amusing branding snafu was in Thailand, where Big Boy, a restaurant chain, put its usual statue (a boy with checkered overalls and cowlick curl) outside its restaurant. Many Thais placed offerings at his feet because they thought it was a Buddha (Frank, 2000).

Strategic Dimensions of Technology

Technology has become pervasive throughout the international marketplace. Some American (e.g., Microsoft, Sun), European (e.g., Ericsson, Siemens, Nokia), and

Asian companies (e.g., Sony, Samsung) are manufacturing and marketing products and services to all four corners of the globe. High-tech products are still considered consumer products. However, they do have some distinctive characteristics (Viardot, 2004):

1. Incorporation of sophisticated technology
2. A high rate of development and improvement
3. A high innovation value for the market

Similar to any company, marketing a high-tech company is part of the overall strategic framework that we've already discussed. It must fit within the overall direction and mission of the company, as well as build on its resources and key competencies. In this case, chief among these competencies is technology.

High-tech companies must take care not to define their missions in terms of their products ("we are a software company"). Instead, they must focus on the market and its customers, because products will come and go but the needs of customers will continue to remain unsatisfied indefinitely. For example, a company's mission should not be to manufacture computers but to "offer the possibility of faster calculations" or "solving customers' needs in data processing."

In 2000, Nokia's strategy was to take a leadership role in creating the mobile information society by combining mobility and the Internet (http://press.nokia.com/PR/200010/793202_5.html). Even more interesting is that Sony's president thinks Sony's mission is to make their products obsolete; otherwise, somebody else will do it.

Technology companies have several choices in their strategic positioning:

1. Be a "first mover." In other words, be the first to do something, using the "early bird catches the worm" principle. Apple's iPod provides an excellent example of this strategy. Apple's iPhone is an even better example.
2. Use the less risky strategy of "innovative imitator." If a firm decides it needs to enter a market after that market has become established (in this case, the PC was firmly entrenched in the marketplace), its managers should define their technology strategy by carefully assessing whether a dominant architectural design has yet emerged. If it has, the firm's technology strategy at entry ought not be to offer innovative architectural concepts in its initial products (Christensen, Suarez, and Utterback, 1998). Hence, Dell computer uses standard components in its computer designs.
3. Project a high-tech image to impress firms.

Because of the quick evolution of technology, the time frames for competitive positioning are much narrower than for nontech firms. The CEO of Alcatel, the giant European telecommunications equipment maker, quipped that it was much easier to understand demand when he was in the oil business. That's not always possible in the tech industry. Because of this, technology firms have to spend more time strategizing than their nontech counterparts. In Chapter 6 and beyond, we will delve into the subjects of product strategy, research and development, and innovation, where we'll concentrate more fully on the product life cycle. In this chapter, it's sufficient just to focus on the strategic elements of the marketing environment for high-tech products. These include the following (Viardot, 2004):

1. Provide an open architecture: Open architecture rather than proprietary architectures will be the future engine for success. Salesforce.com's AppExchange (http://www.salesforce.com/appexchange/) was built on an open architecture to allow other vendors to add on applications, with the express goal of solidifying its lead in the hosted applications market.
2. Be compatible, to generate increasing returns: High-tech solutions are only valuable if there are complementary solutions available (i.e., add-on applications, plug-ins). Increasing returns is why the cellular industry caught on more quickly in Europe than in the United States. In Europe, more than 900 telecommunications vendors and operators backed only one technology (GSM). In the United States, there were four competing technologies.
3. Minimize production costs: The first product by Netscape was a browser based on free resources (Mosaic). The combination of browser technology, a wealth of content, and the marketing strategy of giving the product away for free enabled Netscape to enter the market and secure first-mover and dominant positioning.
4. Go global: Increasing returns on investment follow firms that penetrate one large geographical market after another. SAP, a German company, did just this as it dominated the ERP space. Kazaa, the file-sharing company, has a completely global infrastructure. It is registered in the South Pacific island nation of Vanuatu. Its domain is registered in Australia, the servers are in Denmark, and the software is in Estonia.
5. Invest more than your competitors: One of the reasons for Intel's continuing success is that it has invested in more than 1,000 information technology companies worldwide. Microsoft has an extensive partnership program (https://partner.microsoft.com/global/program/), as shown in Figure 4.1, that runs the gamut from very large firms to small, independent software vendors.
6. Create a supportive network: High-tech firms that work together often achieve higher levels of success than firms that work alone. Witness the success of Wintel, the alliance between Microsoft and Intel.

Linux is a good example of many of these principles. It is being pushed by a wide variety of firms, such as IBM, and has been adopted by many enthusiasts, including managers in some of the world's largest firms. According to market researcher IDC, Linux is expected to register a 26% compound annual growth rate over five

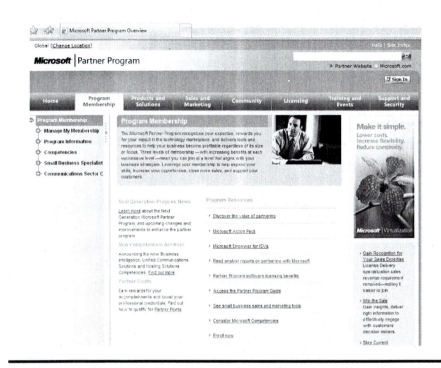

Figure 4.1   Microsoft's partner program.

years. Why has Linux been so successful? It has an open architecture, making it compatible to everything from a mainframe to a cell phone. It comes with almost no production cost. It can be downloaded for free from the Internet.

Whether your firm is high tech or not, managing technology as a core competence is critical. Management must protect and leverage the technology it creates or uses. If yours is a high-tech firm, then these assets must be protected through trademarks and patents, as is true in many other industries (e.g., pharmaceuticals). Marketers are charged with developing new business activities from these very valuable assets. These include the following (Viardot, 2004):

1. **Relabeling:** This is the purchase of finished products or components that are sold under the company's brand name. For example, Dell relabeled Network Appliance's high-end storage servers and sold them under its own brand name.

2. **Licensing:** Yahoo used Web search technology developed and licensed by Google up to the time that it was able to develop its own technology.

3. **Alliances:** These involve two or more parties agreeing to change how they do things for a common purpose. The Airbus was developed using this strategy. The nose was developed by Aerospatiale, the body by MBB, the wings by British Aerospace, and the tail by CASA, with the final assembly completed

by Aerospatiale (http://www.airbus.com/en/corporate/people/company_evolution/). In the 1970s, when the Russian mainframe was a copy of the IBM/360 computer, the different components (e.g., CPU, memory disks, printers) were each produced in a different Eastern Bloc country. The same was true of other industrial products, which nowadays leaves the factories that produced only a part of the whole product deserted and nonoperative.

4. **Joint ventures:** Rather than merge, Dell prefers joint ventures with other companies to expand into new markets. For example, it has a joint venture with Lexmark for printers, EMC Corp. for storage, and Electronic Data Systems for systems integration.

5. **Acquisition:** To boost its product offerings and take an even greater control of the market, Microsoft often buys smaller rivals. It bought Great Plains in 2001. Hewlett-Packard followed the same strategy when it acquired Compaq in 2002. It should be noted that Compaq had previously acquired Digital Equipment Corporation, one of the original computer manufacturers.

Conclusion

In this chapter, we addressed the expanding marketplace. A standardized approach to marketing leads to optimum uniformity in products and programs in the various countries in which sales occur. While this approach minimizes expenses, most companies make changes to fit a specific country's needs to satisfy consumer tastes and increase sales volume. Major problems for standardizing advertising and branding in different countries are translation and legality. The marketing plan must account for the specifics of marketing in the global arena.

The marketing plan must also address growth. This chapter discussed various strategies to achieve this end, including joint ventures, marketing and acquisition, etc., using the high-tech market as the basis of our discussions. The following brief case study draws these two topics together—global market expansion and high-tech marketplace—and demonstrates the power of the ever-expanding marketplace.

Cisco is the world's largest supplier of data networking equipment. It supports sales in over 75 countries and has technical centers in Australia, Belgium, Canada, India, and the United States. International sales accounts for 42% of its revenue. Cisco uses partnerships as an important component of its growth strategy, along with internal development and acquisitions. Cisco's worldwide alliances assist it in achieving its many objectives by enabling the company to meet customer needs that fall outside its area of core competencies. For example, Cisco established a joint venture with the Singaporean company ePic. This joint venture enables the two to use their complementary technology for an Internet video-monitoring service. Alliances are an important aspect of Cisco's international strategy as well. It uses these partnerships to extend its ability to service customers in more markets around the world. This strategy has permitted Cisco to boost its competitiveness through innovative products, strong distribution, and a global service network (Daniels, Radebaugh, and Sullivan, 2004).

References

Cattaui, M. L. (2000). Responsible business conduct in a global economy. Organization for Economic Cooperation and Development. *OECD Observer*, vol. 221/222, pp. 18–20.

Christensen, C. M., Suarez, F. F., and Utterback, J. M. (1998). Strategies for survival in fast-changing industries. *Management Science*, vol. 44, no. 12.

Daniels, J. D., Radebaugh, L. H., and Sullivan, D. P. (2004). *International Business*. Upper Saddle River, NJ: Pearson Prentice Hall.

Dawar, N., and Chattopadhyay, A. (2000). The new language of emerging markets. *Financial Times*, November 11.

Frank, R. (2000). Big Boy's adventures in Thailand. *Wall Street Journal*, April 12.

Freedland, J. (2005). Half of all children aged four don't know their own name, but two thirds of three-year-olds can recognise the McDonald's golden arches. *Guardian*, October.

Mitchell, A. (2003). Closing the gap between the ethical and profitable. *Marketing Week*, vol. 32, October 16.

Viardot, E. (2004). *Successful Marketing Strategy for High-Tech Firms*. London: Artech House.

Chapter 5

Market Research

Marketing research involves collecting and analyzing information and using it to make marketing decisions. Marketing research helps identify the need for a product, who needs it, and what features the product should have to meet those needs. Marketing research is also useful in other marketing tasks, for example, identifying the consumer and the appropriate advertising channel (e.g., television commercial, direct mail, salesperson).

The Marketing Research Process

The marketing research process is akin to the five-step application of the scientific method, as shown in Figure 5.1 (Perreault and McCarthy, 2005):

Step 1 is defining the problem: The manager and the researcher determine the key decision issues requiring information.

Step 2 is analyzing the situation: A study of information that is available in the problem area.

Step 3 is getting problem-specific data: The collection of data that is customized to the decision maker's unique needs.

Step 4 is interpreting the data: The process of deciding what it all means; it is the transformation of raw data into useful information.

Step 5 is solving the problem: The delivery of recommendations to the marketing manager, who is ultimately responsible for implementing the recommendations.

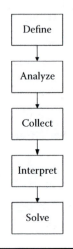

Figure 5.1 The marketing research process.

Step 1: Defining the Problem

Finding the right problem almost solves the problem, in many cases. For example, the problem might involve determining who would buy a new product, or defining the features of that product, or trying to increase sales of an existing product. Marketing research is required to investigate questions about the product's function and appearance, how it is distributed, who is targeted to buy it, and how it's priced. The first step also involves defining the research objective and the type of research that will be performed (i.e., exploratory, descriptive, or casual).

Steps 2 and 3: Analyzing the Situation and Getting Problem-Specific Data

Secondary data is information that has already been collected or published. It is different from **primary data**, which is new information specifically collected to solve a current problem. In other words, secondary data is information that has already been gathered for some other purpose, but which might be useful to the researcher. Primary data is custom-designed to the researcher's immediate need. Examples of secondary data sources from inside the company are financial information from the accounting department, or reports from the field sales force. Information from outside the company might include government information, trade association studies, or information available in magazine or journal articles.

There are two categories of data that can be collected during research: qualitative and quantitative. These categories can be used together or independently, depending on the type of problem and the resources available to conduct the research.

Qualitative research aims for in-depth, detailed responses—not yes or no answers. Asking people questions in an open-ended fashion allows them to elaborate on their answers. So, the main advantage of qualitative questioning is the depth of responses obtained. It tends to work best in research situations that require the generation of a lot of ideas as opposed to firm conclusions. A common qualitative research tactic is the **focus group interview**, which involves interviewing a small group of people in an informal setting. A facilitator leads the discussion. He or she asks open-ended questions on very specific topics that have been structured to take advantage of group dynamics. It is common practice in the technology industry to gather a list of managers, segment the list into a particular geographic area, and then invite a small number (10 or so) to a session. The lure is often a small honorarium and dinner or lunch. Focus groups usually are held in specialized conference rooms where one wall is mirrored. Behind the mirror, however, are observers, one of whom might be filming the session. The focus group members are asked very specific questions, which have been scripted well in advance. Many researchers use focus groups as preparation for more formal quantitative research utilizing a larger, scientifically selected group of respondents.

Quantitative research is the numerical representation of information obtained from research. The results are summarized in numbers, such as percentages, averages, or other statistics. Usually, quantitative research incorporates standardized data collection forms, such as survey questionnaires, which provide fixed responses to questions instead of the open-ended questions typical of many types of qualitative studies.

Step 4: Interpreting the Data

The first question a marketing researcher must answer is, "Is your sample really representative of the population?" A sample is a smaller group selected to represent the larger group (population) of customers. The key here is to use a variety of techniques, including statistical tools, to ensure that the sample selected represents the larger population and to estimate the likelihood that it does not. An interesting discussion that demonstrates the differences between the two approaches can be found at http://www.socialresearchmethods.net/kb/sampnon.htm and http://psychology.ucdavis.edu/rainbow/html/fact_sample.html.

Step 5: Solving the Problem

The marketer should apply the research results to create and fine-tune the marketing strategy planning process.

Target Markets: Segmentation and Evaluation

Segmentation research assists organizations in identifying the most lucrative opportunities. It's used to narrow down a broad set of opportunities to a specific target consumer market and market strategy. Market segmentation is useful in deciding the way in which a marketer will promote the organization's product or service.

Segment marketing concentrates on a large identifiable group within a market, with the following attributes: similar wants, purchasing power, geographic location, buying attitudes, and buying habits. For example, working adults seeking to continue their graduate education may be considered a segment of the graduate education market. There are several ways to segment a consumer market into target markets. Here are some examples:

- **Niche marketing** is more narrowly defined. It's a small market, a subset of a segment. To continue with our previous example, there may be adults who want to go to graduate school but can't get to a physical campus on a regular basis. This means that our working adult graduate segment can be niched into smaller segments: those preferring online classes and those able to attend ground campuses.
- **Local marketing** is tailored to meet the unique needs of a local area (e.g., city, neighborhood, etc.). To continue with our example, some universities might offer more technology-based courses in countries such as Ireland, because of the concentration of technology firms there.
- **Individual marketing** is also known as one-to-one marketing. However, extreme personalization is often too costly and time consuming. Mass customization, which is the ability to prepare individually designed products and communications on a mass basis, solves the time and cost problems of one-to-one marketing. For example, a university might send customized information packets to potential candidates that include preprinted information, but will only send material in which the student has expressed interest.

Each segment "slices" the market in a particular way. The more times you apply a segmentation filter, the more focused your segmentation. The more focused your efforts, the more likely your marketing message and product development will be relevant to your target market. Although segmentation is time consuming, because it requires much research, such preparatory activities are less expensive than creating broad-based marketing programs (i.e., marketing campaigns that go out to the entire population whether the product is relevant to them or not).

There are many ways to segment the population into consumer markets, as shown in Table 5.1 (Schiffman and Kanuk, 2000).

In 1986 Reebok discovered that many consumers who bought running shoes were not athletes. Instead, they bought the shoes for comfort and style. Reebok then developed a marketing plan that directly targeted this segment of the market (Hisrich, Peters, and Shepherd, 2005).

So, as you can see, consumer buying behavior is dependent on many factors. In the previous example, the consumers were buying Reeboks for personal reasons

Table 5.1   Segmentation "Slices"

Segmentation Basis	Definition and Examples
Geographic	The market is divided by location. The theory is that people who live in the same area share similar needs. Examples: region (Africa), city or metro (250,000–500,000 people), density (urban).
Demographic	The vital measurable statistics of a population. Demographics help locate a target market. Examples: age (25–54), sex (F/M), marital status (single), income (50,000 euro), education (college), and occupation (programmer).
Psychological	The inner, intrinsic qualities of the individual consumer. Examples: needs-motivation (shelter, safety), personality (extrovert), perception (low-risk), learning involvement (low-involvement), and attitudes (positive attitude).
Sociocultural	Sociocultural variables divide the market based on stage of family life cycle, social class, etc. Examples: culture (Asian), religion (Hindu), subculture ([American] Indian), social class (upper, middle), and family life cycles (singles, empty nesters).
Psychographic	Also referred to as lifestyle data; includes a composite of consumers' measured activities, interests, and opinions. Consumers respond to a large number of statements that measure activities, such as how they spend their time, what they are interested in, and how they feel about a variety of events. Examples: economy minded, status seekers, outdoor enthusiasts.
Use-related	Categorizes consumers in terms of products/services or brand usage characteristics. Examples: user rate (heavy users, nonusers), brand loyalty (some, none, strong).
Use-situation	Sometimes the occasion or situation determines what consumers will purchase. Examples: time (leisure, work), objective (personal, gift), location (home, work).

Continued

Table 5.1   Segmentation "Slices" (*Continued*)

Segmentation Basis	Definition and Examples
Benefit	Marketers strive to identify the one most important benefit of their product or service that will be most meaningful to consumers. Examples: convenience, social acceptance, long lasting, value for the money.

(comfort and style). There are four factors that are major influencers of consumer buying behavior: cultural, social, personal, and psychological, which are supersets of the segmentation slices shown in Table 5.1.

Understanding consumer behavior is complicated. Understanding consumer behavior across international borders is exponentially more complicated. Marketers need to account for cultural differences within each segment "slice." Remington is a good example. Remington is an American company that makes shavers. For the Japanese market it makes smaller shavers to fit more comfortably into the smaller hands of Japanese consumers. For the British market, where bathrooms have fewer electrical outlets, Remington emphasizes battery-operated shavers.

In the spring of 2005, Reebok, the sneaker manufacturer, offered the richest endorsement deal in hockey history to Canadian teenage hockey phenomenon Sidney Crosby, who is to become the center of Reebok's international marketing campaign—an international sports star for an international consumer group (Thompson, 2005).

Competitive Analysis

Lincoln Financial Group (www.lfg.com) is a 100-year-old company with $119 billion in consolidated assets under management. Competitive analysis is a major component of Lincoln's planning process. Using the information entered by salespeople in the field, Lincoln builds a profile of each competitor's strengths and weaknesses. This is done by identifying the factors that are considered critical for each line of business, and then ranking each competitor's capabilities in that area. At the same time, the same criteria are used to rank Lincoln's own capabilities in these same areas. Using a side-by-side comparison of a competitor versus itself, Lincoln can evaluate whether or not it is weak in the critical factors needed for success in any particular product line. If a perceived weakness is noted, Lincoln formulates a plan to strengthen the company in that particular area. At the same time, the marketing plan is modified to focus on the key strengths while minimizing the weaknesses. One of Lincoln's greatest strengths is the ability to track and process competitor data and then relate it to its own data, further strengthening its own product and marketing plans. Monitoring the moves of a competitor is called competitive analysis.

Competitive analysis helps organizations devise their strategic plans and provide insight into how to craft their performance indicators and marketing plans. One useful technique is to use the company's expert business managers to analyze one competitor at a time to identify strategies and predict future moves (Keyes, 2006, 1992).

Let's review the needed steps for a fictitious company.

Step 1: Preliminary meeting. Once the competitor is chosen, a preliminary meeting is scheduled. It should be attended by all senior managers who might have information or insights to contribute concerning this competitor. This includes the chief executive officer as well as the general manager and managers from sales, marketing, finance, and manufacturing. Attendance of a broader range of staff is important for this technique, since it serves to provide access to many diverse sources of information. This permits the merger of external information sources— as well as internal sources—collected by the organization, such as documents, observations, and personal experiences.

At this meeting, it is agreed that all attendees will spend a specified amount of time collecting more recent information about the competitor. A second meeting is scheduled to review this later information.

Step 2: Information meeting. At this meeting, each attendee will receive an allotment of time to present his or her information to the group.

The group will then perform an analysis of relative strengths/weaknesses. This will be done for all areas of interest uncovered by the information obtained by the group. The analysis will seek to draw conclusions about two criteria. First, is a competitor stronger or weaker than your company? Second, does the area in question have the potential to affect customer behavior?

Unless the area meets both of these criteria, it should not be pursued further either in analysis or discussion. Since managers do not always agree on what areas to include or exclude, it is frequently necessary to appoint a moderator who is not part of the group.

Step 3: Cost analysis. At this point, with areas of concern isolated, it is necessary to perform a comparative cost analysis. The first step here is to prepare a breakdown of costs for each product. This includes labor, manufacturing, cost of goods, distribution, sales, and administration, as well as other relevant items of interest.

At this point, compare the competitor's cost for each of these factors according to the following scale:

Significantly higher
Slightly higher
Slightly lower
Significantly lower

Now, translate these subjective ratings to something a bit more tangible, such as slightly higher being equivalent to 15%. By weighting each of these factors on the basis of its relative contribution to the total product cost, it is now possible to calculate the competitor's total costs.

Step 4: Competitor motivation. This is perhaps the most intangible of the steps. The group must now attempt to analyze its competitor's motivation by determining how the competitor measures success as well as what its objectives and strategies are.

During the research phase, the senior manager and his or her staff gathered considerable information on this topic. By using online databases and Web sites, it is possible to collect information about self-promotions, annual reports, press releases, and the like. In addition, information from former employees, the sales force, investment analysts, suppliers, and mutual clients is extremely useful and broadens the picture.

Based on the senior manager's understanding of the business, the competitor's motivation can be deduced. Motivation can often be deduced by observing how the competitor measures itself. Annual reports are good sources for this information. For example, a competitor that wants to reap the benefits of investment in a particular industry will most likely measure success in terms of return on investment.

Step 5: Total picture. By reviewing information on the competitor's strengths and weaknesses, relative cost structure, and goals and strategies, a total picture of the firm can be created.

Using this information, the group should be able to use individual insights into the process of running a business in a similar industry to determine the competitor's likely next moves. For example, analysis shows that a competitor is stronger in direct sales, has a cost advantage in labor, and is focused on growing from a regional to national firm. The group would draw the conclusion that the competitor will attempt to assemble a direct sales effort nationwide, while positioning itself on the basis of low price.

You can also use a variation of this approach for dealing with the situation in which an outsider enters the marketplace. Here, the aforementioned strategy obviously wouldn't work against these "phantom" competitors.

Using the same group of people gathered to analyze competitor strategy, this exercise requests that the group look at the market in the way an objective third party would. The task is to design a fictitious company that would be able to successfully penetrate the market.

Compare this fictitious company with the competitor firms in the industry to see if any of the traditional competitors can easily adopt this approach. Phantom analysis uncovers a strategy that traditional competitors might easily adopt as a preemptive move. When analysis reveals that an outsider could penetrate the industry by following this strategy, the company should attempt to create additional barriers to entry. This might include forming an alliance with an outside company to pursue the phantom strategy itself.

Hruby's (1989) missing piece analysis also attempts to anticipate competitor moves, but it does this by identifying key weaknesses in the competitor. By concentrating on the competitor's weaknesses, the great wealth of information on that competitor can be turned into usable, action-oriented intelligence.

The methodology for performing Hruby's missing piece analysis is to analyze the strengths and weaknesses of the competitor in six areas. In each of these areas, the competitor is compared to the company performing the analysis:

1. **Product**. Compare the strength of the competitor's product from a consumer point of view.
2. **Manufacturing**. Compare capabilities, cost, and capacity.
3. **Sales and marketing**. How well does the competitor sell a product? Compare positioning, advertising, sales force, and so on.
4. **Finance**. Compare financial resources needed to achieve performance. How strong are these relative to requirements for launching a strong competitive thrust?
5. **Management**. How effective, aggressive, and qualified are the competitor's managers?
6. **Corporate culture**. Examine values and history to determine whether the competitor is likely to enter or to attempt to dominate a market.

The goal of this exercise is to identify weaknesses in each of these areas, as well as to see whether any one of these weaknesses stands out as a major vulnerability. According to Hruby, most companies have a key weakness—or missing piece—that can be exploited.

Performing this technique requires that the competitor be rated in each of the six areas listed. Ratings are done on a scale of 1 to 5, with 1 being very weak, 2 weak/uncompetitive, 3 adequate/average, 4 very strong/competitive, and 5 excellent/superior.

Hruby recommends summarizing the scores in a competitive strengths matrix, as shown in Table 5.2. This matrix lists the names of the competitors down the left-hand side and the competitive areas of interest across the top. Scores are entered into the appropriate cells. The worst score for each competitor should be highlighted. This is their weakest point and should be monitored accordingly.

In our example, Company A and Company B are both weak in the finance area. This means that they do not have enough strength to launch a major advertising campaign to bolster a new product. What this means is that if the company performing this analysis is ready, willing, and able to spend a lot of money, a new product launch would most probably be successful.

Company C scored a 1 in the product category. This means that its product is not as good as that of the company performing the analysis. In this case, an advertising campaign emphasizing product differences would serve to grab some market share from Company C.

Table 5.2 Competitive Strengths Matrix

Competitor		Competitive Areas				
	Area 1: Product	*Area 2: Manufacturing*	*Area 3: Sales and Marketing*	*Area 4: Finance*	*Area 5: Management*	*Area 6: Corporate Culture*
Company A	5	3	4	2	4	3
Company B	4	4	3	2	3	4
Company C	1	3	3	5	2	3
Company D	4	4	4	4	5	4

Note: Key: 1 = weak to 5 = excellent.

Company D, on the other hand, scored strongly in all matrix areas. Given a strong product and an aggressive management team, this company is likely to make an aggressive move, perhaps a new product launch or major advertising for an existing product. It might even reduce costs. Company D certainly bears watching.

Company C, on the other hand, has a weak product but a good financial position. It just might launch a new product. However, its weak management structure might delay any product launch.

In summary, upon analysis of the competitive strengths matrix, one would deduce that a combination of strong financial position and competent management is a mix that indicates a strong likelihood of aggressive action on the part of the competitor. By using this analysis of information obtained from various sources, it is quite possible to keep tabs on what the competition is up to as well as provide a wealth of performance indicators and measures that could be useful for performance management.

Conclusion

In this chapter we addressed marketing research, market segmentation, consumer buying behavior, and competitor analysis. All of these are interrelated topics that are required activities if the organization is to compete effectively in the market.

The Toyota Prius (http://www.toyota-europe.com/cars/new_cars/prius/index.asp) is currently a very hot product, appealing to a growing environmentally conscious consumer group, and those interested in the cost savings a hybrid engine can offer. The Segway Human Transporter (http://www.segway.com/) is also an environment-friendly mode of transportation. So, the marketing research efforts that would have gone into each product's development were probably similar, right? The answer would be no. The Prius is a car, which has an established market and well-understood consumer buying patterns. On the other hand, the Segway is so new a concept that it has no established market and completely unknown consumer appeal. It is not likely that a consumer looking for environment-friendly transportation options would consider the Prius and Segway as viable substitutes. So, how would marketing research differ? It is likely that managers at Toyota would conduct more standard market data analysis and focus groups to gauge consumer interest. Managers at Segway, on the other hand, would probably rely more on field testing and direct sampling. The point here is that the nature of the product will determine the level and type of marketing research activities performed.

References

Hisrich, R. D., Peters, M. P., and Shepherd, D. A. (2005). *Entrepreneurship*, 6th ed. New York: McGraw-Hill.

Hruby, F. M. (1989). Missing piece analysis targets the competitor's weakness. *Marketing News*, January 2.

Keyes, J. (2006). *Knowledge Management, Business Intelligence and Content Management: The IT Practitioner's Guide*. Boca Raton, FL: Auerbach Publications.

Keyes, J. (1992). *InfoTrends: The Competitive Use of Information Technology*. New York: McGraw-Hill.

Perreault, W. D. and McCarthy, E. J. (2005). *Basic Marketing*. New York: McGraw-Hill.

Schiffman, L. G. and Kanuk, L. L. (2000). *Consumer Behavior*, 7th ed. Upper Saddle River, NJ: Prentice Hall.

Thompson, R. (2005). The next one sets record off the ice. *National Post*, March 9.

Chapter 6

Product Strategy

All companies must continually develop new products to compete effectively in today's complex and rapidly changing marketplace. A variety of strategies may be used to maintain the momentum, including the following:

- Discontinuous innovation: New products that create an entirely new market
- New offering category: New market entry into an existing market
- Extensions: Either the product line, a service line, or the brand
- Incremental improvements: Styling, performance, or even price changes

The iPod is an example of discontinuous innovation—creating an entirely new market for downloadable music, providing an aftermarket for iPod attachments, and even spurring the invention of podcasting.

Consumers and organizations are constantly on the lookout for fresh ideas to add convenience and comfort to their lives. However, new product failures rates are high: Some estimate an astonishing 70% failure rate. So, how do we ensure success and avoid being part of this failure statistic?

Market pioneers ("first movers") gain competitive advantage and develop market dominance. However, some ask whether it is always a good idea to be a pioneer. The first-mover advantage may be overwhelmed by copycat profit-taking.

Most products are actually in the maturity stage of their life cycle (see the following section, "The Product Life Cycle"). When sales slow down, overcapacity in the industry intensifies competition. Some companies will abandon weaker products and concentrate on profitable products and the development of new offerings. The company may try to expand the number of brand users by converting nonusers, entering new market segments, or winning competitors' customers. Product modification might also be employed, but it can backfire if proper market research is not performed. If the product is modified to the point where loyal users are upset, then the market share will be further eroded. Coca-Cola is a good example of this. Their much-hyped New Coke product introduction fizzled. There was such an uproar in the marketplace that Coca-Cola was forced to reintroduce the original Coke into the marketplace as Classic Coke (http://www.snopes.com/cokelore/newcoke.asp). As a product matures, margins will thin, so keeping an eye on the entire marketing mix is critical. We will discuss new product development in more detail in Chapters 7 and 8.

The Product Life Cycle

According to Davenport and Prusak (2003), the idealized life cycle of an idea within an organization is called the **P-cycle**, so named because each of its stages starts with the letter *p*: progenitor, pilot, project, program, perspective, and pervasiveness. The authors suggest that successful idea practitioners understand each idea's life cycle, so that they have a good idea as to where it might move next. There is an internal (i.e., within a company) as well as an external life cycle (i.e., the product as it is adopted by the public), and these cycles might differ due to many environmental reasons.

The P-cycle, often discussed in the engineering and innovation management literature, is somewhat similar to the traditional SDLC (systems development life cycle) because both cycles start with someone's bright idea—the **progenitor**. The bright idea may be based on an employee's or other stakeholder's idea (McDonald's popular Big Mac hamburger stemmed from a franchisee's idea) or might be the result of a company's R&D (research and development) efforts. After a feasibility study has been performed, the next stage that the idea (or system) enters is **pilot**. This stage is usually a scaled-down version of the grand idea so that stakeholders can determine if the idea is a fit for the company and whether it will work. Once the idea's potential has been proved, we enter the **project** stage. At this point, a project plan is created and funded, other resources allocated, and work can begin. If successful, the idea (or system) can be implemented and is now referred to as an ongoing **program**. The program may spawn additional projects that are related to the original idea. The program is usually part of a strategic plan so that its goals can be cascaded down throughout the organization and, thus, used within many departments. Over time, the program is embedded within the corporate psyche and becomes firmly entrenched within the operating methods and controls of the company. At the beginning of this rootedness, the idea can be said to be gaining **perspective**. By the time everyone in the company uses the idea on a daily basis, we reach the end state for the P-cycle—**pervasiveness**.

The **external P-cycle** of an idea is similar to the internal P-cycle. Davenport and Prusak (2003) discuss Barbara Ettore's five stages in the external life cycle of an idea: discovery, wild acceptance, digestion, decline, and hard-core. In other words,

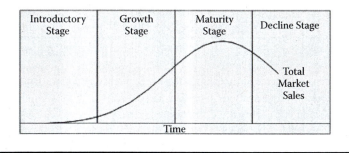

Figure 6.1   The product life cycle (PLC).

when a product is introduced to the public, it first has to be **discovered** and then **accepted**. Early adopters buy the product, like it, and tell others about it. Soon, there is a great buzz about the product, and others start adopting it. One can say that the product has now been **digested** by the marketplace. After a time, the product's use either **declines** and is replaced or becomes a commodity (i.e., **hard-core**).

From a marketing perspective, the P-cycle articulates itself in the **PLC (product life cycle)**, which is the acronym marketers use for the external P-cycle described here. The PLC describes the stages through which a product idea goes from the beginning to the end, as shown in Figure 6.1. As a product advances through the PLC, the marketing mix must advance as well. For example, as a product moves from the introductory phase to the growth phase, the product may be aimed at an entirely different target market. This means that a new marketing strategy must be developed to reach this target market. As you can see, the PLC, the internal P-cycle, and the external P-cycle all describe the same phenomenon from different perspectives: how a product or service is introduced, adopted, and utilized by its public. In this module, our emphasis will be on the PLC.

The PLC consists of four stages:

Introduction: This stage is marked by low sales and little knowledge of the market. This stage is experienced at the beginning of the product's life, immediately after launch.

Growth: This stage reflects the product's growth in the competitive landscape. While sales begin to level off, there is strong product awareness. There is also usually a need to reduce costs in response to pricing pressures from competition. The Apple iPod is an example of a product that moved quickly from the introductory stage to the growth stage. Once into the growth stage of its very popular product, Apple introduced a lower-cost version, the iPod shuffle, to counter moves by competitors. Apple quickly introduced its iPod nano and upgraded its original iPod product with video capabilities. These moves were reactions to competitive pressures (i.e., lower-cost competitors and the introduction of cell phones with similar capabilities) and the company's desire to maintain its first-mover position.

Maturation: This deals with the product's maturity in the competitive land-scape. Although sales begin to level off, there will still be strong product awareness. There is also usually a need to reduce costs in response to pricing pressures. Most PC makers are in this stage of growth. HP, Dell, and Sony all have strong product awareness. However, cutthroat competition has forced all of these manufacturers to reduce their prices and to differentiate them-selves in some other way (e.g., customer service, high-end video, etc.).

Decline: This stage is characterized by the slippage of sales. Good marketers will use this time to rejuvenate and jump-start the life cycle by introducing new versions of the product or product enhancements. Dell Computers may continually lower its prices, but it is also aggressive in introducing new versions of its PC. It recently introduced the Latitude X1, an ultralightweight PC for "road warriors."

Xerox Corporation has long been a leader in office copiers. Its emphasis on manu-facturing efficiency enabled the company to reduce the price of its copiers and, thus, reduce the cost to the customer. However, this class of product is straddling the mat-uration–decline boundary. By reengineering the product, Xerox was able to make key components more accessible and replaceable and, hence, easier to repair in the field. This move enables service technicians to more quickly complete service calls. Therefore, Xerox can be said to have incorporated the design-for-manufacturing approach with the design-for-service mindset, a current trend in maturing industries with declining products. Interestingly, the design-for-service mindset has global implications. With a little advance planning, a product designed in this manner might need only some minor adjustments to be marketable in different countries.

How long the PLC takes and the length of each stage varies according to prod-uct. The cycle may vary from 90 days to 100 years or more. However, there are some definite knowns:

1. PLCs are getting shorter.
2. The first mover makes the (initial) profits.
3. Fads move quickly through the life cycle.

As the product moves to market maturity, the firm must have a competitive advan-tage. Types of competitive advantage are as follows:

1. Quality
2. Low-cost producer
3. Promotional success

Product Life-Cycle Management (PLM)

We can define product life-cycle management (PLM) as a solution that offers the essential requirements and skills that a company requires to manage the life cycle of its product from its development stage until its withdrawal. The PLM is a significant part of any organization's strategy, whether small or large.

As we know, all the products and services offered by any organization have definite life cycles. The life cycle of a product or service can be split into different phases in order to understand the impact of the product or service on the market. Strategic planning is used to analyze market trends and the success of the product. As the market is so flexible, the life cycle of the product varies. The PLM evaluates the changing conditions in which the product is marketed.

Every company is on a hunt to develop successful and innovative products to boost its growth and profitability. It is proved that the success of a new product entirely depends on the product development phase, including cost-effectiveness and market demand. A good and effective PLM will help your business generate more profit by optimizing product life. The PLM would combine product information from supply chains with quality analysis.

The product life cycle (PLC) includes four different stages, as follows:

1. Launching a product is one of the initial stages of the PLC. Marketing trends, cost, sales survey, demand for the product, etc., are evaluated in this stage.
2. It is in the second stage that cost-effectiveness and need for sales increase are evaluated. As the demand and competition increase in the market, public awareness and newer marketing strategies are discussed and analyzed in this stage.
3. In the third stage of the PLC, competitive offerings and the competing products have to be analyzed and examined closely. Product and market analysis are also vital in this stage.
4. Declination of the product from the market is the fourth stage of the PLC. As the profit from the product reduces, the company will have no other option to cut cost except the withdrawal of product.

PLM was first introduced in the fields of medical instrumentation, aerospace, nuclear industries, and military, as quality and safety are the top priorities in these fields. But now, almost all the industries, including electronics, packaged goods, industrial machinery, etc., practice the PLM technique. Effective PLM will enable the company to find out the suitable times to introduce and withdraw a product by analyzing the marketing strategies of competitors and methodologies of developing a new product.

PLM systems enable marketing managers to communicate better and share information, thereby reducing costs as well as increasing efficiency. Errors in product design and marketing can be corrected through effective teamwork facilitated by PLM-oriented teams.

Since PLM promotes best practices, there will be consistency across marketing efforts. PLM provides room for collaboration with suppliers and other departments. In short, PLM functions as the backbone of a successful product and effective marketing.

The Product Development Process

New product development is a specialty in and of itself. There are several key steps necessary to develop a new product or to reposition an existing one, and Table 6.1 highlights these steps.

Moving Ideas off the Conceptual Plane to the Marketplace

The following methodology can be used to bring a product or service to market:

1. Perform market analysis: Prior to developing a product, a market analysis should be performed to see what is "out there" as well as to evaluate what the market would actually want or need within a window or opportunity. Here, the goal is value creation and capture, the tenets of which are pervasive throughout the entire methodology. Miller and Floricel (2004) indicate that value creation and capture involve a range of activities by which products and services are developed and delivered to the marketplace.

2. Assess strengths and weaknesses of competitors in the marketplace: Assess possible phantom competitors. These are companies not in the current marketplace, but those that have the potential to enter the market. For example, Amazon.com was originally just a seller of books. When they entered the e-stores business by selling hardware, it was an unexpected move that produced additional competition for an entrenched industry.

3. Conceptualize the product: This is where you create the idea for the actual product and then execute that idea.

4. Perform financial analysis: Most organizations utilize a breakeven analysis by first preparing a spreadsheet of anticipated costs (e.g., development, marketing, support, etc.). This will enable you to calculate when you will ultimately achieve profitability. This analysis also enables you to "play" with the projected cost of the product, although you are often constrained by what the market will bear as well as what competitors charge for their product. Interestingly, sometimes the innovation is in the cost of the product as much as it is in the feature set. During the Y2K panic, my company developed a set of analytical tools for programmers who needed to find references to dates in their program code. There were many other tools out there. We created a tool that did about 90% of what the other tools did but priced it about 50% lower. We did quite well. The innovation of this product, then, was in the price.

5. Consider alternatives: Other methods of moving a product to market through external means include seeking venture capital, and working with partners and even suppliers.

Table 6.1 Steps for Developing a New Product

Steps	Description
Idea generation and screening	The search for ideas: often developed through market research, environment scanning, or customer wants/needs analysis.
Concept development and testing	If the team uncovers potential concepts, the ideas will be refined into testable product concepts.
Marketing strategy development	Once a product concept has been tested and determined as worth pursuing, initial marketing strategies are developed, including the target market, size, structure, behavior, positioning, sales expectations, market share expectations, and profitability goals.
Business analysis[a]	This stage capitalizes on the initial marketing strategy concepts and incorporates operational and development costs, more realistic profitability projections, revenue projections, and risk analysis.
Product development	Once an acceptable business plan has been approved, R&D or engineering will then develop the actual physical product, which can take months (extremely short) to a decade.
Market testing[b]	Once developed, a product will be test-marketed. In the technology industry, these tests are also called alpha or beta trials.
Commercialization or launch	The product has made it through testing, has been changed, and is now available to the general public with all the appropriate marketing support required.

[a] In some organizations, this step may come prior to marketing strategy development.
[b] Not all companies do this.

Several studies indicate that success in moving products into the marketplace is associated with a number of management determinants. Roberts and Bellotti (1994) list the following, in order of sample usage: (1) use of multifunctional teams, (2) transfer of professionals, (3) early market test, (4) senior sponsors, (5) stronger managerial accountability, (6) total quality management, and (7) simultaneous engineering.

Most companies subscribe to most of these determinants (i.e., 1 through 6). The Defense Advanced Research Project Agency (DARPA) defines the remaining determinant, simultaneous (aka concurrent) engineering, as "a systematic approach to the integrated current design of products and their related processes, including manufacturing and supports. This approach is intended to cause the developers from the outset to consider all the elements of the product life-cycle from conception through disposal, including quality, cost, schedule, and other user equipment." This term was then popularized in the management literature by Backhouse and Brookes (1996). The technique was used successfully by Ford in the 1980s when developing the Saturn model of automobile.

The S-Curve and Continuous Innovation

The **S-curve**, a quantitative trend extrapolation technique used in forecasting, has long been used in the technology industry. Many argue that this analysis is actually more useful to discern where you've been than where you should go (Spencer, 2005). The S-curve is most often used to compare two competitive products in two dimensions, usually, time and performance.

An excellent example of an S-curve can be found in the work of Alexander (2001) and his discussion of the product innovation cycle. He discusses the S-curve of the ubiquitous automobile. In 1900, the automobile was first introduced to the public and became the plaything of the rich. Between 1900 and 1914, it went through the lower curve of the cycle, or the innovation phase, at the end of which Henry Ford introduced the assembly line. Between 1914 and 1928, according to Alexander, the automobile went through its growth phase. It was during this phase that the automobile caught on and was adopted by the general public. By 1928, the automobile was in its maturity phase (the top part of the S-curve), and Ford was seeing leaner, meaner competition.

Essentially, the S-curve is best for defining at what point a new rival has the potential for gaining market share from an established company. Many companies, particularly smaller companies competing with larger, more dominant rivals, use the S-curve to determine if, when, and where they might gain entry to a marketplace. Attackers enjoy important advantages over established rivals: undivided focus, ability to attack talent, freedom from tyranny of those service markets who want your product to stay as is, little bureaucracy, and the lack of a need to protect investments in unrelated skills or assets.

The S-curve can unleash unparalleled creativity when the time for the company to make its entry into the marketplace is realized. It's at this point that the product needs to be exposed in such a way that it effectively competes with the established giant. This stage often translates to reverse-engineering the competitive product and determining which features to adopt into your own product and then, essentially, going one up on them by adding new and novel features and services.

For a company that is a defender of an established technology, the S-curve predicts the point at which its leadership position might decline, as shown in Figure 6.2. Avoiding this point should become the chief focus. Some companies

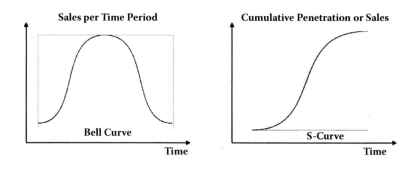

Figure 6.2   The S-curve. It is theorized that innovations will spread through society in an S-curve; the early adopters select the technology first, followed by the majority, until a technology or innovation becomes common.

(e.g., Microsoft) practice what I like to call **continuous innovation**. They practice all the techniques in our textbook as well as some additional ones, such as operating skunk works, acquiring small companies that might become rivals (e.g., Hotmail), and leapfrogging the attacker's technology. This last technique is Microsoft's current tactic with the introduction of its new MSN search engine, which nicely rivals the Google powerhouse.

Organizations strive to create an innovative culture in which opportunities that meet customer needs and address market trends can become reality.

Companies such as IBM are not only looking for product opportunities (e.g., physical goods such as software) but also have successfully added new services (e.g., nonphysical goods such as support services or consulting) to their palette of offerings over the past 20 years, evolving from a products company to an e-business provider. This change required years of strategic planning to ensure that evolving core competencies were aligned with evolving market trends. This effort was worthwhile for IBM, as it might have saved the company from collapsing.

Drucker (2002), a well-known pundit in the field of business, wrote his book on innovation and entrepreneurship more than 20 years ago. In 2002, when his *Harvard Business Review* article was published, his ideas on the subject were just as relevant as they were when he first put pen to paper two decades ago.

Drucker identifies seven sources (four internal to the company and three external) of innovation:

1. **Unexpected occurrences** (internal): Drucker considers unexpected successes and failures to be excellent sources of innovation because most businesses usually ignore them. IBM's first accounting machines, ignored by banks but later sold to libraries, are an example.
2. **Incongruities** (internal): The disconnect between expectations and results often provides opportunities for innovation. The growing market for steel coupled with falling profit margins enabled the invention of the minimill.

3. **Process needs** (internal): Modern advertising permitted the newspaper industry to distribute newspapers at a very low cost and dramatically increase readership (process need).

4. **Industry and market changes** (internal): Deregulation of the telecommunications industry created havoc in the industry but provided ample opportunity for innovation.

5. **Demographic changes** (external): Japanese businesses surveyed changing demographics and determined that the number of people available for blue-collar work is decreasing. They have achieved a leadership position in the area of robotics as a result. However, they are not stopping at robotics for manufacturing. Sony's QRIO robot is an example of the future of robotics.

6. **Changes in perception** (external): Although people are healthier than ever before, according to Drucker, they worry more about their health. This change in perception has been exploited for innovative opportunities. An example is the proliferation of Web-based health sites.

7. **New knowledge** (external): There are two types of innovation based on new knowledge: incremental and disruptive (Managing Creativity and Innovation, 2003). An example of incremental innovation is the Pentium IV chip. There was a Pentium III that preceded it. Therefore, the Pentium IV represents just a slight increment of innovation over its precursor. On the other hand, a radical innovation is something totally new to the world, such as transistor technology. However, technological innovation does have one drawback: It takes much longer to come into effect. For example, while computing machines were available in the early 1900s, it wasn't until the late 1960s that they were commonly used in businesses (http://www.computer.org/computer/timeline/timeline.pdf).

Branding and Positioning

A brand starts developing from the moment it enters the market, sometimes even before the product or service hits the market. In fact, many experts claim that a brand is another term for reputation. Many analysts see brands as the major enduring assets of a company. More than just a name or a symbol, the brand is the buzz generated by the product or service—what the product or service means to the consumer.

Organizations position products for competitive advantage. Once an organization decides which segments to enter, it has to determine its market positioning strategy: the positions it wants to occupy in each market segment. Positioning is usually expressed relative to its competitors. There are a variety of ways to position a product. The ability to spot a positioning opportunity is a sure test of a person's marketing ability. Successful positioning strategies are usually rooted in a product's sustainable competitive advantage. The most common bases for constructing a product positioning strategy are as follows:

1. Specific product features
2. Specific benefits, needs, or solutions
3. A reason to choose an offering over the competition (e.g., cost)

The product positioning process is similar to the competitor analysis process we discussed earlier in Chapter 5. It will be necessary to first identify competing products and their positions in the mind share of consumers, which is usually done based on a sample of customer perceptions. Once all the data are collected, the marketers examine the positions of the competing products vis-à-vis the organization's product with the goal of selecting the optimal position for the product.

Companies often have to balance their brand heritage with changing business strategies. BP (British Petroleum) has successfully repositioned its brand to be a leader in clean energy. Mercedes-Benz has also successfully extended its brand to attract younger, less affluent consumers. Both have attempted to differentiate themselves from the competition by changing their strategy.

Eighty-one-year-old IBM has spent the past several years moving from being a technology product supplier to an on-demand service provider while still investing in and protecting its traditional image (Bulik, 2005; Gerstner, 2002). It managed this transition through very clever advertising campaigns (we will discuss advertising and other marketing communications techniques in seminar 6, Chapter 10). "The Other IBM" was an eight-month campaign highlighting its new business consulting services. "Help Desk" is an ongoing campaign showing how on-demand computing solves real problems and helps real people. IBM has also moved to the leading edge of emerging media through the use of blogging and podcasting.

Branding Checklist

Developing a brand involves formulating a plan. Some guidelines and thoughts for developing this plan are as follows:

1. Determine your budget.
    1.1 Compare marketing budget for your e-business category.
        1.1.1 Use the Securities and Exchange Commission's Edgar system (http://www.sec.gov), and then click on Search Edgar. Use this search method to look up the companies that are in your peer grouping. For example, if Amazon.com is in your peer grouping, by typing in "amazon" in the keyword search field, you will get a listing of all documents that Amazon has filed with the SEC. Review their 10Q and 10K reports to find out some interesting details that may not be widely known.

1.2 Research the marketing campaigns of others in your peer category.

   1:2.1 Obviously, if your marketing department has been paying attention, you already have heard all your competitor's radio and TV spots, seen all their print ads, and gotten a copy of all their direct mail.

   1.2.2 Research the top brands in your category.

   1.2.3 Understand that marketing takes place both online and offline.

1.3 Determine whether your marketing budget is adequate.

   1.3.1 Using the statistics you researched about your peer grouping, deduce an average marketing-to-sales ratio.

   1.3.2 Is your marketing budget adequate in light of list item 1.3.1? If not, investigate alternative means of funding, including selling additional shares of stock, seeking venture capital, seeking loans, partnering and affiliations, and merger.

2. Develop a program for establishing an identity.

  2.1 Convince your staff that it takes time to establish brands. Building a real brand takes years of effort creating an identity for a product or service at every point of contact with the customer, according to Shelly Lazarus, CEO of Ogilvy & Mather Worldwide.

   2.1.1 Hire the best ad agency you can find.

   2.1.2 Decide what it is you stand for. Is it lowest price? Largest selection? Best service? All of the above?

  2.2 Research the failures of other organizations, and do not repeat their mistakes.

   2.2.1 Most analysts, and even venture capitalists, agree that most of the money being expended is wasted. There are many reasons for this: an extremely noisy marketplace with scores of wannabes crowding into the field. The result is multiple brands fighting for dominance in every possible category.

   2.2.2 Realize that brands die quickly on the Web. On the Web, brands are born, force-fed to maturity at a terrifying rate, and then vanish. Some companies even dump a brand and reinvent it using a new name.

  2.3 Develop a strategy for putting across a brand's advantages.

   2.3.1 E*TRADE tries to demonstrate its brand's advantages over others in the overheated online brokerage market by being a financial portal.

  2.4 Establish a consumer advisory committee. You can't brand what you don't understand.

   2.4.1 Determine who your target audience really is. Is it teenage boys, Middle America? At times, a business might have more than one target audience. For example, one consumer credit Web site has two target audiences. One is consumers, and the other is banks (the company's revenue model is to make a small fee on each application forwarded to a bank).

2.4.2 Determine what the target audience wants.

2.4.2.1 The branding attributes required by people are comfort level, personality, ease of use, high security, speed, variety of services, and novelty of services.

2.5 Establish your look.

2.5.1 Consider your logo. Study the look and feel of the majors. New companies have a tendency to make their logos complicated. Microsoft's simple blue logo is a good benchmark.

2.5.2 Create marketing collateral such as stationery.

2.5.3 Decide on your Web site's look and feel. Many dot-coms new to the Web clutter up their sites to look as though they've been around for a while. Companies with presence, such as Amazon, opt for a clean, noncluttered look. Emphasize the following:

2.5.3.1 The look and feel of the site.

2.5.3.2 The tone of the site (i.e., good writing).

2.5.3.3 Make sure the site is efficient and actually works.

2.5.3.4 Make your site easily navigable. It is impossible to find things on most sites where the Web designers force you to surf their way instead of your way.

2.5.4 Review with your customer advisory board.

2.6 Develop your on-air persona.

2.6.1 Avoid the in-your-face advertising that the early adopters ran. Shooting gerbils out of a cannon might get you noticed, but it will not do anything for your brand or image.

2.6.2 Make sure you are targeting the right audience. For example, running radio advertisements on a news program will not attract 18- to 22-year-old males. Just because advertisement rates are cheap at three in the morning doesn't mean that it is effective. There's a reason why advertisement rates are much more expensive during prime time—there's an audience.

2.6.3 Review with your customer advisory board.

3. Make sure you employ your brand in all marketing, sales, and informational endeavors undertaken, including the following:

3.1 Banner advertising: Many doubt the value of the ubiquitous banner ad. Should you use such ads as part of your marketing effort, be careful about how you use them. A bad banner can easily destroy all the careful work you've done creating your brand.

3.2 Newsletters: Both e-mail and paper-based ones can be used.

3.3 Public relations (PR): Make sure your PR company is fully aware of your brand and touts it every chance it gets.

3.4 Classified ads: It is surprising how many people read the help-wanteds. Make sure these small ads are branded too.

3.5 Social networks: With all the noise about Web sites, most people tend to forget that the Internet is about people, and people run like lemmings to join chat groups and newsgroups. You should make sure someone is monitoring, and participating in, any and all chat social networks that pertain to your market.

3.6 Search engines: All search engines are different. Where and how does your company pop up? Investigate search engine marketing tools such as adwords.google.com.

3.7 Back-end and upsell products: You got the attention of a consumer once. Now you have to provide something to lure him or her back.

3.8 Joint ventures and associate programs: It is surprising how many companies expend millions on branding and then don't use the brand when designing their joint venture and associate/affiliate programs. Think of affiliates as your emissaries. Supply them with everything needed to sell your product or service effectively.

Conclusion

Mankin (2004) describes the dimensions of a product or service that will ensure its success:

A. Providing high purchase motivators
   1. It must be less expensive than existing products (**lower price**).
   2. It must provide better features than existing products (**greater benefits**).
B. Eliminating purchase barriers
   3. It must not have any switching or adoption costs (**easy to use**).
   4. It must be readily available (**easy to buy**).

It's hard for a new product to simultaneously excel in all four dimensions (lower price, greater benefits, easy to use, and easy to buy), but Mankin provides an example of one product that came fairly close.

Proctor & Gamble (P&G) began marketing the Crest SpinBrush, an inexpensive electric toothbrush, in 2001. By 2002, it was a market leader. If we examine the four dimensions, we can see why the SpinBrush achieved such a level of success:

1. It was very inexpensive compared to competitors. Most electric toothbrushes had 10 times the price of the SpinBrush (**lower price**).
2. Many consumers found that the SpinBrush delivered better performance than competing products (**greater benefits**).
3. SpinBrush runs on disposable batteries, making it very portable (**easy to use**).

4. P&G's strong distribution capabilities made the SpinBrush ubiquitous in stores. A try-it feature enabled consumers to see the toothbrush in action (**easy to buy**).

This profile, according to Mankin, gave the product a very high probability for market success. The key to marketing, then, is to launch a product that excels in all four dimensions.

References

Alexander, M. A. (2001). The Innovation Wave and Secular Market Trends. [online]. [Accessed on October 20, 2005]. Available from http://www.safehaven.com/article-71.htm.

Backhouse, C. J., and Brookes, N. J. (1996). *Concurrent Engineering*. Hampshire, England: Gower Publishing Limited.

Bulik, B. S. (October 24, 2005). BtoB's best 2005 brands. *B2B: The Magazine for Marketing Strategists*. 24 October.

Davenport, T. H., and Prusak, L. (2003). *What's the Big Idea?* Boston: Harvard Business School Press.

Drucker, P. F. (2002). The discipline of innovation. *Harvard Business Review*, 80(8), pp. 95–102.

Gerstner, L. (2002). *Who Says Elephants Can't Dance? Inside IBM's Historic Turnaround*. New York: HarperCollins.

Mankin, E. (2003). *Managing Creativity and Innovation*. Boston: Harvard Business School Press.

Mankin, E. (2004). Four ways to pick a winning product. Harvard Business School Working Knowledge [online]. Available from: http://hbswk.hbs.edu/item.jhtml?id=4378&t=strategy.

Miller, R., and Floricel, S. (November/December 2004). Value creation and games of innovation. *Research Technology Management*, 47(6).

Roberts, E. B., and Bellotti, P. (December 1994). Managerial Determinants of Industrial R&D Performance: An Analysis of the Global Chemicals/Materials Industry. MIT Sloan: The International Center for Research on the Management of Technology.

Spencer, A. (2005). The Technology S-Curve [online]. [Accessed on October 21, 2005]. Available from http://web.njit.edu/~aspencer/slides/s-curve.ppt.

Chapter 7

Innovation Management

Here is the definition of *innovation* found on Wikipedia (http://en.wikipedia.org/wiki/Innovation): Innovation is either demand-led or supply-pushed, and this topic is considerably debated. Wikipedia is a good example of both definitions of innovation. There was a demand in the marketplace for a free, Web-based encyclopedia. The technology of the Internet and the concept of the wiki, a Web application that lets users add and change content (http://en.wikipedia.org/wiki/Wiki), is an excellent example of supply-pushed innovation. The wiki was conceived and developed by Ward Cunningham in the mid-1990s. Steve Lipscomb's World Poker Tour (Olmstead, 2005) is another example. Poker has taken the world by storm, largely because of Lipscomb's innovative approach to the once seedy concept of the poker tournament.

So, how do you manage to generate this level of innovation and creativity in your company?

Encouraging Innovation

There are two types of innovation:

1. Sustaining—Advances that give our most profitable customers something better, in ways that they define as better
2. Disruptive—Advances that impair or "disrupt" the traditional way in which a company has gone to market and made money, because the innovation offers something our best customers don't want

Most software companies continually enhance their line of software products to provide their customers with the features that they have stated they truly desired.

This is *sustaining* innovation. These companies might also strive to come up with products that are radically different from what their customers want in order to expand their base of customers, compete with the competition, or even jump into a completely new line of business. This is *disruptive* innovation.

Most people equate innovation with a new invention, but it can also refer to a process improvement, continuous improvement, or even new ways to use existing things. Innovation can, and should, occur within every functional area of the enterprise. Good managers are constantly reviewing the internal and external landscape for clues and suggestions regarding what might come next:

1. Research results from R&D—One of the challenges is being alert to market opportunities that might be very different from the inventor's original vision.
2. Competitors' innovations—Microsoft leveraged Apple's breakthrough graphical user interface and ultimately became far more dominant and commercially successful than Apple.
3. Breakthroughs outside industry.
4. Customer requests—A "customer-focused" organization's products and services will reflect a coherent understanding of customer needs.
5. Employee suggestions.
6. Newsgroups and trade journals.
7. Trade shows and networking.

Some experts argue that a company's product architecture mirrors, and is based on, its organizational structure. This is because companies attack that first project or customer opportunity in a certain way, and, if it works, they look to repeat the process; this repetition evolves into a company's "culture." So when we say a company is "bureaucratic," what we are really saying is that it is incapable of organizing differently to address different customer challenges, because it has been so successful with the original model.

There are a variety of workplace structures that promote innovation:

1. Cross-functional teams: Selecting a representative from the various functional areas and assigning them to solve a particular problem can be an effective way to meld quickly a variety of relevant perspectives and also efficiently pass the implementation stress test, avoiding, for example, the possibility that a particular functional group will later try to block a new initiative. Some variations include the following:
   a. "Lightweight project manager" system—Each functional area chooses a person to represent it on the project team. The project manager serves primarily as a coordinator. This function is "lightweight" in that the PM does not have the power to reassign people or reallocate resources.
   b. "Tiger team"—Individuals from various areas are assigned and completely dedicated to the project team, often physically moving into shared

office space together. This does not necessarily require permanent reassignment, but is obviously better suited for longer-term projects with a high level of urgency within the organization.

2. Cross-company teams or industry coalitions: Some companies have developed innovative partnership models to share the costs and risks of these high-profile investments, such as the following:
    a. Customer advisory boards
    b. Executive retreats
    c. Joint ventures
    d. Industry associations

According to Lyon (2002), there are several managerial techniques that can be utilized to spur innovation, as shown in Table 7.1.

The R&D Process

As shown in Figure 7.1, at a very high level, every R&D process will consist of the following:

1. Generation of ideas—From the broadest visioning exercises to specific functionality requirements, the first step is to list the potential options.
2. Evaluation of ideas—Having documented everything from the most practical to the farfetched, the team can then coolly and rationally analyze and prioritize the components, using agreed-upon metrics.
3. Product/service design—These "ideas" are then converted into "requirements," often with very specific technical parameters.

There are two core elements of this longer-term competency-enhancing work. The first is the generation of ideas. Most companies utilize a standard process to make sure that everyone has the time and motivation to contribute. The second element is to promote an environment conductive to innovation. This includes the following:

1. Cultural values and institutional commitment
2. Allocation of resources
3. Linkage with company's business strategy

Creating an "innovation-friendly" environment is time consuming and will require the manager to forego focusing on the "here and how." As Lyon (2002) explains, when there is constant pressure to "hit the numbers" or "make something happen," it is difficult to be farsighted and build in time for you and your team to "create an environment."

Table 7.1 Promoting Innovation

Technique	Definition/Examples
Commitment to problem solving	Ability to ask the "right questions" Build in time for research and analysis
Commitment to openness	Analytical and cultural flexibility
Acceptance of "out-of-box" thinking	Seek out and encourage different viewpoints, even radical ones
Willingness to reinvent products and processes that are already in place	Create a "blank slate" opportunity map, even for processes that appear to be battle tested and working well
Willingness to listen to everyone (employees, customers, vendors)	"Open door" Respect for data and perspective without regard to seniority or insider status
Keeping oneself informed of industry trends	Constantly scanning business publications/trade journals, and clipping articles of interest "FYI" participation with fellow managers
Promotion of diversity, cross-pollination	Forward-thinking team formation, which also attempts to foster diversity Sensitivity to considerations of gender, race, even work style
Change of management policies	Instill energy and "fresh start" by revising established rules
Provision of incentives for all employees, not just researchers/engineers	Compensation schemes to align individual performance with realization of company goals
Use of project management	Clear goals and milestones Tracking tools Expanded communication
Transfer of knowledge within an organization	Commitment to aggregating and reformatting key data for "intelligence" purposes

Table 7.1   Promoting Innovation (*Continued*)

Technique	Definition/Examples
Provision for off-site teaming	Structured meetings and socialization outside the office to reinforce bonds between key team members
Provision for off-site training	Development of individuals through education and experiential learning to master new competencies
Use of simple visual models	Simple but compelling frameworks and schematics to clarify core beliefs
Use of the Internet for research	Fluency and access to Web sites (e.g., competitor home pages)
Development of processes for implementing new products and ideas	Structured ideation and productization process Clear release criteria Senior management buy-in
Champion products	Identify and prioritize those products that represent the best possible chance for commercial success Personally engage and encourage contributors to strategic initiatives

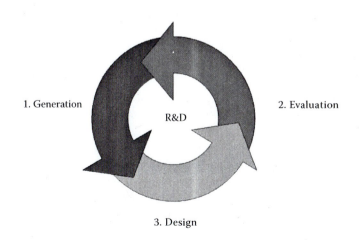

Figure 7.1   The R&D process.

Managing innovation is a bit different from creating an environment that promotes it. This refers to the service- or product-specific initiative, whether it is a new car or a streamlined manufacturing process. The big question is, how do we make this process come together on time and under budget? There are two main phases to the successful management of innovation:

The first phase seeks to stress-test the proposal with a variety of operational and financial benchmarks, such as the following:

1. Is the innovation "real"? Is this "next great thing" dramatic enough to justify the costs, financial and otherwise? Does it clearly and demonstrably distance you from your competitors? And can it be easily duplicated once it becomes public knowledge?
2. Can the innovation be realized? Does the organization have the resources? This is where you figure out whether the rubber meets the road. You need to ask whether you have the capabilities and functional expertise to realize this vision. Many organizations come up with a multitude of ideas. Upon further examination, they often find that they just do not have the resources to implement the vast majority of their ideas. This might lead them to become innovative in a different way as they search for partners. In other words, some organizations try to couple their brains with someone else's brawn!
3. Is the innovation worth it? Does the innovation fit into the organization's mission and strategic plan? ROI (return on investment) is the most frequently used quantitative measure used to help plan and assess new initiatives. Probably more useful, however, is ROM (return on management), which poses a fundamental question: What should the CEO and the management team focus on? Research extending over a period of 10 years led to the concept of return on management (Strassman, 1996). This ratio is calculated by first isolating the management value-added of a company, and then dividing it by the company's total management costs:

$$\text{Return on management} = F(\text{management value-added}/\text{management costs})$$

Management value-added is that which remains after every contributor to a firm's inputs gets paid. If management value-added is greater than management costs, one can conclude that managerial efforts are productive because the managerial outputs exceed managerial inputs.

Another way of looking at the return-on-management ratio (R-O-M productivity index) is to view it as a measure of productivity. It answers the question of how many surplus dollars you get for every dollar paid for management.

The second phase, design, is the process by which these ideas and concepts get distilled into an actual product design, for example, a Web site map or a prototype. Many mistakes are made by delegating this process to lower-level functional experts, when in fact some of these decisions go a long way toward determining the product's ultimate acceptance in the marketplace.

Lyon (2002) postulates that most of the outward signs of excellence and creativity that we associate with the most innovative companies are a result of a culture and related values that encourage and support managers who use their specific initiatives to also reinforce and strengthen the company's processes. When these processes become "repeatable," they become the rule instead of the exception, which of course makes it easier for the next manager to "be innovative."

Kuczmarski (2001) points to Capital One as a company that uses a model based on continuous innovation. They utilize a patented Information-Based Strategy (IBS) that enables the company to expand its mature credit card business by tailoring more than 16,000 different product combinations to customers' needs. They are able to embrace high degrees of risk because they base their innovations on customer needs. The company tests new ideas against existing customers or possibly a separate grouping of prospects.

Measuring Innovation

A wealth of metrics can be derived from the preceding discussions. Other innovation metrics to consider include the following:

1. Return on innovation investment—Number of customers who view the brand as innovative divided by the total number of potential customers
2. Brand innovation quotient—Number of repeat purchasers divided by total number of purchasers
3. Pipeline process flow—Measures number of products at every stage of development (i.e., concept development, business analysis, prototype, test, launch)
4. Innovation loyalty—Number of repeat purchases made before switching to a competitor

Citibank long had an Innovation Index (Tucker, 2002). This index measured revenues derived from new products, but Citibank deemed this index insufficient to meet their needs. They created an Innovation Initiative, staffed by a special task force. This group was challenged to come up with more meaningful metrics that could be used to track progress and be easily integrated into Citibank's balanced scorecard. The task force eventually developed a set of metrics that included new revenue from innovation, successful transfer of products from one country or region to another, the number and type of ideas in the pipeline, and time from idea to profit.

The Six Steps for Increasing Creativity

The six steps for increasing creativity described in the following subsections are but a starting point for creating the innovative organization. All of this, however, still relies on the CEO being an advocate for innovation management.

Step 1: Make Sure Your Company's Goals Are Consistent with Your Value System

This is an interesting perspective in an era of few good jobs and trends toward outsourcing and offshoring.

In 2004, Elizabeth Lukin presented her results of a study about how Australians look at work. She found the following, which is consistent with other U.S. studies:

1. Job insecurity is a big issue.
2. More and more permanent jobs are being replaced by temporary jobs.
3. Employees are battling unrealistic expectations, increased workloads, and lack of staff.

She concludes her discussion by saying that very few people can imagine their situation improving substantially. In fact, many believe things will only get worse. They see the gap between rich and poor growing, and they feel that they don't know where all this change will lead.

Managers need to realize that many, if not most, employees will harbor some or all of these feelings. Given the dire job situation, they might opt to stay put rather than, as the Harvard text suggests, find a company whose goals match their values. Therefore, it is up to the manager to somehow ameliorate the level of anxiety that accompanies these feelings in such a way that creativity is not stifled.

Step 2: Pursue Self-Initiated Activity by Choosing High-Motivation Projects

Few employees get to choose their own task assignments. However, savvy managers need to be aware that creativity is greatly enhanced when employees are motivated to do their jobs.

The better companies try to fit the employee to the task by creating a skills database. These permit managers to rapidly locate an employee who has the skills—and the motivation—to fulfill a particular work requirement.

However, there will always be those times when the task the employee is expected to complete is simply not one he or she is especially interested in. At this point, the wise IT manager will use a variety of motivating techniques.

Based on a study at Wichita State University, the top five motivating techniques are the following:

1. Manager personally congratulates employee who does a good job.
2. Manager writes personal notes about good performance.
3. Organization uses performance as basis for promotion.
4. Manager publicly recognizes employee for good performance.
5. Manager holds morale-building meetings to celebrate successes.

One doesn't have to actually give an award for recognition to happen. Giving your attention is just as effective. The Hawthorne Effect states that the act of measuring (paying attention) will itself change behavior. Nelson and Blanchard (1994) suggest the following low-cost rewards recognition techniques:

1. Make a photo collage about a successful project that shows the people who worked on it, its stages of development, and its completion and presentation.
2. Create a "yearbook" to be displayed in the lobby that contains each employee's photograph, along with his or her best achievement of the year.
3. Establish a place to display memos, posters, photos, and so on, recognizing progress toward goals and thanking individual employees for their help.
4. Develop a "Behind the Scenes Award" specifically for those whose actions are not usually in the limelight.
5. Say thanks to your boss, your peers, and your employees when they have performed a task well or have done something to help you.
6. Make a thank-you card by hand.
7. Cover the person's desk with balloons.
8. Bake a batch of chocolate-chip cookies for the person.
9. Make and deliver a fruit basket to the person.
10. Tape a candy bar for the typist in the middle of a long report with a note saying, "halfway there."
11. Give a person a candle with a note saying, "No one holds a candle to you."
12. Give a person a heart sticker with a note saying, "Thanks for caring."
13. Purchase a plaque, stuffed animal, anything fun or meaningful, and give it to an employee at a staff meeting with specific praise. That employee displays it for a while, then gives it to another employee at a staff meeting in recognition of an accomplishment.
14. Call an employee into your office (or stop by his or her office) just to thank him or her; don't discuss any other issue.
15. Post a thank-you note on the employee's office door.
16. Send an e-mail thank-you card.
17. Praise people immediately. Encourage them to keep up the good work.
18. Greet employees by name when you pass them in the hall.
19. Make sure you give credit to the employee or group that came up with an idea being used.
20. Acknowledge individual achievements by using employees' names when preparing status reports.

McCarthy and Allen (2000) suggest that you set up your employees for success. When you give someone a new assignment, tell the employee why you are trusting him or her with this new challenge. "I want you to handle this because I like the way you tackled that problem I gave you last week." They also suggest that you never steal an employee's thunder. When an employee tells you about an accomplishment, resist the temptation to describe something similar that you achieved. They also suggest that you never use sarcasm, even in a teasing way. Resist the temptation to say something like, "It's about time you gave me this report on time." Deal with the "late" problem by setting a specific time the report is due. If it's done on time, make a positive comment about timeliness.

Step 3: Take Advantage of Unofficial Activity

I know of few people who have the luxury of working on unofficial projects in larger companies. However, this is actually quite a good idea. Management should allow slack time to be used for creative purposes. Channels should be put in place such that any great idea nurtured during slack time has an equal opportunity to be presented for possible funding.

Step 4: Be Open to Serendipity

Scotchgard was actually invented by accident. It is very important that a manager be open to this sort of novel product development opportunity. 3M researchers were trying to develop a new kind of rubber for jet aircraft fuel lines when one of the lab assistants accidentally dropped a glass bottle that contained a batch of synthetic latex. Some of the latex mixture splashed on the assistant's canvas tennis shoes. The researchers observed that the accidental spill on a white tennis shoe would not wash off nor would solvent remove it. The area resisted soiling. They recognized the commercial potential of its application to fabrics during manufacture and by the consumer at home.

Step 5: Diversify Your Stimuli

The authors recommend rotating into every job you are capable of doing to induce intellectual cross-pollination. This is not a new technique, as it has been practiced for years in the high-tech industry. Rotating jobs is also a tenet of quality management systems, including ISO 9001 (http://standardsgroup.asq.org/news/psi/0207-PSIQA02.pdf).

Step 6: Create Opportunities for Information Communication (Meet and Greet)

Salespeople are natural networkers. These folks sign up for every event and learn a great deal by doing so. Other employees are somewhat less motivated to leave the office to attend industrywide gatherings, particularly if they are as older and have additional familial responsibilities.

Rewarding Employees for Innovative Ideas

Intrinsic rewards appeal to a person's desire for self-actualization, curiosity, joy, and interest in the work. Extrinsic rewards appeal to a person's desire for attainment— for example, money, stock options, days offs, tickets to ballgames, etc. Intrinsic rewards are intangible, while extrinsic rewards are quite tangible. As one of my employees says, "Show me the money."

Many of the motivation techniques discussed in this chapter could be considered intrinsic rewards. Extrinsic reward systems are more difficult to implement, as there are usually budget considerations to deal with. In many companies, the methodology used to grant yearly raises can even be considered countermotivational. When I worked for the New York Stock Exchange, employees were rated on a scale of 1 to 5. The largest "rewards" (i.e., raises) were granted to the 5s. However, we were told to rate our employees using a bell-shaped curve. The result is that some 5s were cheated out of their fair share of the reward system.

This topic is so important that more than a few books have been written on the subject. Wilson (2002) talks about the use of spot bonuses, team celebrations, innovative employee benefits, and flex compensation. Pearce and Robinson (2005) discuss the subject of executive compensation in their textbook on strategic management, now in its ninth edition. Ideas that work for the senior managers should also work for the employee who greatly contributes to the profitability or competitive advantage of the firm:

1. Stock option grants
2. Restricted stock plan
3. Bonus income deferred, sometimes referred to as "golden handcuffs"
4. Cash based on accounting performance measures

Couger et al. (1991) suggest a process for generating innovation through a series of bottom-up creativity techniques. A brief list of the best of these techniques follows:

1. **Brainstorming**. This technique is perhaps the most familiar of all the techniques discussed here. It is used to generate a large number of ideas in a short time.
2. **Blue slip**. Ideas are individually generated and recorded on a 3″ × 5″ sheet of blue paper. People anonymously share ideas in order to make people feel more at ease. Since each idea is on a separate piece of blue paper, the sorting and grouping of similar ideas is facilitated.
3. **Extrapolation**. A technique or approach, already used by the organization, is stretched to apply to a new problem.

4. **Progressive abstraction technique**. By moving through progressively higher levels of abstraction, it is possible to generate alternative problem definitions from an original problem. When a problem is enlarged in a systematic way, it is possible to generate many new definitions that can then be evaluated for their usefulness and feasibility. Once an appropriate level of abstraction is reached, possible solutions are more easily identified.

5. **5Ws and H technique**. This technique is the traditional, and journalistic, approach of who-what-where-when-why-how. Use of this technique serves to expand a person's view of the problem and assists in verifying that all related aspects of the problem have been addressed and considered.

6. **Force field analysis technique**. The name of this technique comes from its ability to identify forces contributing to or hindering a solution to a problem. This technique stimulates creative thinking in three ways: (1) it defines direction, (2) identifies strengths that can be maximized, and (3) identifies weaknesses that can be minimized.

7. **Problem reversal**. Reversing a problem statement often provides a different framework for analysis. For example, in attempting to come up with ways to improve productivity, try considering the opposite—how to decrease productivity.

8. **Associations/Image technique**. Most of us have played the game, at one time or another, in which a person names a person, place, or thing and then asks for the first thing that pops into the second person's mind. The process of combining and linking is another way of expanding the solution space.

9. **Wishful thinking**. This technique enables people to loosen analytical parameters to consider a larger set of alternatives than they might ordinarily consider. By injecting a degree of fantasy into the process, the result just might be a new and unique approach.

Conclusion

Harari (1993), a professor at the University of San Francisco and a management consultant, relates an interesting experience with one of his clients. While he was waiting for an appointment with this particular client, he overheard two of the manager's clerical assistants calling customers and asking them how they liked the company's product. Professor Harari reflected that it was no wonder this manager had such a good reputation. When he finally met with her, he offered his congratulations on her ability to delegate the customer service task to her staff. "What are you talking about?" she asked, bewildered. "Why, your secretaries are calling up customers on their own," Harari replied. "Oh, really? Is that what they're doing?," she laughed. "You mean you didn't delegate that task to them?" "No," she said. "I didn't even know they were doing it. Listen, Oren, my job is to get everyone on my team to think creatively in pursuit of the same goal. So what I do is talk to people regularly about why we exist as a company and as a team. That means we talk straight about our common purpose and the high standards we want to achieve. I call these our goal lines. Then we talk regularly about some broad constraints we have to work with them, like budgets, ethics, policies, and legalities. Those are our sidelines."

"It's like a sport. Once we agree on the goal lines and sidelines, I leave it to my people to figure out how to best get from here to there. I'm available and attentive when they need feedback. Sometimes I praise; sometimes I criticize—but always constructively, I hope. We get together periodically and talk about who's been trying what, and we give constructive feedback to one another. I know that sounds overly simplistic, but I assure you that is my basic management philosophy."

"And that's why I don't know what my assistants are doing, because it's obviously something they decided to try for the first time this week. I happen to think it's a great idea, because it's within the playing field and helps keep high standards for being number one in our industry. I will tell you something else: I don't even know what they intend to do with the data they're collecting, but I know they'll do the right thing."

"Here's my secret: I don't know what my people are doing, but because I work face to face with them as a coach, I know that whenever it is they're doing is exactly what I'd want them to be doing if I knew what they were doing!"

The Harari story is one of my favorites because it encapsulates into one very brief story exactly what it is a good manager is supposed to do to encourage innovative thinking in his or her employees.

References

Couger, J. D., McIntyre, S. C., Higgins, L. F., and Snow, T. A. (1991, September). Using a bottom-up approach to creativity improvement in IS development. *Journal of Systems Management*, 23–36.

Harari, O. (1993, November). Stop empowering your people. *Management Review*, 26–29.

Kuczmarski, T. (2001, Spring). Five fatal flaws of innovation metrics: Measuring innovation may seem complicated, but it doesn't need to be. *Marketing Management*.

Lyon, S. (2002, July). Managing Innovation. Lecture.

McCarthy, M., and J. Allen. (2000). *You Made My Day: Creating Co-Worker Recognition and Relationships*. New York: L-F Books.

Nelson, B. and K. Blanchard (1994). *1001 Ways to Reward Employees*. New York: Workman Publishing Co.

Olmstead, L. (2005, May). How Steve Lipscomb reinvented poker and built the hottest business in America. *Inc.*, pp. 80–92.

Pearce, H. A. & Robinson, R.B. (2005). *Strategic Management: Formulation, Implementation and Control*, ninth edition. New York: McGraw-Hill-Irwin.

Strassmann, P. (1996). Introduction to ROM Analysis: Linking Management Productivity and Information Technology. http://www.strassmann.com/consulting/ROM-intro/Intro_to_ROM.html.

Tucker, R. (2002). *Driving Growth through Innovation*. Pub Group West.

Wilson, T.B. (2002). *Innovative Reward Systems for the Changing Marketplace*. New York: McGraw-Hill.

Chapter 8

The IT Product Development Cycle

An IT company's most valuable asset isn't its machinery or equipment, communication systems, or influence in the market. It's the thought capital: an army of creative thinkers, whose ideas can be converted into noteworthy products or services. So how does an IT company go about developing a new product or service, and what challenges does an IT manager face while dealing with marketing issues during each stage of development?

New Product or Service Introduction

New products or services in the IT sector can enter the market under different categories. Take, for example, IBM. Some of its products or services are new to the market (example: Open Services for Lifecycle Collaboration, which aims to simplify association across delivery life cycle of software), some are novel to the IT company itself (example: utilization of blade technology in making high-performance computing systems), and some are completely novel and create totally new markets (example: Go Green with IBM Web 2.0 solutions). Some new products are just modified versions of existing products, while some are completely original, as shown in Figure 8.1.

These various categories of product introduction can be explained using commonly used software as an example, as shown in Table 8.1.

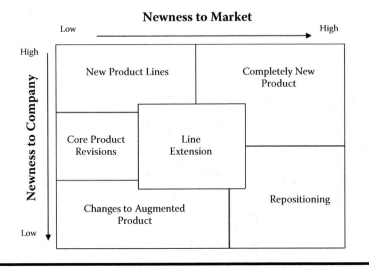

Figure 8.1 Categorization of new products or services.

Table 8.1 Product Introduction Methodologies

New Product Category	Example
Changes to augmented product	Adding a new language to the existing vocabulary program to extend its market reach
Core product revision	Introducing a new vocabulary program with the software interface redesigned for a new look and new options
Line extensions	Creating a vocabulary program based on original source code that caters to the scientific community
Repositioning	Changing market strategy by offering deals to schools for classroom use
Completely new	Launching a program that assists children in learning math

Figure 8.2   The IT product development process.

The IT Product Development Process

The development process, as shown in Figure 8.2, of any IT product or service involves eight stages:

- Idea generation
- Idea screening
- Concept development and testing
- Marketing strategy development
- Business analysis
- Product development
- Market testing
- Commercialization

Let us now look at the market challenges surfacing at each stage of the development process.

Idea Generation

The new product or service development process begins with the hunt for ideas. Management has to delineate product and market scope as well as the new product's objectives. They should state how much effort should be dedicated to making breakthrough products or services, modifying already existing products or services, and copying competitors' products or services. New product ideas can come from many sources: customers, R&D, competitors, channel members, employees, and top management. The highest percentage of ideas for new industrial products originates from customers. IT companies can discover a lot by analyzing their lead users, users who recognize early that the product needs to be improved, since they are the ones making more advanced use of the company's products or services. Apple has been consistently picked as the Top Innovator due to its capability to time and again come up with innovative concepts anticipating customer wants.

Successful companies have established a company culture that encourages every employee to seek new ways of improving production. Tata Consultancy Services (TCS), a top Indian IT firm, and other such firms give pecuniary, vacation, or appreciation awards to people who come up with the best ideas.

Top management is also a rich resource of ideas. A number of company leaders, such as Steve Jobs, CEO and cofounder of Apple, take personal responsibility for technical, scientific, and industrial novelty in their companies. On the other hand, Lewis Platt, former CEO of Hewlett-Packard, believed senior management's responsibility is to construct an atmosphere that encourages managers to generate fresh development opportunities and take measured amount of risks. Under Platt's leadership, HP had been structured as a assortment of extremely independent entrepreneurial businesses.

New-product or service ideas can also come from other sources as well, including marketing research firms, patent attorneys, inventors and industrial publications, advertising agencies, industrial consultants, and university and commercial R&D centers. However, the product or service idea is not likely to receive serious consideration unless it has a strong advocate.

Idea Screening

Any company can attract good ideas by organizing itself properly. An IT manager should inspire the employees to come up with innovative ideas. Ideas can be noted and analyzed regularly by a committee, which categorizes them into promising ideas, marginal ideas, and rejects. Every promising idea can be analyzed further and implemented accordingly. The company should reward employees submitting the best ideas.

Some companies tremble when they think about the ideas they ignored: Xerox observed the potential of Chester Carlson's copying machine, but Eastman Kodak and IBM did not. According to IBM, the market potential of personal computers was very small. These mistakes must be avoided at all cost by managers.

The intention of screening is to get rid of poor ideas early on. The underlying principle is that product development costs rise considerably with every succeeding development stage. The executive committee can review every idea alongside a set of criteria:

1. Is the product meeting a need?
2. Will it put forward greater value?
3. Is it possible for it to be distinctively advertised?
4. Does the company have crucial acquaintance and resources?
5. Is the new product capable of delivering the expected sales volume, profit, and sales growth?

Concept Development and Testing

Promising ideas should be polished into testable entities. A product concept is an elaborated version of the idea articulated in significant customer requisites, whereas a product idea is just a potential product to be offered to the market by the company.

The difference lies in the fact that customers buy product concepts and not product ideas. By asking and answering certain questions, each of the product ideas can be converted into several concepts. Questions might be as follows:

1. Who will be using this product?
2. What principal advantage should this product offer?
3. How will consumers exploit this product?

By providing answers to such questions, several concepts can be formed and accordingly be tested.

Marketing Strategy Development

Once concept development and testing is done, the manager must develop an introductory marketing strategy for launching the new product. This strategy consists of three parts:

1. Describing the target market's behavior, size and structure; the market share, sales, and profit goals sought in the initial years and the intended product positioning
2. Outlining distribution strategy, planned price, and marketing budget for the initial years
3. Describing the marketing-mix tactics over time and long-run profit and sales goals

Business Analysis

After concept development and marketing strategy, management has to evaluate the proposal's business charisma. Cost, sales, and profit projections need to be prepared to agree on whether they suit company objectives without which the product concept cannot be moved to the development stage. The business document will ultimately be revised and expanded upon as new information is received.

Evaluation of Total Sales

Sales needs to be estimated by the management; will they be high enough to generate a profit? Total sales will include first-time sales, repeat sales, and replacement sales. This evaluation depends on whether the product is a one-time purchase (such as a company-specific tailor-made business continuity and resiliency service), an occasionally purchased product (such as workstations), or a repeatedly purchased product (such as storage systems and servers):

1. For one-time purchased products, sales rise at the start, reach a peak, and subsequently fall to zero as the list of potential buyers is exhausted. The curve does not fall to zero if new customers keep entering the market.
2. Occasionally purchased products demonstrate replacement cycles marked by obsolescence associated with changing features, styles, and performance or by physical wearing out of products. For such products, sales forecasting has to be done by estimating replacement sales and first-time sales separately.
3. With repeatedly purchased products, the number of first-time customers initially increases and then decreases gradually as smaller number of buyers are left (assuming that the population is fixed). Repeat purchases take place soon, provided the product is satisfactory. The sales curve ultimately falls to an area of little variation, showing steady repeat-purchase volume.

Evaluation of Profits and Costs

Once the sales are evaluated, management should evaluate expected profits and costs. These estimations are done by the various departments involved in new product development, such as R&D, development, marketing, and finance departments.

Product Development

Once the product concept is analyzed, it is moved to the R&D or engineering department to be transformed into a physical entity. This involves a significant increase in investment, which is large when compared to the costs involved in the previous stages. Whether the product idea can be converted into a commercially and technically feasible product is determined by the company at this point.

A list of required consumer attributes is developed through market research and transformed into a list of engineering attributes that the company engineers can utilize. Example: Customers of a new operating system may demand a particular security feature. Engineers can transform this into the required firewalls, inbuilt antivirus programs, and other engineering attributes. This methodology improves communication between engineers, marketers, and the development people. The R&D department develops multiple versions of the product concept in its quest to find a prototype that meets the key attributes embodied in the product concept statement, can be produced within the budgeted development costs, and performs safely under standard use and conditions.

Apple assumes the worst handling by its customers and hence subjects its laptop computers to a series of rigorous, if odd, tests: It submerges the computers in sodas such as Pepsi, smudges them with mayonnaise, and even bakes them in ovens at temperatures of around 140°F or more to replicate the heat of a typical car trunk.

Market Testing

At this point the product is ready to be given a brand name and proper packaging, after which it can be put to a market test. The new product has to be launched in a measurable locale so that it becomes easy to discern the market size and how dealers and customers react to using, handling, and repurchasing the product.

Not all products or services require market testing. Some products or services do not require mass distribution; hence, it would be needless for the product or service to be market tested. When a new product or service is developed, say, an Integrated Communications Service for a particular client, testing by the client itself solves the purpose.

Market testing can provide much relevant information regarding marketing strategy effectiveness, buyers, dealers, and even market potential. IT products and services generally go through alpha testing, which is done within the company, and beta testing, which is done with customers. The purpose of beta testing is to monitor how the product or service is used by test customers, which might uncover unforeseen issues of maintenance and servicing. The company also gets the opportunity to observe how important the product or service is to the customer's business, which can be used to determine pricing.

Test customers also enjoy several benefits: They get to influence product design, gain familiarity with the new product developed ahead of competitors, get price discounts in return for assistance, and boost their status as technical pioneers. Beta test results must be carefully interpreted, because only select test customers are utilized and the tests are to some extent tailored to each site. Another risk is that the test customers who are not impressed with the product may reveal unfavorable information about it.

Commercialization

Once the company decides to finally enter the market, that is, to go forward with commercialization, it will encounter the biggest expenses to date. The first task is to build or rent a full-scale development facility. Commercialization requires the following factors to be taken into consideration.

When (Timing)

Market entry timing is a critical issue when a new product is to be launched. This is made particularly tricky when a competitor is launching a similar product or service. There are several ways to handle this:

1. First entry: Have the first-mover advantage of gaining reputational leadership and locking up key distributors and customers. A pitfall is that the product's image can be negatively affected if the product is hurried to market before it is properly debugged.
2. Parallel entry: Both the firm and its competitor's entry into the market might coincide. There might be a benefit to this. Since two companies are coming up with a similar new product, the market may pay more attention.
3. Late entry: The firm might delay its launch and wait for the competitor to launch the product first. In this situation, the competitor bears the cost of educating the market about the benefits of the product. Many faults might be revealed in the competitor's product, which can be avoided by the late entrant. Market size can be better estimated.

The timing decision involves some additional considerations. The company might delay the launch until the old product's stock is drawn down if a new product is replacing an older product. The product launch might be postponed until the right season arrives if the product is highly seasonal.

Where (Geographic Strategy)

The company has to make a decision whether to launch the new product in a single locality, a single region, multiple regions, nationally, or internationally.

Some researchers have observed that products designed solely for the domestic market generally have a high failure rate, low growth, and low market share. In contrast, products intended for the international market, or at least those that include neighboring countries, achieve considerably more profits, both abroad as well as at home. The recommendation is that IT companies should have a global focus in planning and developing new products.

The company should develop a planning spreadsheet to help select potential markets. In choosing these rollout markets, the candidate markets can be listed as rows, and rollout attractiveness criteria can be listed as columns. The key evaluation criteria are the company's local reputation, market potential, cost of communication media, competitive penetration, cost of filling the pipeline, and influence of area on other areas. The existence of tough competition will impact the rollout strategy. IT companies are rolling out progressively more new products concurrently across the world, rather than nationwide or even regionally.

To Whom (Target-Market Prospects)

The company generally aims its initial promotion and distribution to the best prospect groups within the rollout markets. The company must first profile the primary prospects, who would ideally have the following features: They will generally be early adopters, opinion leaders, heavy users, and be reached at a low cost. Some groups possess all these features, whereas others don't. The best prospect groups should be selected by the manager from the various prospect groups, by rating the different prospect groups on these features. The intent is to generate strong sales as early as possible.

Many companies are surprised to learn who really buys their product and why. Households dramatically increased their purchase of computers when the CD-ROM multimedia feature was introduced.

How (Introductory Market Strategy)

When launching a new product into the rollout markets, a proper action plan needs to be developed. Apple made its reentry into the PC business in 1998 after a break of 14 years with its very competitive iMac. The company launched the iMac with a gigantic marketing blitz.

Apple staged a spectacular launch for its new machine iMac, the egg-shaped sleek computer with one-touch access to the Internet. For beginners, the iMac was a secret until May 6, 1998, when Steve Jobs unveiled the new machine to the mesmerized reporters. By the time the machine went on sale in August, the buzz continued to mount, online and offline. Computer retailers stimulated Midnight Madness sales with 20-foot-high inflatable iMacs floating above the stores on the weekend of the launch. Steve Jobs individually signed five "golden" tickets and positioned them in the boxes of five iMacs, with the winner getting a free iMac every year for the next five years. iMac countdown was begun at radio stations across the country. With a $100 million ad campaign, Apple amplified these efforts. This was its biggest ad campaign to promote iMac through TV, radio, print, and billboards. Images of iMac alongside slogans such as "Mental Floss" and "I think, therefore iMac" were featured as part of the campaign.

Conclusion

The development of an IT product or service goes through eight phases: idea generation, idea screening, concept development and testing, marketing strategy development, business analysis, product development, market testing, and commercialization. Those of you who are IT developers probably find this set of phases similar to the systems development life cycle (SDLC) that is used to develop a computer system from an idea through to an implemented system. You wouldn't be far wrong. The difference here is that marketing concepts are infused throughout the eight steps so that what is ultimately developed is something that can be successfully marketed.

Chapter 9

Pricing Products

In February of 2005, Maytag—a home and commercial appliance company with a presence in markets around the world and sales operations in Canada, Australia, Mexico, Puerto Rico, and the United Kingdom—launched the Skybox with great fanfare (http://gizmodo.com/archives/maytag-skybox-019629.php). Skybox is a personal beverage vendor, or a beverage vending machine, that does not require any money. It holds 64 cans or 32 bottles, which it chills and dispenses by the touch of a selection button. It can also be customized with the logo of one's favorite sports team. At around $500, the Skybox did not represent tremendous value. After all, you might get a basic refrigerator (in the Unites States) for far less. But was value ever the point? More likely, the point was to create a sensation, to create that hot new product that nobody actually needs, probably, but that they crave and have to have before their neighbor does. The price likely reflects that the Skybox is an indulgence—more of a trophy than a functional appliance. Indeed, the marketing blurb on the Skybox Web site emphasizes the bragging rights.

One purpose of marketing is to facilitate an exchange between a buyer and a seller. Price is the value that is exchanged for products in a typical marketing transaction, although barter (i.e., the exchange of products or services) might also be used. As demonstrated in the Skybox example, buyers' willingness to pay a particular price is dependent on their perception of the value of the product to them.

As we saw in Chapters 6, 7, and 8, product development is a time-consuming and often expensive process. The organization must have a way to recoup these expenses as well as earn a profit. Price, therefore, is a key element in the marketing mix because it relates directly to total revenue:

$$\text{Profits} = \text{Total revenues} - \text{Total costs}$$

or

Profits = (Prices × Quantities sold) − Total costs (Pride and Ferrell, 2003)

Many firms set a price by just adding a standard markup to the average cost of the products they sell (i.e., cost-plus pricing). Also typical is breakeven analysis, used during activities such as software development project planning.

Products for which R&D costs are high and product life is short utilize a pricing model in which an attempt is made to recoup costs at the beginning of a product's sales cycle. The pharmaceutical industry in the United States is a good example of this. The typical cost to produce a new drug (from discovery through commercialization) ranges from $900 million to $1.2 billion. Pharmaceuticals only have a specific period of time—usually the duration of their patent, which is typically 20 years—before their drug is permitted to be reformulated as a generic by competitor firms. Therefore, the pharmaceuticals often price their drugs aggressively. Indeed, some would say that many pharmaceutical companies engage in predatory pricing.

More managers are realizing that they should set prices by evaluating the effect of a price decision not only on profit margin for a given item but also on demand and, therefore, on sales volume, costs, and total profit.

In order to estimate demand, marketers need to know how to evaluate a customer's price sensitivity. Asking a series of questions may help:

1. *Are there alternate ways of meeting a need?* If there are, the consumer is more price sensitive. Price elasticity comes into play here. This is a measure of the magnitude of consumer response to a change in price. Products that have few good substitutes generally have lower price elasticity than products with many substitutes.
2. *Is it easy to compare prices?* If so, the ease of comparison tends to increase price sensitivity.
3. *Who pays the bill?* People are less price sensitive if someone else pays or if they share the cost with someone else.
4. *How great is the total expenditure?* If it is large, marketers may try to break the expenditure into smaller pieces.
5. *How significant is the end benefit?* Consumers will be less price sensitive if they perceive the end benefit from purchasing the product to be substantial.

Factors Affecting Pricing Decisions

The process of determining price depends on a number of generic factors, as shown in Figure 9.1.

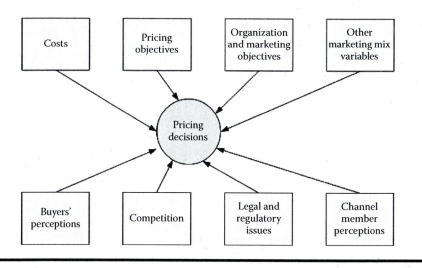

Figure 9.1   Factors affecting pricing decisions (Pride and Ferrell, 2003).

1. **Costs**. Most markets are price sensitive. Marketers usually examine all costs to determine the "floor" price of the product (i.e., the price below which the product should not be priced). Costs include R&D, distribution, and marketing. As we will see in the following section, a firm may sell products below cost to match competition, generate volume, or introduce a new product.

2. **Pricing objectives**. The price of a product may depend on a variety of objectives. The firm might want to target a particular return on investment and to undercut competition, so it could price the product below competing brands.

3. **Organization and marketing objectives**. The price of a product is usually aligned with the organization's mission, strategies, and goals. For example, if the organization has positioned itself as the producer of quality luxury cars, then it will usually price its products at the high end of the market.

4. **Other marketing mix variables**. The price of a product is also dependent on other marketing mix variables such as production, promotion, and distribution. Premium-priced products are usually distributed through selective distribution methods (e.g., boutiques), while economy-priced products are sold through intensive distribution (e.g., cut-rate discount stores).

5. **Buyers' perceptions**. Value-conscious consumers are concerned about price and quality. Price-conscious consumers, on the other hand, are usually on the lookout for lower prices. Prestige-sensitive consumers have a tendency to purchase only those products that promote their image and status.

6. **Competition**. Price cannot be set in a vacuum. It is critical that a marketer be very aware of competitor pricing models. Some organizations are quite aggressive in matching, or even undercutting, competitors' prices. This strategy requires the marketer to first assess how competitors will respond to the change in prices. As we discuss in the McDonald's–Burger King

example in the following text, some price-cutting can lead to price wars where no one wins.

7. **Legal and regulatory issues**. Governments have an active hand in price determination. To curb inflation, the government may invoke price controls. In certain instances, price freezes have been instituted. In other cases, governments have dictated the price itself.

8. **Channel member perceptions**. The marketing channel is a group of individuals or organizations that moves the product from the seller to the buyer. There are a variety of channel members (e.g., distributor, reseller, value-added reseller, etc.). Value-added resellers add value to the original product by selling it with an add-in or set of services. Channel members (often called *partners*) have their own expectations that must be figured into the pricing policy. For example, channel members often expect to receive large discounts so that they may resell the product at a reasonable profit.

Pricing Strategy

Almost every business transaction in our modern economy involves an exchange of money—the price—for something of (perceived) value. Guided by the company's objectives, marketing managers must develop a set of pricing objectives and policies. The pricing objectives and policies should spell out the following:

- How flexible prices will be
- At what level prices will be set over the product life cycle
- To whom and when discounts and allowances will be given

With all the analysis that goes into a pricing strategy and policy, as we have already mentioned, price cannot be set in a vacuum. Even perceived-value pricing must at least take into account competitive pricing. Regardless of whether competitors' prices are used as a benchmark to set prices, competitive pricing information should be gathered continually and used as market landscape reference points.

Setting a single price is also rare. Pricing structures that reflect variations in geographical demand and costs, market-segment requirements, purchase timing, order levels, delivery frequency, guarantees, service contracts, and other factors are much more common. Many companies have some sort of "buy more for less" program. In both consumer and business-to-business marketing, companies recognize that they can save overhead with higher volume sales. A price reduction to those customers who buy large quantities or to those who pay their bills on time is common. Whatever the context, price setting is obviously not a one-time event; it is a process closely tied to market positioning.

Price changes often involve much more than just a simple price tag change. Many times this involves repositioning the entire brand in a new market. Companies have pursued price cuts in an attempt to make themselves more competitive. This can be risky. The day a company announces its price cuts, consumers may not be the only stakeholders to react. Investors will interpret the change as well and may not reward price cuts.

In the early 1990s, Taco Bell, which operates 280 restaurants worldwide, decided to introduce a value menu to boost its volume. This did indeed boost sales. In the late 1990s, the company introduced a better-quality menu at higher prices. However, consumers continue to resist the nonvalue menu.

Promotional pricing strategies, the chosen strategy of many fast-food chains, are often tricky and sometimes disastrous. McDonald's introduced its Dollar Menu only to be undercut by Burger King's somewhat less than a dollar menu. The resulting competition was one of the reasons for declining profitability for both chains for a period of time.

Aligning price with marketplace positioning strategy affords managers of all types of products and services a strategy that clearly differentiates their brands on a variable that is important and noticeable to customers. Price and quality perceptions of cars is a good example. Higher-priced cars are perceived to possess high quality. Similarly, higher-quality cars are assumed to be much higher priced. Quality, similar to many offering characteristics, is a complex variable. Therefore, it is simpler to communicate price differences rather than quality differences to customers. Consumers assume that there is a relationship between price and quality.

Normally, the higher the price, the lower the demand. However, in the case of prestige goods and psychologically priced products (e.g., face cream that promises to reduce your age by 10 years), consumers are not as sensitive to the higher pricing, and demand is not as negatively affected. Buyers are generally less price sensitive when the product cannot be compared very easily to substitutes.

Pricing policies affect aspects of the marketing mix, as marketing managers use strategy planning to support the information communicated to consumers through the product's price. Two types of profit-oriented objectives are common:

1. **Target return objective**. Target profit pricing sets specific guidelines for a level of profit. Prices may be linked to a percentage of sales or return on investment. Some companies just want satisfactory profits that ensure the firm's survival and provide adequate returns to shareholders.
2. **Profit maximization objective**. The firm sets prices to seek as much profit as possible. This objective may be used to recoup high investment costs, or it may be simply a matter of company policy. Profit maximization can be socially responsible, as it does not always lead to high prices. Prices that are initially high during market introduction can go down in the later stages of the product life cycle, thus expanding sales and profits.

With sales-oriented objectives, pricing supports the objective of increasing sales without regard to their effects on profit. Sales growth does not necessarily mean big profits, because marketers may overlook the costs associated with delivering those sales. Market share growth objectives are popular. Coupled with a long-run view of the overall market growth rate and attention to costs, this approach can lead to long-term competitive advantages.

Price policies usually lead to administered prices with price-flexibility policies:

1. **One-price policy.** The same price for everyone. It is common with frequently purchased, inexpensive items. It can be more convenient, entail lower transaction costs, and maintain goodwill with customers.
2. **Flexible-price policy.** Offering different prices for different customers. Pricing databases make flexible pricing easier, less costly, and less time consuming because they contain information about different customers. Salespeople can also adjust prices to take into account the competition, the firm's relationship with a customer, and the customer's bargaining ability. However, too much price cutting may erode profits. A flexible-price policy may cause customers who do not get the lowest price to feel resentful.

Two of the major price-level policies are price skimming and price penetration:

1. **Skimming price policy.** Tries to sell to the top of the market by feeling out demand at a high price before aiming at more price-sensitive customers. For example, EasyJet sells only through the Internet. The earlier you buy, the cheaper (by far) the price. Skimming has critics, who charge that this policy should not be used for products that have important social consequences (e.g., prescription drugs). When well executed, price moves down the demand curve when each price-linked segment is nearly exhausted. The new price and new features should attract a new target market and help maximize profits over the course of the product's life cycle.
2. **Penetration price policy.** Tries to sell the whole market and achieve volume at a low price. When the elite market is small, this policy can be more effective than skimming. A penetration policy typically aims at setting a price low enough to discourage competition. If successful, large volume may help producers lower costs further, leading to still lower prices.

The Internet's Effect on Pricing

The late 1990s saw the stunning rise of numerous businesses that employed the Internet in their business models. Priceline.com was one of these companies, and, while the Internet was crucial to its rise to prominence, what really drove the company's business model was exploiting the economics of the airline industry. Similar to the pharmaceuticals mentioned earlier, the airline business is a high fixed-cost business, given the cost to purchase planes and maintain the large infrastructure needed to ferry passengers around the world. Once the infrastructure is in place, it costs very little to add passengers. In addition, an airline seat on a flight is a perishable commodity in that if it is not used, it is gone forever, representing a lost opportunity. Given this, the airlines have an incentive to accept any revenue—no matter how small—rather than suffer the lost opportunity of flying a plane with empty seats. So, why didn't people wait around until a flight was about to fly and then offer to buy a seat for a low amount of money? The reason is that there was no efficient way to aggregate real-time data and match it with real-time customer demand in a way that was efficient and convenient. The technologies behind e-business made these tasks doable in an efficient manner, but it was the underlying economics of the airline business that created the opportunity for Priceline.com to offer its service.

Similar to its airline partners, Priceline.com has a high-fixed-cost, low-variable-cost model. Once the tremendous costs of software development have been absorbed, there is almost no cost to processing incremental transactions through their system. So long as there is sufficient and growing transaction volume, Priceline.com can maintain and expand profitability.

In the aftermath of September 11, 2001, airlines drastically cut back their capacity as demand dried up. This meant that the number of potential transactions that would fall into Priceline.com's market niche of moving surplus inventory eroded as well. Priceline.com initiated per-transaction service fees to make up for the short fall. However, this eroded its perception among consumers as the lowest-cost source for discount travel, making the company more vulnerable to new competition.

The Ethics of Pricing

The area of pricing is an ethical minefield. The fact that prices are set by markets and can vary across time and geography, often significantly, is still upsetting to many in our society and arouses accusations of unethical behavior. It is frustrating to be faced with prices for gasoline, housing, and steel, to name a few, that were drastically lower within recent memory. This is the free market system; most of society has accepted its workings, but the free market system is based on rules and grounded in certain assumptions. These can be violated or distorted to certain advantage. Herein lie the ethical concerns. For example, the notion of having access to full information, fairly represented, is a foundational principle of transactions in the free market. Yet, often transactions occur in which one party will violate this tenet and misrepresent the details of the proposed transaction, which obfuscates the market determination of price. Anytime there is an information imbalance or other distortion of the market determination of price that leads to the seller's advantage, the seller's intent and ethics can be called into question.

Pricing in a Global Environment

Operating in a global environment presents both complexities as well as opportunities to firms engaged in new product development. With access to markets, labor, and materials from around the globe, the economic factors influencing new-product decisions have multiplied. Ideas that might have once been infeasible may be reconsidered, given the ability to manufacture or source materials from around the globe. However, they can also restrict pricing approaches. For example, could a German manufacturer continue to command prestige pricing on a product after moving production from Germany to, say, Latvia? Readers have probably experienced this as well. If you are reading an international edition of our textbook, it probably carries a message that you are not allowed to resell the book in the United States or Canada, since your cost was probably less expensive than the cost to a student in the United States. Even cheaper are textbooks printed in India, using lower-quality paper and ink. These books can only be sold in India.

New markets around the world expand the size of the overall market, making certain projects worth pursuing that might not have been worth pursuing previously. For example, additional, incremental volume that could be achieved in foreign markets might make a penetration pricing model for a new and unproven product more feasible.

Conclusion

Over the life of a product or service, it is likely that there will be one or more price increases. How marketing handles price increases is a good case study in the psychology of price-setting in general. The right strategy for increasing prices can result in increased customer satisfaction and fewer defections. There are several approaches to raising prices (Docters et al., 2004):

1. Use brute force—just insist on a higher price
2. Change the value, and increase the price
3. Price more completely by charging for previously free services
4. Adjust the roles of buyers and sellers in the marketplace
5. Leverage the price structure so that customers grow into a higher or better price level

All of these approaches require the marketer to understand customer value and economic dynamics. In all cases, raising prices will change the relationship between the cost and the value provided. It should always be remembered that customers want to be treated fairly. A price increase with no explanation or justification violates this sense of fairness. Rising gasoline prices in the United States prompted a congressional inquiry as outraged consumers questioned why the petroleum industry's profitability should grow astronomically at their expense. Their sense of fairness was violated.

The best way to persuade customers to pay more is to convince them that there is more value to be had at the higher price. We discussed the Crest SpinBrush in Chapter 6. This toothbrush is two to three times the price of an average toothbrush, but it offers many more features. Hence, the public accepted the price increase.

Another tactic is to reduce the quality or size of a product but maintain the same price. This is commonly seen on supermarket shelves where, for example, a can of tuna fish may have decreased in size but retained the same price.

Ultimately, pricing is a combination of science and art, requiring an understanding of consumer psychology, competitors' actions, and the product itself—past, present, and future.

Some companies deal with the vagaries of the pricing process by creating a specialized pricing organization within the company. A study of the pharmaceutical industry showed that a formal pricing department had a marked impact on pricing (Docters et al., 2004). Companies with pricing departments discounted less frequently and had very narrow price spreads for a particular product compared to companies without a pricing department.

References

Docters, R. G., Reopel, M. R., Sun, J. M., and Tanny, S. M. (2004). Brute force or stealthy inroads? The subtleties of effective price increases. *Journal of Business Strategy*, 25(3).

Pride, W., and Ferrell, O. C. (2003). *Marketing: Concepts and Strategies*. New York: Houghton Mifflin.

Chapter 10

Communications Strategies

Think for a minute about Microsoft and Apple. What do you know about these companies, and where did you learn about them? Maybe you saw a commercial on television, or read an article in the newspaper, or talked to your next-door neighbor who bought an iPod or iPhone. The impressions that you have about these companies are the result of branding, which we introduced in depth in Chapter 4. Marketing professionals who work for these companies spend a great deal of time and money to ensure you have the right impression of their brands so that when you buy a PC you'll ask for Microsoft software, or you'll think of Apple when you want to listen to music.

McDonald's developed an ad campaign around the tagline "I'm lovin' it," which it purchased from a German ad agency. The tagline was translated into different languages and is, or soon will be, used in over a hundred countries around the world—demonstrating that marketing campaigns can indeed be global. Coca-Cola's "Taste of Life" is another example. In both cases, these U.S.-based companies had to pay careful attention to cultural and language differences as they translated their American campaigns for use in foreign markets.

Each of these companies has gone to great lengths to influence your opinion. Successful brands use a variety of integrated marketing communication (IMC) methods and tools to build relationships with customers. In this chapter, you'll learn about these methods, including why they're important and how best to apply them.

Developing an Integrated Marketing Communications Program

IMC is the intentional coordination and blending of a firm's communications efforts to create a single message for a specific target audience that is complete and consistent, that is, a single voice. Think about it: Aren't you able to recognize a Nike ad even before you see the swoosh symbol (http://www.nike.com/main.html)? This kind of immediate recognition does not happen by accident—it's deliberate.

Most marketers ask themselves the following questions when developing an IMC:

Who is the target audience?
> Think about it in terms of who they are (single mom, CEO, teenager, etc.) as well as how they would like to be communicated with. Do they like telemarketers? A personal sales representative? E-mail? Print advertising?

What are the objectives?
> Do you want to sell something? Improve your company's reputation? Repeat sales?

What are the key communication messages?
> What does your customer value? Is it ease of ordering? Customer service? Hassle-free warrantees?

What is the message?
> Make sure to take the time to develop a creative message that resonates with your audience.

Which communications vehicles should be used?
> Back in the dark ages (before the Web), companies printed everything. Now, many firms find it is much more cost-effective to publish brochures and product information on their Web sites.

What can you afford?
> Understand how much things are going to cost—it all adds up. Be sure that you know what you can and can't afford before signing on the dotted line.

What's the best way to manage materials?
> No customer likes out-of-date information. Be sure to keep your materials, whether brochures or Web materials, up to date with the most current information available.

Promotion

When one thinks of marketing, some kind of promotional activity is usually the first thing that comes to mind. Promotion is defined as the communication of information between the seller and potential buyer to influence attitudes and behavior. The marketing manager's main promotional job is to tell target customers that the right **product** is available at the right **place**, at the right **price**.

There are three basic promotional objectives:

■ Inform
■ Persuade
■ Remind

There are several generic categories of promotional marketing communications (Perreault and McCarthy, 2005):

Mass selling: Communicating with large numbers of potential customers at the same time. When the target market is large and scattered, mass selling can be less expensive than personal selling. Advertising is the main form of mass selling. Advertising includes the use of traditional media such as magazines, newspapers, radio and TV, signs and direct mail, as well as new media such as the Internet.

Personal selling: Direct, face-to-face communication between sellers and customers. Although salespeople are included in most marketing mixes, personal selling can be very expensive.

Sales promotion: Refers to promotional activities—other than advertising, public relations, and personal selling—that stimulate interest, trial, or purchase by final customers or others in the sales channel. Most promotional efforts are designed to produce immediate results. Examples include contests, trade shows, events, etc.

Public relations: Essentially, PR is product release as news story. Often considered a stepchild to other marketing communication techniques, nevertheless, public relations, can be very effective and economical.

Promotional efforts create demand for an organization's products. The basic promotion objectives and adoption process can best be represented in the following AIDA model (http://www.ciadvertising.org/studies/student/97_fall/theory/hierarchy/early.html).

1. Attention: Get the customer's attention
2. Interest: Hold their interest
3. Desire: Arouse desire
4. Action: Obtain action, such as a purchase

Advertising campaigns can appeal to very specific groups of people through careful selection of words, images, and symbols. Marketers must provide advertisers with accurate target market information. Marketing managers should specify the kinds of advertising (from the many types available) that will best support over-all marketing objectives. Marketing managers should specify to the advertiser which media should be used to reach the target market; different target markets may use different media. While an advertising agency may develop the "creative" message—including some specific advertising copy—the marketing manager should specify the direction of this copy thrust and its link to specific promotional objectives.

Advertising objectives should be specific and related to the overall marketing strategy. Marketing managers set the overall direction for the advertising campaign, which may incorporate one or more of the following types of objectives:

Position brands: Advertising can communicate product benefits to position the brand relative to others in the mind of the consumer.

Introduce new products: Advertising can make target markets aware of new products and their benefits. Marketing managers can specify the percentage of the market that should be aware of the product after a specific period of time.

Obtain outlets: Advertising tells customers where they can buy the product and may help encourage merchants to carry it.

Provide ongoing contact: Advertising can be a "virtual salesperson," reminding customers about the product and keeping in touch with them.

Prepare the way for salespeople: Advertising may serve to "prime the pump" in advance of a sales call. Salespeople can then reference the ad in their presentation.

Get immediate action: Advertising can be a good way to announce time-dated deals, discounts, or other availability requiring immediate customer action.

Maintain relationships: Advertising can help maintain relationships with satisfied customers and confirm their original purchase decision.

Measuring advertising effectiveness is often difficult. In addition, advertising effectiveness needs to be considered in relation to its specific objective. For example, an ad campaign designed to increase awareness should not be judged a failure because it does not increase desire for the product. The effectiveness of advertising is hard to separate from the effects of other elements in the mix. For example, a great advertisement cannot be faulted for failing to sell a poor product.

Traditional Marketing Strategies

A variety of traditional marketing techniques are used by most marketers. Among them are advertising, sales promotion, and public relations.

Print Advertising

If you're going after a particular industry, then you don't want to advertise in a general-interest magazine. Popular consumer magazines attract large, fragmented audiences. What you don't want is diversity. You want 100% of the readership to be interested in what you offer. A study by Opinion Research Corporation (http://opinionresearch.com/) found that 40% of business customers cited trade publications as their chief source of information about particular products or services.

Given the focus of your degree program, let's say you're interested in targeting the computer industry. There are literally dozens of publications to choose from. The goal is to find the magazines that provide you with the largest audience at the lowest possible price. Marketers have access to various directories that provide this sort of information. Standard Rate and Data (http://www.srds.com) provides information on over 100,000 international media properties.

Ad rate is based on the ad size, whether color is used, and the number of times it is run. Although trade magazines are less expensive than business or consumer magazines, ads are still expensive. A full-page color ad might run for $6,000 a month, while a full-page color ad in a major business magazine can cost four times that amount. The unfortunate thing about advertising is that you can't really do it just once. As with direct mail, repetition is needed for it to work. You also need repetition to get the lowest rates.

The actual ad is usually created by an advertising agency hired to write the copy and develop the look and feel of the advertisement. Advertising is as much of an art form as it is a business. Creativity in advertising can create a "buzz" about a particular product or company, as demonstrated by these award-winning magazine ads: (http://www.adforum.com/).

Radio and Television Advertising

Like print advertising, radio and television advertising strives to make a product, company, or service stand out in a crowded marketplace. Creativity, as demonstrated by these award-winning spots (http://www.andyawards.com/winners/index.php), is the key component. The most famous of all television ads was aired during the Super Bowl in 1984. Aptly entitled "1984," directed by Ridley Scott, and ultimately named the "Commercial of the Decade," the futuristic ad startled viewers, who rushed out to buy the Macintosh. Ted Friedman's paper (http://www.duke.edu/~tlove/mac.htm) for the Society for the History of Technology Convention is worth reading.

Public Relations

Most companies have fully staffed public relations (PR) departments to handle relations with the press. The chief function of this department is to encourage the press to publish favorable articles about the company, its products, and its employees. In some cases, PR may also act as the first line of defense when damage control is needed (e.g., a defective product might lead to bad publicity, which requires all of the talents of the PR department to counter).

The mastheads (usually the first few pages) of all magazines and newspapers list everyone who edits and writes for a publication; some even include e-mail addresses. Alternatively, a list of media contacts can be purchased from various sources, such as Standard Rate and Data mentioned earlier. PR departments rigorously maintain their press databases and use them to send out press releases on new product launches, product enhancements, media tours, and other events.

While paper press releases are still mailed out on a regular basis, it is quite common for press releases also to be e-mailed or faxed to editors and writers. Most companies use press release newswires, such as PRWeb (www.prweb.com), for this purpose. In addition, most companies also publish press releases on the public relations portals of their Web sites, as Microsoft does here (http://www.microsoft.com/presspass/press/2005/nov05/11-21Xbox360LaunchFrenzyPR.mspx).

In our very global, interconnected world, it is also not uncommon for press releases to be simultaneously released in a wide variety of languages (http://www.microsoft.com/presspass/internat.mspx). Aside from maintaining press releases on PR portals, other information, such as product information, executive profiles, case studies, brochures, and contact information, is made available.

Marketing in the Digital Age

E-marketing is thought of as the place on the Internet "where the rubber meets the road." In the precommercial days of the Internet, Web sites were places for academics and researchers. That's changed rather dramatically. Today, the Web is the largest commercial marketplace in the world. The vast majority of companies have Web sites, and many are actively engaged in some sort of e-commerce, whether it be B2B (business to business), B2C (business to consumer), or another model.

You should review your company's e-marketing efforts. Does your company have a Web site? Are banner ads being used? How about pop-ups and pop-unders, e-mail, or Web communities? How is the success of these efforts being measured? You might also want to ask whether the Internet is being used effectively as a competitive analysis vehicle. Much information about your competitors can be found online. Is your company using appropriate searching methodologies and tools to stay on top of the market?

X10 popped into everyone's consciousness during the summer of 2001. It began benignly enough with a few trial pop-under ads. Then, all of a sudden, millions of Internet users were bombarded with a continual stream of X10 pop-unders.

X10.com was a small company with an interesting product. X10's tiny, wireless video camera is another in the long line of inexpensive technology gadgets that people just love to buy. The problem the little-known company had was in getting the word out.

At the time, most marketers used banner ads and pop-ups to market to potential customers. Banner ads, graphics usually placed at the top or the side of a Web page, were the original medium for e-marketing advertising. Pop-ups, small ads that pop up on top of your Internet browser, quickly followed suit and became one of the more popular e-marketing techniques. They are now ubiquitous.

X10 has the dubious distinction of being the pop-under pioneer. Pop-unders are similar to pop-ups, except that they pop under your browser, not on top of it. You don't actually notice them until you close your browser. This annoyed so many people that the X10 ads were followed by a storm of protest. Still, in the tradition of "any publicity is good publicity," the X10 pop-unders got results. Numbers from Jupiter Media Metrix (Carroll, 2001) show that the pop-unders launched X10.com into one of the most visited sites on the Web.

X10 may have been the guinea pig for the pop-under, but it is ad-server companies that have turned a mere annoyance into an ethical dilemma. Ad-server companies contract with firms to display ads to customers who might be interested in their products. Displaying an ad to a consumer who is already interested is far more effective than displaying an ad to everyone. How do they do this?

Online behavioral marketing uses software to track the Web-surfing habits of consumers. Many times, unbeknown to the consumer, tracking software is downloaded to his or her PC and proceeds to record what sites the consumer is viewing. Often called spyware or adware, the tracking software relays this information back to the ad-server company, which uses the information to send pop-up and pop-under ads to targeted consumers. So, for example, if you have adware installed on your PC and you visit google.com to do a search on car rental companies, you might wind up with pop-ups for Avis on your computer.

Online behavioral tracking software raises some interesting questions. Is it ethical to download tracking software onto a consumer's computer without his or her knowledge? Tracking software often comes bundled with game-playing or music-downloading software. For the most part, unless the consumer reads the legal agreement, he or she does not usually know that tracking software is being downloaded. A second ethical question is the propriety of popping up an ad over a competitive Web site. Hertz Corporation sued Gator.com for doing just that. Adware-enriched consumers visiting the Hertz Web site were often greeted with advertisements from competitors such as Avis. Effective? Yes. Ethical? No. Interestingly, Gator.com rebranded itself as Claria in 2003. In October 2008, Claria (rebranded as Jelly Cloud) shut down.

Cutting-Edge Internet Marketing Strategies

You're probably familiar with Internet-based advertising. Who hasn't been annoyed by a pop-up or pop-under ad or one of those ubiquitous banner ads? Rich media is also being used for its multimedia capabilities. It is even possible to pay for premium placement on the first page of search engine results (http://adwords.google.com). Other Internet-based marketing techniques that you are probably familiar with include affiliate programs, e-mail marketing, and link exchanges.

Recently, companies have taken to using the Internet in new and exciting ways to help manage issues facing them in traditional advertising media. In 2006/2007, companies started to recognize the power of search, video, and Web 2.0 for advertising. BMW, for example, was able to use word-of-mouth marketing and the Internet to generate buzz for its products by creating extended commercials that were only available online. Part advertising, part entertainment, these commercials created quite a stir among an audience that generally is overburdened with advertising noise.

The basis of this idea is viral marketing, which is good old-fashioned word-of-mouth advertising, or creating a "buzz" with a high-tech twist. Companies create online movies or commercials that can only be viewed at a Web site and downloaded. Interested consumers can then e-mail the actual ad or a link to the site to their friends. Word travels fast, and the excitement builds. The BMW ads (at http://www.bmwusa.com/Standard/Content/Uniquely/TVAndNewMedia/BMWFilms.aspx) were the pioneering effort and have since been copied. For this type of marketing to work, the ad has to be unique and it has to capture the interest of the audience so dramatically that viewers can't wait to share it with their friends.

The term *viral marketing* was purportedly coined by venture capitalist Steve Jurvetson to describe Hotmail's practice of appending advertising to the e-mails of their customers. Viral marketing can be quite creative—and crazy. Burger King hired a Miami creative ad agency to come up with a campaign for Burger King's new line of chicken sandwiches. The result is the Subservient Chicken (http://www.subservientchicken.com/). When the Web site was launched, only 20 people were told about it. Burger King says the site has since received 15 million to 20 million hits (Steinberg and Vranica, 2004).

Seth Godin coined the term *idea virus*—the notion that an idea can become contagious. He argues that information and ideas can most effectively spread from customer to customer, rather than business to customer. He urges marketers to create an environment in which their ideas can replicate and spread (Godin, 2001). One of the techniques marketers use is targeting what are referred to as "influentials." However, some feel that spending a billion dollars a year on this effort is not a very good idea.

As companies learn how traditional media is becoming less and less effective because of changes in consumer habits and technology, they look for nontraditional ways to attract the attention of their target audiences. One example is the cell phone industry. Companies competing in this industry have managed to spur demand for phones with everything from color screens to digital cameras! Young people in particular are attracted to the latest colors and functions these phones offer.

XML RSS

Figure 10.1 RSS symbols.

One company that is capitalizing on the "cool" factor is Motorola. They've used nontraditional marketing such as buzz and entertainment marketing. The company knew that it had to think outside the box to capture the attention and interest of the young people who make up its target market. Traditional advertising methods were not going to result in the buzz (and sales) it needed. "Cool" is definitely the next big thing in marketing.

The Internet has been a "cool" marketing medium for close to a decade. As technology changes, marketing inevitably follows the medium. RSS, or Really Simple Syndication, first entered the public's consciousness in 1999 by way of Netscape, which developed it for use on the My Netscape portal. At that time it was known as RDF Site Summary. RSS, part of the XML family, is most frequently used by news Web sites to push headlines, and perhaps multimedia files, to subscribers. Web-based readers make these feeds available to Web browsers, although client-side downloadable software also exists for this purpose. Web pages providing RSS feeds are usually designated with one of the symbols shown in Figure 10.1.

Companies use RSS feeds to keep the public in the loop about what's going on within the company, the RSS feed serving much the same function as a press release. Information on creating your own RSS feed can be found at http://searchenginewatch.com/sereport/article.php/2175271.

RSS is also used by that new generation of commentators that marketers are also trying to reach—the blogger. While the vast majority of blogs are read only by a handful of family friends, there are quite a few that have become influential in their respective fields. Indeed, some have even earned press credentials. It is estimated that there are well over 50 million bloggers online!

Unfortunately, there is also a negative side to blogging. Some bloggers are using their highly public forums to attack companies. Technorati (http://www.technorati.com/), a firm in San Francisco, tracks the content of 52 million active blogs, with 67,000 new blog entries posted each hour. What they are finding is that a certain percentage of these blogs are used for attacking people and companies. Unfortunately, some of the "attack blogs," as they have come to be known, are funded by competitors (Lyons, 2005). One blog, Groklaw, exists primarily to bash software maker SCO Group in its Linux patent lawsuit against IBM.

The blogosphere, therefore, needs to become part of the marketing communications strategy, using a three-step strategy as follows:

1. Monitor the blogosphere to locate blog smears early, before they can spread.
2. Start a blog. Sun's acerbic president, Jonathan Schwartz, uses his to reach employees, the press, and the public (http://blogs.sun.com/roller/page/jonathan).

3. Build a "blogswarm" by reaching out to key bloggers to get them on board. Some companies have even started to pay key bloggers for posting favorable commentary in their blogs. Marqui, a small software shop, paid 21 bloggers $800 per month to post items about the company, while requiring them to disclose the payments (Lyons, 2005).

It is said that Digg (www.digg.com) is revolutionizing the economics of publishing. Its more than 300,000 members submit links to interesting items on the Internet. Users then vote on them, with the top choices rising to the top of Digg's homepage. If you can get a few thousand people to "digg" your offering (i.e., article, video, white paper, etc.), you can generate far more traffic than even the hottest marketing campaign (Gillin, 2006).

RSS feeds and blogs were just the beginning, however. Apple's iPod has spawned yet another novel marketing opportunity. Podcasting, creating audio files that can be downloaded to a computer or MP3 player, was named among 24/7 Real Media's 10 predictions at the ad:tech conference for online advertising trends that will have the greatest impact (Krol, 2005). BearingPoint, a global consulting firm, uses podcasts as a prospecting tool to reach new clients. General Motors has also dabbled in podcasting and insists that it has secured twice as much readership as for its newsletter (Krol, 2005).

Second Life (www.secondlife.com) is a subscription-based 3-D world in which real-life advertisers, such as Warner Brothers and Adidas, have set up shop (http://www.businessweek.com/magazine/content/06_48/b4011413.htm?chan=search). BrandPort (www.brandport.com) is a new Internet-based advertising medium where advertisers pay consumers to view ads.

Video is also now a reality. YouTube's acquisition by Google for $1.65 billion of Google stock emphasizes the importance of this medium. Online video advertising will grow to 8% in 2010 (Booker, 2006). According to Booker (2006), the next phase of this phenomenon will be video that appear to be similar to those unedited "reality" videos that have become so popular. He provides the example of two different videos. In one, the CEO is droning on about his vision for the future. In the other, the CEO is walking through one of the company's factories, talking off the cuff with his employees about their jobs and the company's future. Which would you rather watch? Companies on the cutting edge are turning to "viral video" for everything from advertising to recruiting to training.

WOMM is a type of marketing strategy that functions through an individual's personal recommendations of a particular product/service or brand. WOMM spreads outside a formalized setting from one person to another, without the involvement of advertisers.

A recommendation from a person one is familiar with and someone whom one can trust is the easiest pathway to a product or service sale, link, or new subscriber. This is because recommendations are usually supposed to be incentive-free, in contrast to the apparent driving force of advertisers, who usually overpromise in a bid to boost sales.

If a company wants to sell more of its products or services, it should acquire a greater number of affiliate commissions or simply increase the number of new supporters for its site. WOMM is one of the most potent ways to do so. There isn't a better method of promoting the brand than to encourage a crowd of supporters continually chatting about or referencing it offline or online, through links or conversations.

WOMM Strategies

1. **Leverage existing social networks**. Online social networks have a strongly interwoven set of members who can assist in increasing a product's brand awareness. Example: Facebook, Orkut, MySpace, etc.
2. **Target the influencers**. Search for persons who are authorities or trend-setters in a specified domain. These people should generally be folks having a large and loyal audience and plethora of personal connections. Once these people spread the message you want, the site or product/service will effortlessly be spread across the targeted audience. Example: celebrities, popular webmasters and bloggers, power users on social networks, etc.
3. **Exclusivity and scarcity**. Launching virally by offering a restricted number of Web site invites, temporal discounts, or limited-edition products, in combination with influencer marketing, is an excellent way to increase brand awareness for new products or services. Curiosity is generated by exclusivity and consistent demand, and conversation results from scarcity in production.
4. **Micro-market**. Providing individuals with highly customizable products along with scarcity and use of social networks can generate word-of-mouth exposure.
5. **Industry marketing**. Focus on the people who have the potential to build your brand instead of focusing directly on customers. Make your mark within a niche community to leverage connections and build relationships. One needs to become a reputable brand that is recommended by other players in the same industry.

Using WOMM Services: P&G Tremor and BzzAgent

P&G Tremor creates and implements proprietary WOM promotion campaigns targeting teens and mothers. Driven by P&G's marketing and consumer insight expertise, such campaigns have the potential to accomplish the following:

1. Identify people who are most likely to discuss your products or services with others.
2. Determine significant customer insights that form the basis of discussions customers are most likely to share.

3. Develop a plan with 10 to 12 customer touch-points (both offline and online) that help customers slot in with and own the product or service scheme.
4. Generate outcomes of large scale using their panels of 250,000 teens and 450,000 women with kids.
5. Measure the impact of Tremor on the client's business by using control markets.

BzzAgent launched in 2001 with the aim of helping marketers harness the power of word of mouth. This company allows people to get early knowledge of new products or services, share their opinions about them with persons they know, and report such actions and opinions so marketers can directly see the results. This community brings marketers and consumers together to systematize and track WOM. It uses a three-step methodology:

1. Selection of a challenge medium, such as TV, print, radio, etc., to measure against BzzAgent
2. Execution of the WOMM campaign
3. Measuring results in terms of brand awareness, brand favorability, purchase intent, and purchase

WOMM Methodology

In WOMM, there are five steps:

1. **Talkers**—Find people who will talk.
2. **Topics**—Give people reasons to talk.
3. **Tools**—Help the message spread.
4. **Taking part**—Join conversation.
5. **Tracking**—Measure and understand what people are saying.

Talkers are people who highly recommend your product or service. They may not necessarily be customers. They could be third parties as well. How can you identify the talkers? Try to identify the satisfied customers and offer them enhanced service quality. People never forget a brand if they receive great service and will recommend the product to others as well. Visit online fan clubs, blogs, and social networks to identify the potential talkers.

Make sure the topic is attractive enough to entice more customers. It may not necessarily be a marketing message, because marketing messages are not word-of-mouth friendly. Try to give accurate reasons for people to talk about you. They are special offers, great service, trendy products, new features, etc.

Tools help the message to spread. A "tell a friend" form on a Web site is a highly recommended tool that all companies serious about marketing need to implement.

Others are viral e-mails, blogs, handouts, samples, online brochures, message boards, online communities, etc.

Try to join the conversation if it seems relevant to the product or service. Example: If a positive conversation is going on in a forum, join and say thank you. If it's negative, apologize. This will help the potential customers to identify how well one is engaged and also create a buzz about the product.

Try to measure and understand what people are saying. Search blogs, read message boards, and listen to feedback. Use advanced measurement tools to evaluate everything.

Some final points to note about WOMM:

1. Happy customers are the best advertisers.
2. Customers do marketing for the company for free.
3. Negative WOM is an opportunity; companies have to listen and learn.
4. People are already talking; the only job is to join the conversation.
5. Visibility is a key factor.
6. If it's not worth talking about, it's not worth doing it.
7. Honest marketing always makes more money.

Search Engine Marketing

Search engine marketing (SEM) is a type of Internet marketing whose objective is to promote Web sites or links to various IT products or services by increasing their visibility in result pages of search engines. Various SEM methods are search engine optimization (SEO), contextual advertising, paid inclusion, paid placement, etc.

Search Engine Optimization

SEO is the most extensively used SEM method. It is the process through which quality and quantity of traffic to a particular link or a Web site from search engines is improved via algorithmic or organic search results. Generally, a site is more frequently visited if it ranks higher, that is, if it is displayed earlier in the search results. Image search, industry-specific vertical search, and local search engines are also the different kinds of searches targeted. A visit to www.google.com/webmasters will enable you to submit your Web site for indexing. You can also have your Web site analyzed by Google's search engine, which identifies the top search terms that lead to your Web site.

The basic idea is to analyze what people generally search for and how specific search engines work. Web sites are then optimized by editing their content and HTML coding. This results in removal of barriers to the indexing activities of search engines and also increases a Web site's relevance to specific keywords.

SEO is used extensively these days by many IT companies to market their products or services. Search engines have been the most widely used Internet tool for finding Web sites and links to products and information, and the trend will continue at least for the foreseeable future.

The top ten search results are most often used by the people using search engines. For a site to be successful, it really needs to be on the first page. Most optimally, it should be found in the top three results. The probability of being clicked increases if the site is ranked high. A site does more business with more traffic, but this ranking has to be maintained for ongoing results.

Search engine optimization requires much work. Various aspects have to be changed on the site or added in order to get good results from the search engine. A lot of information needs to be gathered about the keyword phrases that are popular in regard to the Web site's theme or niche. Various studies on eye tracking have found that a search results page is scanned by searchers from the top to the bottom and from the left to the right. Therefore, to increase the number of visitors to the site, a top position is required.

After building a high-quality site, it is important to be sure that the products or services are named in such a way that people can easily find them. One should be sure to use names that potential customers would actually think of typing into a search engine. This type of marketing can be understood by comparing putting up a billboard in a cornfield in the middle of nowhere to having your advertising in the middle of Times Square. So, instead of naming the product "I love this special laptop," one should try using a name that people would actually search for.

It is best to test the search terms in several ways. First, they can be tried in the search engine and if the right Web sites show up, you know that you are on the right track. After searching, it is important to check to see how many people are searching for the products. This can be done through search suggestion tools provided by the major paid search engines. They suggest phrases that they deem to be a logical choice compared to what marketing managers put into the request form. This will provide guidance based on what people are actually searching for. The estimations they provide are just that, estimations, and can vary dramatically. Thus, it's important to try these phrases and see how well they perform.

So, the manager should be sure to understand how the products, categories, and services are labeled. This can make a very large impact on the traffic. An additional option is collaboration with other Web sites to get page transfers and link exchanges. The more the incoming and outgoing traffic generated by the Web site, the better the rank it is given by the search engines.

The secret to SEO is timing. A search engine marketing strategy should consider what to optimize, when to optimize it, and how to optimize the parameters necessary to achieve high search engine rankings for customers.

Some considerations:

1. The focus should be on bringing in quality traffic to the Web site.
2. The emphasis should be on analyzing and reporting of various results as an addition to the marketing strategy and its employment.

3. A comprehensive strategy of combining SEO strategies together with ground-breaking new advertising programs should be employed to maximize success.
4. It should be cost-effective.

Findings from a Microsoft study of marketing managers demonstrate the problems of search engine marketing:

1. Nearly 9 in 10 (89%) feared keywords may become too expensive.
2. Eighty-one percent of the respondents questioned if paid search marketing is the best use of their marketing budgets.
3. One-quarter of respondents believe paid search marketing is too complex.
4. Twenty-one percent thought it would be too time-consuming.
5. Thirty-five percent felt they would need an agency to help set up a search marketing campaign.

Depending on the advertiser's motives, other Web promotion strategies might be more effective, and SEM might not necessarily be an appropriate strategy. Heavy dependence on search engine traffic is not considered wise, as their algorithms keep changing. There is no guarantee of continued referral. A business might sustain large losses if these search engines discontinue sending traffic.

Google

Google is the most sought-after search engine in the world and will continue to be for a long time to come. Google search optimization has to be a component of an IT company's marketing campaign if it is entering the field of SEM. The current search engine market is dominated by Google, partly because of its extensive results, and more significantly because of its "organized" appearance. MSN and Yahoo! are cluttered with so much information that they confuse a typical Internet user.

Google launched its AdWords product back in 2000, and it is now its flagship advertising product with a total revenue of $16.4 billion in 2007. Through this program of Google, advertisers decide the keywords that would trigger their ads and accordingly pay per click. Further advancements in the product, such as the introduction of Placement Targeted Advertisements in 2003, help place the ads on what Google sees as relevant sites within its content network. Google Advertising Professional Program was launched in 2005. This program certifies companies and individuals who have completed AdWords training by passing an exam. These professionals were the need of the hour because of the complexity of AdWords and the amount of money at stake.

Integrated into AdWords is Google Analytics, which shows the advertisers how their site was discovered by people, how it was explored, and how a viewer's experience can be enhanced. It also gives inputs regarding how to enhance their Web site's ROI, how to increase conversions and, eventually, increase the amount of money made through the Web. Google Analytics tracks viewers through the Web site and also keeps a check on the performance of companies' various promotional strategies, be it the e-mail campaigns, using AdWords, or any other online marketing program. Advertisers get an idea as to which keywords are actually working, which type of ad text is most effective, and where the viewers are dropping off during the process of conversion by looking at myriad reports containing relevant information.

The Placement Performance Report is an AdWords report that provides site-by-site performance metrics for the ads across the Google content network. This report delivers increased transparency and control to help an advertiser meet ROI objectives on the Google content network by providing increased visibility into performance metrics such as clicks, impressions, cost, and conversions on a site-by-site basis. It can assist the advertiser in making informed decisions on improving its campaign's ROI and help in identifying high-value placements to target more aggressively and low-value sites that require content optimization or exclusion.

Google's content network has tens of thousands of Web sites, blogs, and news pages that display advertisements in partnership with the Google AdWords program. The marketing reach of such advertisements can be expanded to potential customers—that is, the targeted audience—who visit these sites on a regular basis as and when the advertiser chooses to advertise on the content network. This is the largest network for contextual advertising in the world. Advertisers have the option of themselves hand-picking sites from the content network, or relying on Google's established ad targeting capability to show the ads on the Web site pages that are most relevant to their products and services. Google's content network has a reach in over 100 countries comprising more than 75% of unique Internet users interacting in more than 20 languages. So when a marketing manager decides to use Google's search network, as well as Google's content network, the company has the potential to reach three out of every four unique Internet users in the world.

Search and content are different worlds with different audiences. Successful advertisers keep this in mind as they create their ads for the content network. When done right, content advertising reaches a completely new audience of customers who are browsing, researching, and ready to learn about a company's product on thousands of sites around the Web. Contextual targeting on the content network is not done at the keyword level but at the ad group level. So, when Google is deciding whether to display an ad on a particular content page, it evaluates all the keywords related to the content and the ad group.

Therefore, it becomes important that all the keywords in an ad group fit in with a universal subject matter. Ads are shown to those users who search through these keywords for a Web site on the search network. On the other hand, in the content network, when users research links of interest to them and look through Web sites that are related to certain keywords, the related ads are shown. Various changes to the ad text, keywords, and account structure might be required to derive the maximum benefit from content network advertising since the users on this network have a different mindset than users on search.

Some general tips for advertisers using SEM:

1. Give visitors the information they're looking for.
2. Make sure that other sites link to yours.
3. Make the site easily accessible.

SEM strategy formulation is a critical marketing technique that is often ignored by companies entering online marketing. A marketing manager should consider and understand all the alternatives, and only then develop a plan with the aim of achieving the desired results and making the best use of each marketing dollar.

Virtual Trade Shows

Like almost everything else these days, trade show producers are using the Web to get in touch with a larger audience of global viewers. For IT products or services, virtual trade shows become even more important as most of the targeted audience already spends a lot of their time on the Internet. A virtual trade show allows participants, no matter where they are located geographically, to connect and exchange information with one another via the Internet through an online environment that exists for a restricted time period.

While the wizardry of avatars and three-dimensional graphics gave virtual trade shows a "wow" appeal in their early days, companies have shifted their priorities to improving usability for participants and measurability for exhibitors, which makes virtual trade shows much more attractive nowadays.

Companies such as IBM, Cisco, and others are taking their trade shows and conferences virtual. Some, such as IBM, have used the virtual world Second Life for such events, but virtual trade shows take it a step further. Unlike Second Life shows, events are more professional and created for a business environment—there are no actual avatars. However, participants can upload a picture, chat with booth representatives, and attend sessions.

After submitting an online registration, participants are provided online name badges. Various other control features limit and monitor traffic flow and participation. Advancements in technology allow virtual entities to actually imitate real-world trade show booths with displays and company information. Thus, companies try to digitally replicate everything a customer would get at a face-to-face event. Tailored content is uploaded by the exhibitors to appeal to their target viewers. Communication can be established with the exhibitor with the click of a mouse through e-mail, instant messaging, or a voice call. Audio messages and product demonstrations can be given with the help of multimedia. Elliot Markowitz, Nielsen Business Media's editorial director of Webcasts and digital events, says,

"First, we have three to four Webcasts, because the content drives the audience. Second is the virtual trade show floor where exhibitors can house anything they would house in a regular booth, as long as it's downloadable. Third, we facilitate live interaction through chat between attendees and exhibitors, but the attendee, not the exhibitor, must initiate the conversation in the booths. Finally, we create networking opportunities, such as live forums, so attendees can meet and talk to one another."

A survey was recently conducted by United Business Media's InformationWeek Business Technology Network (IWBTM) of 545 professional IT buyers. They found that they are attending an average of one virtual event per quarter. Sixty-two percent of the professionals agree that virtual trade shows are an efficient use of time, enabling them to see a variety of technologies in one place. Eighty-two percent said that they considered virtual events to be a valuable source for learning about new technologies.

A major advantage of virtual trade shows is that they can save a lot of money over conventional trade shows as they can be conducted anywhere in the world just by the use of a computer without the expenditure of convention centers, lodging, travel, meals, trade show displays, etc. Bottom line: Virtual events are cheaper than flying in customers or team members from around the world. Other advantages include the following:

1. The market of accessible customers. A business may be local, but the customers may be global.
2. Business on the Internet is 24/7. This allows a company to service its customers when they are not physically present. "Work while you sleep" takes on a new meaning when a company takes this new route of doing business on the Internet.
3. Tired of answering the same questions over and over? A Web site helps to move customers smoothly along the presales process because it will answer the most frequently asked questions, which are already posted on the Web site. All content created for online events become mini Web sites in themselves, and user's questions, social media elements such as blogs, etc., are very valuable to leverage to other marketing arenas.
4. At conventional trade shows, customers can only review the products by looking at them at the show location. Using the virtual trade show format, information is available to anyone 24 hours a day.
5. Additional dimensions can be added to the business as products or services can be described in a better way through sound, pictures, and electronic files. Virtual shows can comprise a display hall with trade show displays and booths to exhibit information and products or services much like conventional trade shows. These shows can host virtual seminars, Web conferences, and educational presentations. The Web allows for limitless scenarios with combinations of sound, video, and text.

6. Participants also have the benefit of live interaction between company representatives and other users.
7. Virtual trade shows can also benefit the employees of an IT organization as they offer a wide variety of educational experiences via online seminars, conferences, and classes. They can be as extravagant as live video conferences or as simple as online text courses. Participants can instantly view as well as download information from unlimited sources. Text, images, sounds, and videos can all be integrated to improve the educational experience.
8. Virtual trade shows are excessively transparent. Every mouse click can be tracked and, thus, measured.

Virtual trade shows have the option of either being stand-alone online shows or being used in combination with real-world shows. Either way, they are becoming part of today's IT companies' marketing strategies to reach the global community.

Conclusion

As a marketing professional, designing key messages is a big part of the job. Content is still king when it comes to communication, although how, where, and when to communicate are also very important. The *what* has got to be paramount. Saying too much, too little, or just giving the wrong message altogether will be disastrous.

Consider the communications issues surrounding the Exxon Valdez events. On March 24, 1989, an Exxon tanker ran aground and was dumping gummy crude oil into the water just outside of Valdez, Alaska. The first message was sent when CEO Lawrence Rawl decided against making a trip immediately to Valdez, and instead opted to stay in New York. The second message rang loud and clear but was not until one week following the spill. Exxon's words were then too little, too late, and the message mostly blamed others in defensive, argumentative language. Now this is noted as a communications textbook case study of what not to do when information is needed in a crisis.

A crisis is not the only time messages must be clear. Planned communications must include plenty of planning around the *what*—the message. One of the new key trends in messaging is personalization. Marketers are always striving for relevance (creating meaningful messages that add value for each customer). Proctor & Gamble (P&G) is one consumer products company that is on the edge of messaging in a personalized way. Central to P&G's online branding efforts is the idea of relevance. They have used micro-sites and personalization techniques to communicate with their target markets. For instance, one of P&G's brands, Cover Girl, asks consumers questions around hair and cosmetics that generate personal profiles, and then offers specific advice and promotions via the Web based on those profiles.

Advertising is a multibillion-dollar industry. More advertisers are using risky creative tactics to try to get attention and break through ad clutter. They can be effective, but they can also break the bank with no return or even negative reactions. Advertising is classified in many different ways, but there are three general aims to ads: They either aim to inform, to persuade, or to remind. Part of marketing management is thinking through the aim prior to creating advertising. It should not be left to an ad agency to do this.

Since you have extensively evaluated *to whom* with segmenting and targeting, and have the rough draft message of *what* in your messaging, the next question is *how*. Media selection is deciding which will most successfully meet your objectives and metrics. You are generally looking for the best and most exposure per dollar. *Best* and *most* exposure is measured in terms of reach (the number of different persons or households exposed to a particular media schedule at once during a specific time period), frequency (the number of times within the specified time period that an average person or household is exposed to the message), and impact (the qualitative value of an exposure through a given medium).

Media planners and marketing managers then make their choices by considering variables such as cost and application to message, but most importantly, target-market media habits are considered (i.e., does the segment we want to reach generally watch TV prime time, cable late at night, or only listen to talk radio? And do they really read the newspaper? Do they shop/browse online, or are they only on the computer working?).

References

Booker, E. (2006). Do you see video in your future? I do. *BtoB: The Magazine for Marketing Strategists*, October 9.

Carroll, J. (2001). Ending the pop-under ad scourge. *Digital Marketing*, November, p. 11.

Gillin, P. (2006). Link blogs growing huge without overhead. *BtoB: The Magazine for Marketing Strategists*, October 9.

Godin, S. (2001). *Unleashing the Ideavirus*. New York: Hyperion.

Krol, C. (2005). Podcasting call lures advertisers. *BtoB: The Magazine for Marketing Strategists*, November 14.

Lyons, D. (2005). Attack of the blogs. *Forbes*, November 14.

Perreault, W. D., and McCarthy, E. J. (2005). *Essentials of Marketing*. New York: McGraw-Hill.

Steinberg, B., and Vranica, S. (2004). Burger King seeks some Web heat. *Wall Street Journal*, April 15.

Chapter 11

Distribution Strategies

A typical consumer can shop in a variety of places ranging from retailers to e-tailers to automatic vending machines and even the home (in-home sales). The results of distribution can be seen on a daily basis. Yesterday, you may have purchased petrol from a garage, a gift at Harrod's, and a book from Amazon.com. Each one of these items was brought to you through a channel of distribution. With the advent of technology, consumers can now act across multiple channels, calling, clicking, or visiting.

Channels of Distribution

There are a variety of strategic decisions related to placing a product or service in the market. Some of these involve the following:

1. Type of marketing channel: direct or indirect
2. Number of channels
3. How the organization will manage the channels
4. Type of physical distribution facilities needed
5. Customer service level desired
6. Degree of market exposure desired
7. Middlemen or facilitators needed

A direct marketing channel has no intermediaries. For example, a craftsperson sells his or her wares at a crafts fair; that is, the goods move directly from the producer to the consumer. An indirect marketing channel is one in which there are one or more intermediary levels, for example, from producer to wholesaler to retailer to consumer. While the indirect channel is the one most often used by producers, the direct channel has its advantages. Fewer intermediaries means that the producer has greater control over the product. It also means that the cost to the consumer is lower and revenues are higher for the producer. Since there are fewer layers between consumer and producer, the latter can react more quickly to consumer requests and be more responsive to changes in the market. For the most part, however, a large producer will only use the direct channel if suitable intermediaries are not available.

When making decisions concerning place or marketing channel, an organization must consider which form of exposure best fits its marketing objectives. There are three general approaches to market exposure:

1. **Intensive:** An example of this would be a company launching a product worldwide through the retail market.
2. **Selective:** A company distributes a product in certain regions of the world.
3. **Exclusive:** A company distributes a product to specific dealers.

For example, a small software company launches a software product. It uses an intensive distribution method by getting its product into computer and office supply stores in the United States. To do this, it uses a distributor such as Ingram Micro (http://www.ingrammicro.com/). It markets globally by working with dealers, usually referred to as resellers, in different countries, each of whom has exclusive rights to sell the product in its territory. In each case, the software company will enter into an agreement stipulating how much the distributor or reseller will earn for each product sold, as shown in this example.

Marketing channels also play an important role in determining the cost of a product. Distribution, transportation, and customer service are cost factors. Many companies fail to consider the cost of lost sales when customers use competing products or when access to a product is denied. To be successful, organizations need to be able to interact with customers in multiple locations through multiple channels, when and where customers want to interact.

The channels chosen ultimately affect all the other marketing decisions, and channels are not mutually exclusive, so sometimes the toughest decisions for managers are those regarding which channels will complement one another most effectively. Marketing channels have changed drastically in the past decade. The Internet has been a major driving factor in that change, as has been the rapid flow of information in general. For instance, having a fancy Web site with nothing behind it won't work today, and managing a brick-and-mortar facility with no Web presence is probably not ideal in most industries either. Failing to integrate channels that enrich the buying experience for customers can be a serious drawback. Doing it right can create a definitive edge.

As we discussed in Chapter 2, the success of Amazon.com came as a big surprise to Barnes & Noble. Who would have thought that a no-name virtual start-up would soon outpace and outsell the biggest bookseller in the world? Competing with a first mover, particularly one as creative and dynamic as Amazon.com, isn't easy. This is where having multiple distribution channels can help.

Selling Intermediaries

Some producers choose to sell directly to consumers. The Internet has made this approach much more manageable, but a direct channel is not always the ideal setup for a manufacturer. Many firms prefer a set of intermediaries, all performing a variety of functions between them and consumers. These intermediaries serve as marketing channels and take on the roles of merchant, agent, facilitator, partner, etc. For instance, wholesalers are used when they become more efficient at selling or promoting the product, buying and assortment building, bulk breaking, warehousing, transportation, financing, risk bearing, or providing market information or management services.

Not all companies can master placement well. Organizations in almost all industries now realize that they need strategic partners if they hope to be effective. Forging partnerships and putting together synergistic programs do require a significant investment of time and leadership support up front, but they can result in economies of scale, bulk lead generation, sustained growth, and brand strength and stature. Many of the world's top airlines have formed alliances. By integrating collaborative distribution strategies that share reservation systems and routes, each strategic alliance member gains access to a broader market, can reduce capital expenses, and can achieve better utilization and capacity rates.

Strategic partners can also act as sales channels. While it makes sense for some manufacturers and service providers to distribute directly to consumers through their own sales forces, strategic partners may be a much more efficient option. Companies give creative thought to finding partners that might build on their strengths and offset their weaknesses. Well-managed alliances allow companies to realize greater impact at lower cost. To keep their strategic partnerships thriving, corporations have to develop organizational structures to support them and have come to view the ability to form and manage partnerships as a core skill in itself.

Disney employs a team of alliance executives, and Xerox has a strategic alliance group as well. The software industry sets an example for the importance and value of creating, managing, and monitoring partnerships. HP/Compaq, Intel, Microsoft, and Oracle all have elevated their alliance marketing and business development groups, expecting return on investment (ROI) from strategic investments in relationships with partners. Many small companies have grown almost solely from alliances with complementary technology groups and companies, creating a high-tech culture over the past 20 years that relies on "co-opetition" rather than strictly head-to-head competition. As globalization and technology enable rapid change, even sector leaders cannot maintain leadership positions without forming strategic partnerships with entities that complement or leverage their capabilities and resources.

Distribution can also be the strategic key to new and emerging markets. Access to distribution is often critical to success in emerging international markets, and it cannot be taken for granted. There is no substitute for a detailed understanding of the unique characteristics of a region's distribution system and how it is evolving. New markets do not necessarily need to be overseas. Sometimes, an opportunity emerges within a brand's current distribution channel—a boom in the value segment of any given product category sold through a supermarket, for example. If a low-cost distribution channel creates an opportunity, companies must consider offering their products through that channel. Specialty superstores have created category-dominant outlets with price-sensitive customers and significant economies of scale. This type of vertical extension promises increased volume and economies of scale, but the risk of moving down market might be loss of brand equity and stature.

New channels may also be important decisions when introducing new brands. When Toyota launched Lexus, the new luxury vehicles could easily have been sold through Toyota dealerships, but the strategic brand decision was made to set up entirely new channels—Lexus dealers that specialize in the Lexus brand.

Many other companies that rely on customer retention have taken similar steps in creating new channels suited to the needs of loyal customers. State Farm Insurance could have sold insurance through independent agents, the way almost every other agency did years ago. Instead, it chose to develop quality relationships with its own agents, who in turn were developing relationships with end-user clients.

These current business examples tell us quite a bit about good decisions, but the hardest part of the issue of placement (i.e., distribution) is determining the optimal channel for each specific product or service. Certainly, in each specific business case, there are pros and cons to distribution models used in other settings. What must be considered is the impact that placement has on the other three strategic components of the marketing mix (product, pricing, and promotion)—and what cannot be forgotten is the customer.

A well-constructed channel and distribution plan results in a strong strategic foundation for any organization. Certainly, when the entire supply chain is integrated and communicating, customers are more satisfied, companies are more efficient, and all stakeholders can win.

The Supply Chain

What we will discuss here is known as the supply chain (see Figure 11.1), which is a logistics network that consists of raw materials, work in progress, finished goods, packaging, warehouses, distribution centers, distributors, resellers, dealers, and customers, that is, everything from product inception to delivery of the product to the consumer.

According to Stanford University's Warren Hausman, "The battleground of the next decade will be supply chain vs. supply chain" (Birchfield, 2002). What Hausman is alluding to is that to gain competitive advantage, companies will have to provide their products through the customers' preferred purchasing channels,

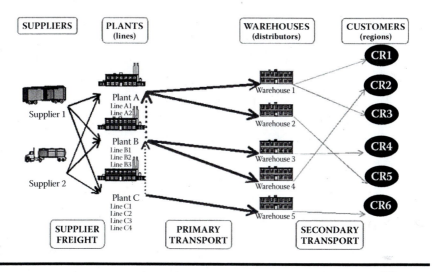

Figure 11.1   Depiction of a typical supply chain.

whether this be online, through a catalog, or in a retail store. As a result, companies will need to deal with the impact of multiple channels and the variations that the supply chain will have to accommodate.

Throughout the 1980s and 1990s, manufacturing companies turned to lean production techniques, such as just in time (JIT), to lower in-process inventory and its associated costs. JIT is actually demand driven; that is, the product is manufactured only when needed rather than manufactured in mass quantities and then shipped to a warehouse to gather dust.

Indeed, many manufacturing companies actually outsourced their warehousing, production, and freight processes during this period. With the advent of e-business and supply chain management methodologies and technologies, producers are able to make products to order and on demand. Fisher & Paykel, an appliance manufacturer located in New Zealand, operates a demand-drive supply chain (Birchfield, 2002). New Zealanders shopping for a fridge go to a local store where an order is taken. That order is transmitted to an F&P factory, where the product is assembled and delivered within three days.

One of the companies often cited in the literature on supply chain management is the Spanish apparel giant Zara. The company has consistently exhibited high returns and sales growth compared to its competitors. The reason for its success is extensive use of sales and demographic data, which lets the company create new products based on what it sees as trends in the market and price them aggressively.

Italian fashion house Benetton also uses supply chain management to increase its manufacturing efficiency. For example, it often manufactures clothing in a gray stock color, only dying these to different colors when it sees what is selling in its shops.

Multichannel Distribution

Once a producer decides to sell using different channels, it must make some decisions:

1. How many warehouses should be used?
2. How should inventory be allocated among channels?

There are many ways to set up multichannel distribution. The method ultimately selected will be based on product characteristics, retail locations, vendors' locations, and customer demographics. How one handles distribution is also dependent on the type of packaging used. Products may be packaged differently for different markets. How a product is packaged is determined by what the customer wants and what the distributor needs. For example, a reseller may not accept a particular form of packaging because it does not conform to the requirements it has for storing products. The International Standards Organization (ISO) identifies a wide variety of packaging types:

1. One facility for all channels: Some producers maintain their entire inventory in one location. This is the most economical method and allows for tighter control over inventory.
2. Different facilities for different channels: Some producers separate retail and direct-to-customer operations to ensure that they do not interfere with each other's flow. They might also take this approach to make sure that the warehouse is closer to a particular channel.
3. Multiple multichannel facilities: Larger businesses often opt for this methodology because it leads to quicker order turnaround. Obviously, multiple warehouses lead to higher costs as well. In addition, the logistics to support this methodology have the most complexity.
4. One channel fulfilled in-house, one channel outsourced: In this method, the dominant channel might be fulfilled in-house, while others are outsourced to third-party fulfillment centers. Amazon.com's annual report indicates that this is one of their techniques for order fulfillment: "We fulfill customer orders in a number of ways, including through our U.S. and international fulfillment centers and warehouses; through fulfillment centers operated under co-sourcing arrangements, including our fulfillment center supporting www.amazon.co.jp; through outsourced fulfillment providers, including our fulfillment provider supporting www.amazon.ca; and through other third-party fulfillment arrangements."

In reviewing these four methods of setting up multichannel distribution, the reader should be aware that there are two distinctly different types of marketing systems. A vertical marketing system (VMS) is a distribution channel structure in which everyone (i.e., producers, wholesalers, etc.) acts as a unified system. Either one channel member owns the others, is affiliated with the others, or has so much power that everyone has agreed to cooperate. The all-powerful Wal-Mart, and its many suppliers, is a good example of this type of structure.

A channel arrangement in which at least two unrelated companies agree to join together to follow a new marketing opportunity is referred to as a horizontal marketing system. An example of this is when a bank and a supermarket agree to have the bank's ATMs located at the supermarket's locations.

Packaging

Software can be sold in a variety of ways. It can be transferred to CDs and sold through stores, or sold online via mail delivery. It can be downloaded, or even sold as a Web-based service—SaaS, or software as a service.

Packaging refers to the product's container, label, and graphic design. Packaging is concerned with more than merely containing the product. It is something referred to as the fifth *P* in the marketing mix. Packaging has the following basic functions:

1. Protection of contents from damage and deterioration
2. Provision of product information
3. Promotion of corporate identity
4. Sales promotion
5. Adds to the appeal of the product

Labeling is a packaging ingredient used to distinguish a product, and to display product information and legally required information. Labeling is integral to packaging but must confirm to regulations and ethical controls. It should be informative, truthful, and distinctive.

Packaging is often what sells the product. Seth Godin, author of many marketing books, stresses that most products are invisible. This means that products need to be made remarkable if they are to be sold. In his book *Purple Cow*, he stresses that it is better "to be the purple cow in a field of monochrome Holsteins."

Partnership Techniques

There are several partnering techniques companies can use to expand the reach of their product or service market via available distribution channels.

Sponsorships: Sponsoring a site is much like advertising on a site except that you really do get more bang for the buck. For this methodology to work, you are going to have to do research in order to determine just which Web sites your potential customers frequent, so that you can consider sponsoring those sites.

One way to do this is an online survey. If you already have regular visitors to your site, ask them where they spend most of their time on the Web. If your site receives few visitors or is not yet off the ground, then a telemarketing survey not only has the advantage of finding out which sites people visit but also lets you inform them of your site's launch.

What a sponsorship gets you is a small ad with the words "brought to you by [your company name]" and a link to your site. Costs for sponsorships vary widely, but be ready to pay about 20% over and above the cost of a banner ad on the same page.

Content partnerships: A wide variety of brand and not-quite brand names enable companies to provide content. One example is the *Wall Street Journal* (http://public.wsj.com/partner/).

In November 2008, it was announced that Yellowbook's video advertisers would be showcased on YouTube via a content partnership agreement between the two. This is indeed an interesting partnership as yellow pages publishers attempt to transition their business online, and YouTube continues its attempt to generate revenue for Google.

E-commerce partnerships: Amazon has its own mall. Instead of revving up your selling site, you might want to investigate this. Amazon also handles fulfillment (http://aws.amazon.com/fws/).

Distribution partnerships: Back around the turn of the millennium, my company entered into a massive number of distribution agreements with consultants overseas. The purpose was to sell our Y2K products in as many countries as possible, in as short a time as possible.

Affiliates

Affiliate marketing is a marketing model in which the profits are shared between the online merchants and online salespeople. It is an online advertising medium in which advertisers who publish their products to increase sales pay a percentage to the publishers, who own the Web sites, e-mail newsletters, maintain blogs, etc. Affiliates directly and indirectly promote the sale of products or services. The publisher is paid only if the product is sold or the service hired. Though it's a low-risk proposition, it is a competitive field in which both the advertiser and the publisher are rewarded for result-oriented services.

Affiliate marketing is one of the more popular and effective forms of marketing. Profit and sales compensation are usually based on sales, Web site hits, and Web site registrations. In this mode of marketing, the online merchants are generally referred to as affiliate merchants, and the people involved in the promotion of sales are simply referred to as affiliates. Thus, we can define affiliate marketing in simple terms as "pay for performance." A number of affiliate networks are available at http://www.webaffiliatesdirectory.com/.

Revenue sharing and getting commissions for sales is the basic premise behind this form of marketing. We can actually trace the introduction of affiliate marketing to the adult industry, where each click on the Web site advertisements generated payment to an affiliate. These adult Web sites were the first to adopt the now widely used cost-per-click program.

The first nonadult Web site to introduce affiliate marketing was CDNOW in 1994. Their concept was entirely different from that of the adult Web sites. They adopted the concept of click per sale. They listed the reviews and details of popular musical albums and gave visitors the opportunity to buy the musical albums online. Those who were interested could buy the product by clicking on the link provided by CDNOW.

There are four types of compensation models used in affiliate marketing: pay per impression, pay per click, pay per lead, and pay per sale. Due to fraudulent activities (i.e., overblown number of clicks or impressions), compensation models such as pay per click and pay per impression are less popular among advertisers.

Google launched AdSense in 2003 (http://adsense.google.com), and its introduction provided a newer dimension to affiliate marketing, especially online sales promotions. It provides useful links and popularizes merchants' Web sites by adding their advertisements in different publishers' Web sites.

Amazon.com has some hundreds of thousands of affiliate Web sites. The key is to make it easy for the affiliate to earn commissions. Amazon.com provides a set of utilities that makes it simple for a Web-site owner to create his or her own bookstore. What he or she is really doing is providing links to the book on Amazon's site. The link contains affiliate-identifying information. For each link that leads to a sale, the affiliate earns a commission. Amazon.com treats its affiliates with kid gloves, which means paying on time and providing good services.

eLetter, now zairmail, is an example of a smaller company that followed the affiliate path and increased its sales dramatically as a result. eLetter is an online service bureau that enables a company or individual to upload both a letter and a mailing list. eLetter handles printing as well as mailing, saving you lots of money on small-run jobs.

eLetter's affiliate programs prove that it is not just the large, well-known companies that can profit from this technique. eLetter's program is similar to Amazon's. By placing a link on your own Web site, you are entitled to a commission should any of your visitors hyperlink to the eLetter Web site and then place an order (http://www.zairmail.com/cendix/affiliates/).

From eLetter's point of view, this is money well spent. Customers willingly act as salespeople to get a commission. All they really have to do is place an image and some code on their own Web sites and they are in business.

Acquisitions

It is enough to read the business section of any newspaper to appreciate the prevalence of acquisitions as a method of broadening one's exposure and sales base. There are two ways of looking at the acquisition process. One might want to acquire a company. In this scenario, you have to be very clear about exactly what you want to accomplish. Is it entry into a market you are not now in? Is it additional customers or contracts and projects in the pipeline? Is it a specific proprietary technology?

The flip side of the acquisition process is making your company an acquisition target. This is the tack that many small business companies take. In fact, this is the specific reason why they are in existence at all. A small company I was working with in the New Jersey area had just this goal. They knew that they were far too small to compete with the majors. Their goal became to generate enough buzz about their product so that they would become a viable acquisition target.

Whether you want to acquire or be acquired, the steps to take are much the same. If your goal is to be acquired, then read through the following checklist and take action (if you want to do the acquiring, make sure the following checklist applies to the object of your desires):

1. Generate a buzz about your product or service. This might require the services of a good marketing company and certainly that of a talented public relations agency.

2. Make sure your business plan is up to date and accurate. It is interesting to find that a great majority of businesses don't take the time to keep their plans up to date. Most businesses change over time. What you wrote in your initial business plan is usually quite different from the business that finally takes root. Since the business plan document is what the acquiring company will use to understand your mission and goals, make the effort to keep the plan current.

3. It is a good idea to develop a sales-planning document. Identify in it your strengths, competencies, proprietary technologies and techniques, etc.; list your key people; and identify future plans and expectations and virtually anything else you can think of that will make your company saleable.

4. It is a safe bet that the acquiring company will want an audited financial statement; so, save time by making sure you already have one at hand. Make sure your numbers are accurate. Too many Internet companies rely on puffery when it comes to projections, and too many auditors miss this problem entirely. For example, it has become quite prevalent for Web companies to swap ad space and then cite it as revenue. While this is perfectly legal, the Securities and Exchange Commission (SEC) itself is becoming uncomfortable with the practice, believing that there is a serious potential of misleading investors. On the other hand, do everything you can to make sure your figures are palatable. You might want to forgo that very expensive advertising campaign or the hiring of 10 new employees since these activities will drain your bottom line. In fact, defer everything you can so that your numbers are as robust as you can make them.

5. Determine your selling price. Will this be a cash or stock transaction, or a combination of the two? The vast majority of net acquisitions are stock transactions. Indeed, it is not unusual to see a small company acquiring a larger company purely because it is generally a "no money down" situation. The ultimate price of the company is based on a combination of the company's current and projected sales and assets. Many service companies have few assets other than their people, but product companies have the product (and all of the equipment needed to make that product); so, using a selling price that is based solely on yearly sales would result in the underpricing of your company. Take a look at sales of similar companies over the past few years. This will give you a handle on what you can expect to sell the company for.

6. Employees are most surely an asset. What plan do you have in place for retaining them? A savvy acquirer will ask this question.

7. Resolve any open tax or legal issues. Few companies look desirable with unresolved legal and financial issues still open and on the table.

8. If the company is a subsidiary of another, larger company, then make sure the links between the two companies are clear and in the open. The acquiring company is going to take a good long look at the financial transactions between the two companies. Could it just be that the parent company has been providing loans to the subsidiary to make its bottom line look better than it should?

9. Provide a blueprint for corporate financial performance. The CFO needs to take charge and answer the following questions:
   a. Has the company's financial performance varied over the past three years? If so, why?
   b. What is the value of the company now?
   c. Can this value be replicated in the future? How?

10. Be prepared to provide information about the real drivers of the company:
   a. Price sensitivity
   b. Major customers
   c. Manufacturing costs
   d. Product development cycle
   e. Chief competitors
   f. Key employees

Joint Ventures

A joint venture is the easiest of partnership techniques in that it will not require your company to merge with or acquire another company—or be acquired by another company. A joint venture consists of two or more companies joining forces for a particular purpose. The Ford–Yahoo! partnership is a good example of a joint venture. Ford and Yahoo! built a site on Yahoo! that offered Ford car owners a number of services such as owner guides, recall notifications, credit account information, service reminders, and vehicle maintenance logs. As part of the deal, Ford bought banner ads on Yahoo! for Ford brands and sponsored special promotions.

Negotiating the Sharing of Information

Information partnerships between companies run the gamut from links between suppliers and customers to joint ventures between companies in the same industry to collaboration on research and development (R&D) or marketing.

In all of these partnerships, the common entity is a shared information resource. Sharing information will require exacting managerial efforts because widely dispersed companies, out of necessity, must provide a commonality in the areas of data definitions, relationships, and even search patterns.

Even well into the 2000s, companies are having difficulty in creating internal information resources common to all divisions within a single company. Thus, attempting to develop an intercompany information resource is even more difficult. Flexibility, cooperation, and computer power are the keywords of a workable and mutually profitable partnership. The optimum approach to a strategic alliance is one of adapting to great change. This ability to accommodate is the deciding factor between success and failure. A partnership is only as successful as the partners' abilities to make it work, which requires each partner to change more than just the way business is performed. The partners may have to change their corporate culture as well.

For an information services department bearing the brunt of development of the new relationship, the joint venture, strategic partnership, merger, or acquisition means having to accommodate clients who are external to the company. Developing a negotiating game plan can be of invaluable assistance:

1. Standardize the terms that all companies use. Greenwood Mills located in Greenwood, South Carolina, found that standardization of jargon was a necessity if they were to successfully implement a system that linked the textile company to its suppliers and customers. They were used to keeping track of material using standard sizes such as 36 or 38 inches, but their customers were using a more sophisticated numerically controlled fabric-measurement system. Greenwood also found that they had a jargon problem in the naming of colors. Greenwood designated names for shades, while their customers used a value that described the amount of variance from a standard color.

2. Choose a board of directors. In joint venture partnerships, all partners are created equal. This, of course, is just theory. In practice, it is possible that the internal admin groups will wind up being beholden to several masters. Since the partnership is formed around a joint goal, the many-master approach will lower efficiency. Information must serve one master only. In joint partnerships, this can be accomplished through the election of a board of directors,

the function of which is to oversee information services efforts. The board should have equal representation from all partners. Their function is to determine both the short- and long-term plans of the information services group. This includes the determination of priorities of all development projects as well as resolution of all political confrontations.

3. In situations where a firm has formed an alliance with one or more companies in which the firm permits utilization of a proprietary information system by those companies, it is reasonable to expect requests for modification to that system. Given the great number of requests that can be generated from multiple groups of people, it would be wise to appoint a user liaison to that system. This liaison would be responsible for taking requests for change, and then working with all concerned to see if change is desirable and when and if it can be accommodated.

4. Determine boundaries of exchange. Data links between two companies can be unidirectional or bidirectional. A supplier posting new product information may require only a one-way link. Most e-commerce systems exhibit a two-way link. Vendors can supply customers with information about products, and customers can place orders.

5. Eliminate redundancies. In a joint venture, separate firms, each having its own computer systems, join forces for a common goal. In such cases, there may be a desire for each firm to retain its own independent information services group. Efficiencies are lowered when a processing function is performed more than once. In addition, redundant data often become inconsistent. For example, a group of three firms uploads market data to its respective marketing research departments for analyses. Each marketing research department has its own computer system. It is possible that three possible results will be obtained because of the differences in data processing. Additionally, the longer the raw data sit in diverse databases, the stronger the chance that the data will be altered and, thus, differ from those in their sister databases.

6. It is recommended that all data be processed in one location to negate these potentialities. This calls for creation of a joint processing center servicing the legitimate needs of the partnership.

7. Allow for varying levels of sophistication. In building information systems for multiple partners, it should be remembered that each partner will exhibit a particular level of sophistication, with its own set of requirements. Many firms develop a joint system with multiple interfaces. One for the least-sophisticated users, one for the average user, and one for an extremely knowledgeable, or power, user.

8. Be ready to compromise. In a single-user system, the user can tailor the system for a specific purpose. This is usually not possible in jointly held systems. Although many of the problems of partnership systems can be resolved through the use of a board of directors, companies involved in the process should be ready to compromise on some of their specific requirements.

The partnering techniques just discussed assist companies in making efficient decisions:

1. Attack new markets.
2. Improve time to market.
3. Add new skill sets.

Ultimately, the most successful companies are those that are most adept at strategic alliances. For a partnership to work, both sides must have committed champions. Both sides must demonstrate significant tangible benefits for the other side to be committed. Finally, both sides must have adequate resources assigned within each group. Ultimately, partnerships are really a matter of survival. Eat or be eaten!

Conclusion

MBNA, a large U.S.-based financial conglomerate, is a company that has come to understand the importance of strategic channels. After segmenting its market by professional and affinity groups, it found that in the long term the most successful way to market credit card offerings was through these groups. While MBNA's competitors continued to try to refine direct mail and other mass marketing efforts, MBNA created an entirely new channel. The extra expense was significant, but it greatly improved the quality of new customers acquired and allowed the company to compete more aggressively in a market that was approaching saturation.

Other firms have found that superior distribution strategies can be the basis of sustained competitive advantage. Supply chain management has been at the heart of Wal-Mart's success over the past two decades. The key to achieving its goals has been to make inventory management the core of its competitive advantage. Wal-Mart's cross-docking and zero-inventory management strategies enable it to achieve economies that come with purchasing full truckloads of goods, while avoiding the usual inventory and handling costs. Strong communication and transportation systems keep these strategies going. Suppliers, distribution centers, and storefronts are constantly in contact, and the distribution strategy remains an ongoing, ever-evolving process. In fact, distribution must evolve as business environments evolve. DeBeers is another firm whose distribution strategy has enabled continued competition through industry evolution. In spite of market pressures from all over the world, DeBeers continued to exert a powerful influence on the worldwide distribution of diamonds throughout the past decade by strategically realigning its distribution with overall corporate goals.

References

Birchfield, D. (2002, March). Supply chains deliver competitive advantage. *New Zealand Management*, 49(2).

Chapter 12

Marketing Implementation and Control

With good marketing strategies and plans, the marketing manager and the organization are prepared for a marketing effort. However, for a successful marketing effort, good implementation (putting plans into operation) is critical. An important aspect of implementation is establishing measurements and controls. These provide feedback that helps the marketer understand the effectiveness of plans and implementation, and to plan for the future. Advances in information technology are allowing marketers faster access to information, leading to better implementation and control.

Marketing Control

Marketing control has been referred to as the reverse side of planning. It focuses on the use of accounting and financial data. Control is accomplished by continuous feedback known as feedback control, but it is important to realize that control reports will not affect change in performance, as change will take place only when managers initiate relevant actions. An extension of the feedback method is "adaptive control" once set by environmental factors a variance between results and preset standards, plans must be modified to reduce this variance. There are many definitions and terms related to marketing control, such as marketing information system (centralized), designed to generate, store, and disseminate an orderly flow of essential information to managers; marketing decision support systems (decentralized), allowing managers to interact directly with the database, which has built-in mathematical models; and contingency plan, a plan that occurs when changes take place.

Marketing planning and marketing control are counterbalancing processes that go hand in hand. Control should focus on key variables with quicker implementation measures provided by IT and understanding the impact of these key variables as well as predicting the impact of their changing and desired end results.

A marketing plan should be monitored as it progresses. This is required to make sure that the adopted measures are contributing toward the goals of the plan. Should any assumptions change, then the marketing plan needs to be adjusted to attain the desired results. Various control measures that should be implemented include the following:

1. Identify key metrics based on critical success factors, so that effectiveness can be measured.
2. Constantly evaluate contribution margin, so that appropriate adjustments can be made to the product mix.
3. Produce regular dashboards or scorecards to monitor or review with management and finance regarding spend, effectiveness, and impact.
4. Risk of exceeding thresholds should be managed and mitigated.
5. Be prepared to revisit, assess impact, and make changes when a situation arises.

Plan and perform regular sales analysis. Frequent sales analysis can illustrate trends and allow marketing managers to validate their assumptions. Lack of such analysis would result in poor forecasts or incorrect decisions.

Plan and perform a marketing audit, so that a third party can review and provide independent perspective about effectiveness.

Feedback Improves the Marketing Management Process

Computers linked to checkout scanners, intranets, and decision-support systems give today's marketing manager fast feedback. Among these tools are customer relationship management (CRM) and data mining, in conjunction with data warehousing. Fast feedback can be a competitive advantage, but the marketing manager must take charge to ensure that the necessary data are collected.

New information technologies offer speed and detail. It is possible for marketing managers to get information they require instantly. Computers can provide almost any level of detail, in any form the manager wants. With some marketing programs, such as TV shopping networks, marketing managers can see the "real-time" or instantaneous effects of manipulating the 4Ps: product, price, place, and promotion. Implementing a marketing plan may involve different operational decisions and activities. When these elements are executed well, customers get what is intended. If the plan is good, customer satisfaction and repeat purchases should result. However, poor implementation may alienate customers.

Good Implementation Builds Relationships with Customers

Information technology can improve marketing plan implementation, which is important in meeting customer expectations. Through interactive customer data-bases, using CRM software, data mining, and data warehousing, as mentioned earlier, marketers can track purchase patterns, update prices, and even suggest product alternatives.

These tools help to build relationships with customers by helping them com-municate indirectly what they want. Service-quality research indicates that cus-tomers appreciate clear communication with marketers and, therefore, marketers can manage customer expectations by good communication. When a product or service fulfills customer expectations, they are more satisfied. If customer expecta-tions are not fulfilled, however, marketers should give clear, honest explanations for the disappointing interaction.

Sales Analysis Shows What's Happening in the Market

Sales analysis is a detailed breakdown of a company's sales records. Over time, repeated analyses can illustrate trends and allow managers to check their hypoth-eses and assumptions. Without this information, marketers may make poor sales forecasts or poor decisions.

Computer technology can make sales analysis easier and less expensive than it used to be. There are many types of analyses that a marketer may want to use, but some typical breakdowns include the following:

1. Geographic region—country, state, county, city, or sales representative's territory
2. Product, package size, grade, or color
3. Customer size
4. Customer type or class of trade
5. Price or discount class
6. Method of sale—online, telephone, or sales representatives
7. Financial arrangement—cash or charge
8. Size of order
9. Commission class

Sales analyses that provide too much data can overwhelm a manager. Breakdowns should be directly tied to decisions that need to be made.

Marketing Cost Analysis

Marketing cost analysis is a technique for determining, and ensuring, that money is spent for a specific marketing purpose, which leads to desired results. Knowing where money goes helps managers determine whether a given activity is being performed adequately or cost-effectively.

It often makes sense to allocate costs to specific customers and products. This lets managers directly analyze the profitability of the firm's target markets. Should all costs be allocated?

Cost allocation can be tricky, especially as some costs are likely to be common to several products and customers. Two basic approaches are possible:

Full-cost approach: All costs are allocated to products, customers, or other categories, including fixed and common costs—so everything costs something. Profitability can be determined easily by subtracting costs from sales. This method assumes that costs have been allocated correctly.

Contribution-margin approach: Not all costs are allocated in all situations. This approach focuses on variable costs and allocates them, leaving fixed costs unallocated. So, it ignores some costs to get results. It can be more illustrative of actual product or departmental performance since it assumes that fixed costs remain separate from individual product areas. It may also help managers to avoid conflict over the allocation of fixed costs.

The URL http://www.bplans.com/spv/3206/7.cfm#1070000 provides an example of a complete business plan for a company intending to sell online skating products. This hyperlink will take you to the financial section of the business plan, which includes business ratios.

Balanced Scorecard

One technique that is seeing increasing popularity is the balanced scorecard. Heralded by the *Harvard Business Review* as one of the most significant management ideas of the past 75 years, balanced scorecard has been implemented in companies to both measure and manage the marketing effort.

Robert S. Kaplan and David P. Norton developed the balanced scorecard approach in the early 1990s to compensate for the perceived shortcomings of using only financial metrics to judge performance. They recognized that in this new economy it was also necessary to value intangible assets. Because of this, they urged companies to measure such esoteric factors as quality and customer satisfaction. By the mid-1990s, balanced scorecard became the hallmark of a well-run company. Kaplan and Norton often compare their approach to managing a company to that of pilots viewing assorted instrument panels in an airplane cockpit—both have a need to monitor multiple aspects of their working environment.

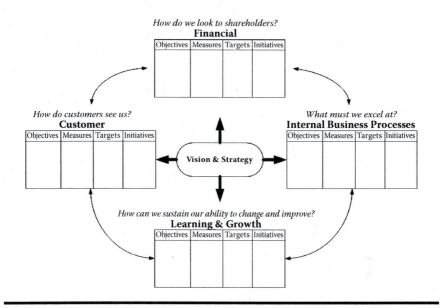

Figure 12.1 The balanced scorecard and its four perspectives (Kaplan and Norton, 1996).

In the scorecard scenario, as shown in Figure 12.1, a company organizes its business goals into four perspectives: financial, customer, internal process, and learning or growth. The company then determines cause–effect relationships—for example, satisfied customers buy more goods, which increases revenue. Next, the company lists measures for each goal, pinpoints targets, and identifies projects and other initiatives to help reach those targets. A scorecard for strategic marketing could contain the objectives and measures shown in Table 12.1.

Marketing Math

A marketing plan is a document that spells out in detail the steps needed to accomplish a specific marketing objective. A company must initially review the macroenvironment and then carry out a market research study followed by a customer analysis. Next, the company should evaluate resources and objectives. Pricing and marketing costs are required to develop the cost analysis.

Marketing requires the expenditures of funds to be budgeted, reflecting sales and profit goals, and the financial condition of the business. The three most commonly used methods are the following:

1. **Percentage of sales approach**: A fixed percentage of predicted sales is allocated to marketing, based on past results or on management judgment.

Table 12.1   Sample Marketing Scorecard

Strategic Objectives	Strategic Measures
Financial: • F.1 Return on capital • F.2 Cash flow • F.3 Profitability • F.4 Profitability growth • F.5 Reliability of performance	Financial: • ROCE • Cash flow • Net margin • Volume growth rate versus industry • Profit forecast reliability • Sales backlog
Customer: • C.1 Value for money • C.2 Competitive price • C.3 Customer satisfaction	Customer: • Customer ranking survey • Pricing index • Customer satisfaction index • Mystery shopping rating
Internal: 1.1 Marketing • Product and service development • Shape customer requirement 1.2 Manufacturing • Lower manufacturing cost • Improve project management 1.3 Logistics • Reduce delivery costs • Inventory management 1.4 Quality	Internal: • Pioneer percentage of product portfolio • Hours with customer on new work • Total expenses per unit versus competition • Safety incident index • Delivered cost per unit • Inventory level compared to plan and output rate • Rework
Innovation and learning: • 1L.1 Innovate products and services • 1L.2 Time to market • 1L.3 Empowered workforce • 1L.4 Access to strategic information • 1L.5 Continuous improvement	Innovation and learning: • Percentage revenue from pioneer products • Cycle time versus industry norm • Staff attitude survey • Strategic information availability • Number of employee suggestions

2. **All you can afford approach**: Marketing budgets are set on the basis of fund availability.
3. **Task or objective approach**: Marketing objectives are clearly stated and then expenditures to attain these objectives are determined.

A sales forecast and an expense forecast are required for developing projected income statements and budgeting. Three alternative income statements based on pessimistic, most likely, and optimistic assumptions are developed for evaluation. Financial impact evaluation requires an in-depth look at sales forecast and expense forecast. For example, the total budget for the billing analysis for a new product might reach 60% of the annual promotional budget, and the budget distribution will be approximately 20% allocation to billing, 30% to customer surveys, and 50% to new business development and new product implementation.

The size of a marketing budget is determined by the cost of producing the ads, placing the required number of those ads in the media, and paying the agency for its services. If the brand is entering an existing market, then CLV is finally calculated by subtracting the acquisition cost from the amount just calculated. In markets where there is a strong relationship between the volume of advertising, referred to as share of voice (SOV), and market share of the market (SOM), the budget is set by specifying the market share required and budgeting the same percentage of the product category.

Additional methods used, such as "affordable method," calculate a certain percentage of sales, and "competitive parity" method is a budget that is set to match that of the main competitor. However, because determining advertising budgeting is such an inexact science, it is always advisable to use more than one method to set an ad budget.

Marketing Financial Analysis

There are three types of costs that are important in the marketing cost analysis process:

1. Fixed
2. Variable
3. Semivariable

These can be measured by the effective efficiency method, which uses factors such as customer profitability analysis (CPA) and financial ratios. The CPA involves the analysis of revenues earned from the customers, and financial ratios can be used to measure the performance of a company using profitability ratios, liquidity ratios, leverage ratios, and activity ratios.

Marketing decisions are coming under increasing scrutiny, and marketing managers must be accountable for the financial implications of their actions. A sound marketing plan will have a detailed breakup of projected expenses as percentages of overall projected sales. The marketing plan should at least contain the following budgetary analysis:

Breakeven analysis. It determines the unit volume and sales needed to be profitable, given a particular price and cost structure. At the breakeven point, the total revenue equals the total costs and, hence, the profit is zero. Above the breakeven point the company will start making profits, and below the point the company will lose money. The breakeven volume can be calculated using the following formula:

Breakeven volume = Fixed costs/(Price – Unit variable cost)

Contribution margin. It is the unit contribution divided by the selling price, where unit contribution is the amount that each unit contributes to covering fixed costs. Understanding contribution margin is very helpful, as it determines the amount to cover costs. Contribution margin is also represented as follows:

Contribution margin = (Total sales – Total variable costs)/Total sales

Pro forma (or projected) profit and loss statement. This statement shows projected revenues less budgeted expenses and estimates the projected net profit for an organization, product, or brand during a specific period. This statement also includes direct product manufacturing costs, marketing expenses budgeted to attain a given sales forecast, and other overheads. Based on the pro forma statement, the following can be budgeted:
Gross margin percentage. This is defined as the percentage of net sales remaining after the cost of goods or services sold. This is given by the following formula:

Gross margin percentage = Gross margin/Net sales

Net margin percentage. This is defined as the percentage of each dollar going to profit. This is given by the following formula:

Net margin percentage = Net profit/Net sales

Return on investment (ROI). This is defined as the ratio of net profits to total investment. ROI is used to compare alternatives when making decisions on investments. A positive ROI is preferred.
Benefit-cost ratio (BCR). This is defined as the ratio of total revenue to total cost.

$$BCR = \text{Total revenue/Total cost}$$

If BCR > 1, then the business is profitable, whereas BCR < 1 means the company is losing money.

Expense structure ratio. This is defined as the ratio of fixed cost to the total cost.

Net marketing contribution (NMC). This is defined as a measure of marketing profitability, which includes only components of profitability controlled by marketing. This is given by the following formula:

$$NMC = \text{Net sales} - \text{Cost of goods sold} = \text{Marketing expenses}$$

Marketing return on sales (or marketing ROS). This is defined as the percentage of net sales attributable to net marketing contribution. This is given by the following formula:

$$\text{Marketing ROS} = NMC/\text{Net sales}$$

Marketing return on investment (or marketing ROI). This is defined as the ratio of net marketing contribution to the marketing expenses. This is given by the following formula:

$$\text{Marketing ROI} = NMC/\text{Total marketing expenses}$$

Customer lifetime value (or CLV). Customer lifetime value represents how much a customer is worth. This allows marketing departments to focus on how much they are willing to spend to acquire and maintain customers, and if the marketing plan and budget are able to achieve the requested results. Customer lifetime value can be calculated as a function of the following parameters:

p_t—the price paid by a consumer at time t
c_t—the cost of servicing the customer at time t
i—the discount rate or cost of capital for the firm
r_t—the probability of consumer repeat buying at time t
AC—the acquisition cost
T—the time horizon for estimating CLV

The formula assumes the calculation of the customer margin, by subtracting the cost of servicing the customer from the price paid by the customer so far. The result is then multiplied by the probability of consumer repeat buying and divided by the discount rate of the firm. CLV is finally calculated by subtracting the acquisition cost from Figure 12.1. This is summarized in the following formula:

$$CLV = \Sigma \ [((p_t - c_t)^* \ r_t \ ) \ / \ (1 + i)^t \ ] - AC \ \text{for time t} = 0 \ \text{to} \ T$$

Control Analysis

Control involves the monitoring and evaluation of actual and planned results in order to keep operations on course. It takes three basic forms: sales standards, cost standards, and profit standards. The tools used are sales analysis, cost analysis, and profit analysis.

Sales analysis is the breakdown and evaluation of sales data to determine the effectiveness of the marketing effort. These are dependants of the product or service, the market and the customer, and the information needed to assess performance.

Cost analysis involves the breakdown and restriction of marketing costs, such as direct and indirect costs, to evaluate the efficiency of the marketing effort. Direct costs may be specific to sales and marketing activities, while indirect costs are allocated to common overheads such as marketing managers' salary, travel allowance expense, company car, and advertising; direct cost items could be sales commissions, shipping and packaging costs, promotional items, and advertising.

Profit analysis is the breakdown and evaluation of sales revenue and cost charges by activity. Profitability is measured by the contribution margin of individual products and the contribution of the total marketing effort to overall company profits.

The marketing manager uses a wide variety of tools to achieve these ends. For example, to track online ad impressions via the AdWords service, Google's Campaign Management Analytics function provides important information such as bounce rate and average time on site. Google provides instructive advice about all of these settings. For example, they explain bounce rate to mean the percentage of single-page visits or visits in which the person left your site from the entrance (landing) page. Use this metric to measure visit quality—a high bounce rate generally indicates that site entrance pages are not relevant to your visitors. The more compelling your landing pages, the more visitors will stay on your site and convert. You can minimize bounce rates by tailoring landing pages to each keyword and ad that you run. Landing pages should provide the information and services that were promised in the ad copy.

AdWords Analytics also provides some segmentation statistics, as shown in Figure 12.2.

Markups and Markdowns

To stay in business, it is critical that the concepts of markups and markdowns be well understood. As discussed in Chapter 9, a markup is the percentage of the cost (or selling price) that is added to the cost to arrive at the final selling price. Aside from ensuring profitability, markups may be used because of the value added via services or products. A markdown is a percentage reduction from the selling price. Consumers love markdowns; sellers love markups.

As a product moves through the distribution channel, a markup is usually added as it passes through each channel. For example, the producer's cost to manufacture

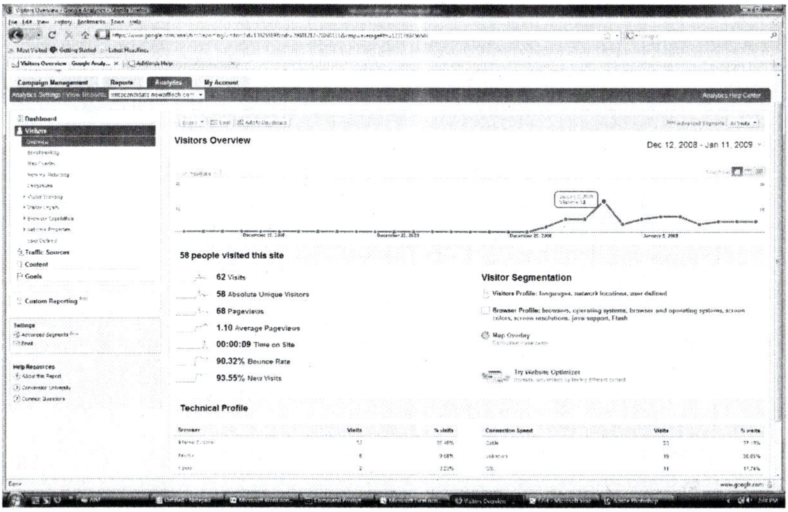

Figure 12.2   AdWord Analytics for a new service my company is providing.

a product is $20. The producer marks this up to $25. The product next hits the wholesale outlet, which marks the product up by $10 to $35. The retailer gets the product for $35 and marks it up by $15 to arrive at a final selling price of $50. Should the retailer experience problems in selling the product, match competitive pricing from another retailer, wish to lure shoppers for the holiday season, etc., it might mark down the product. At times, the retailer might mark down the product close to its cost.

The key is achieving maximum profitability. This is referred to as gross margin.

Marketing Audit

The marketing manager is usually responsible for day-to-day implementation of marketing plans and tactics, as well as planning and control. As a result, the manager may not have time to evaluate effectiveness. While crises arise, planning and control must go on.

A marketing audit is a systematic, critical, and unbiased review and appraisal of the basic objectives of the marketing function. In addition, the marketing audit evaluates the organization, methods, procedures, and people employed to implement the policies. Other key aspects of the audit include the following:

1. Detailed examination of the firm's current marketing plans
2. Use of the marketing strategy planning framework—working backward to evaluate the plans that have been implemented

3. Evaluation of the quality of the effort
4. Involvement of consumers, competitors, channel members, and employees

Marketing audits are often necessary because managers can easily become so directly tied to the strategies they developed that an outside view is needed to measure effectiveness.

Marketing Manager Evaluation

As indicated in Chapter 1, there are two levels of marketing:

Micro level—how firms run
Macro level—how the whole system works

We must evaluate marketing at two levels as well:

1. **A nation's objectives** affect the evaluation of marketing. Depending on the sociopolitical structure and policies prevalent in a nation, its social and economic objectives may differ.
2. **Consumer satisfaction** is the objective in most capitalist countries. This objective is derived from a market-based economic system, and it implies that political freedom and economic freedom go hand in hand.

In many countries, people have the right to live and to satisfy their economic and social needs as they choose. Since customer satisfaction is such an important objective, marketing's effectiveness must be measured by how well it satisfies consumers.

However, there are limits to this type of measure:

1. To some extent, satisfaction depends on individual aspirations. A standard of living or a level of performance that is satisfactory today may not be so in the future.
2. Consumer satisfaction is also highly personal. Therefore, looking at the average satisfaction level of a whole society does not provide a complete picture for evaluating macro-marketing effectiveness.

On the other hand, there are many measures of micro-marketing effectiveness. Firms use attitude research, comment cards, e-mail surveys, consumer feedback, and other methods to measure effectiveness. Repeat purchase and profitability measures also provide some rough indicators of satisfaction. Therefore, evaluating marketing effectiveness is difficult, but not impossible.

Conclusion

The most important output of implementing a marketing process effectively can be the organization's appropriate response to multiple futures. We cannot always be certain of the future, but we can gather and use information wisely to plan contingent strategic positions and courses of action.

History is one overlooked knowledge source that would be beneficial when planning for the future. Organizations must assess their successes as well as their failures, then acquire knowledge that is instrumental in creating profitable future situations. For instance, IBM's 360 computer series (one of the most profitable and popular it ever built) was based on the failed technology of its predecessor: the Stretch computer. Similarly, by managing knowledge gained from the failed initial 737 and 747 Boeing launches, the subsequent 757 and 767 were highly successful, error-free launches. Managing knowledge about market trends is probably the most important factor when looking at multiple futures. Microsoft saw the future wave of personal computers and captured the opportunity. GE anticipated the need for networked exchange throughout industries. All of these success stories relied on focusing on the future, as any manager knows that current success can last only so long.

References

Kaplan, R. S., and Norton, D. P. (1996). *The Balanced Scorecard: Translating Strategy into Action*. Cambridge: Harvard University Press.

Chapter 13

Social Networking and the Sales Strategy

Nowadays, social networks such as LinkedIn, Facebook, and MySpace have become popular platforms where one can share values, ideas, and friendships. They have transformed the social structure; one can discuss or popularize marketing strategies, likes, dislikes, trading concepts, etc. Some social networks have a great influence in solving critical issues and can help individuals achieve their goals and dreams.

Even major political parties utilize the popularity of such social networks. We have seen the great influence of social networks in the last U.S. presidential election, where candidates made their presence felt on all the social network sites. Half of the election campaigns were done through social networks. It indicates the widespread popularity of these modern social forums.

Do you still think that these social networks have no real value? The Twitter (twitter.com) service has made Dell $1 million in revenue through sales alerts in 2008 alone.

Why Social Network

Almost everyone in our modern world is part of one or more social networks. Many factors influence the popularity of these networks. These range from the influence of friendship to the attractive and free world of communication:

Friendship: Recent studies show that the urge for friendship is one of the influential factors that attract people to social networks. Those who are searching for friendship and those who already have a large group of friends use these social networks as a common platform to find new realms of friendship, and an opportunity to expand and maintain their social circles.

Social influence: As these social networks become the new modes of communication and the dominant window for friendship, everyone is in a hurry to join. This is due to the social influence these networks have on their members. Many seem to be addicted to these new technologies and behaviors. As a result, social networks spread like an epidemic.

Correlation: Another factor that influences the widespread use of the social network is correlation. People are getting acquainted with similar kinds of people—that is, those who have similar visions, thoughts, interests, etc. Thus, social networks provide a platform for similar-minded people to build new relationships. Correlation in social networks is affected by two factors:

Homophily: In most cases, people who are in similar professions are likely to become friends after they get to know each other. For example, two scientists will soon become friends, as they have common interests and visions.

External factors: External factors too will build correlation. People who are living in the same area or locality can easily be affected by their common interests.

Psychological factors: Most people like to present themselves under the cover of a mask. Online social networks provide them such masks. While building a profile, users can sidestep questions that may affect their security. They can hide their original personality by not providing their personal data. Social networks such as Second Life even provide the ability to create an alternate personality through use of an animated avatar. Thus, a short, fat, 40-year-old man can live a second life as a svelte, 20-something female.

It is everyone's basic desire to share his or her thoughts and visions with others. Some people may feel a kind of suffocation if they cannot express their ideas. These online social networks provide them an opportunity to express their thoughts, visions, and dreams, even if they are weird. There are no limitations for them. Social networks encourage people to express views on different issues. Anyone can join in these social networks, and there is no age, gender, race, or other requirement.

Group segment and easy mode of communication: In most social networks, various kinds of groups are available for people to join. They can join any group having similar-minded people as members. Some networks offer the opportunity to create new groups. One can create his or her own group and invite colleagues, customers, and clients. Thus, they can communicate with one another very quickly and maintain their relationships for a long time. Even a single message can be sent to many using the facilities of social networks in the group setup.

Advanced technologies: Almost all the online social networks enhance their sites with multimedia. As people are always looking for something new, these social networks are competing to provide the service of advanced technologies to their users. Some of the new features that attract users toward the social networks are as follows:

Photos: This facility is one of the influential factors that attracts people in online social networking. One can share any number of photos and invite others to see them. This entertains both the publisher and the viewer.

Videos: Videos of any category can be posted in online social networking. They range from clips dating back to one's school days to the latest fashion trends. Some social network sites have come up with interactive video facilities.

Scraps: This has become one the cheapest and quickest ways of messaging. Multiple scrape-sending facilities are very useful, as a single user can send the same message to many people without wasting time.

Chatting modes: Some of the online social network sites come with chatting facilities to attract more users.

Marketing opportunities: As we know, marketing has transformed into newer forms from its traditional modes. People are using social networks as a means to market their products. They market their product easily and effectively by forming separate groups for different people using opinion polls and other interactive applications.

Brand Advertising on Social Networks

Social networks have always been a vital aspect of people's social lives and communications. Thus, there is a growing educational and commercial interest in the role of **virtual** social networks in the field of brand advertising. Present-day users of social networks range from the inhabitants of Second Life® (a virtual reality meeting place) to the modish, youthful users of MySpace, to the business users who post their experiences with different kind of IT products or services on business social networking Web sites such as LinkedIn®. Such networking Web sites create an excellent scope for brand advertising, as they're trendy, fresh, extensively covered in the press, used by tech-savvy folks, and symbolize both an opportunity and a threat to conventional advertisers.

Basic social networking has always been around in the form of message boards, instant messaging, and newsgroups. These have helped develop awareness about various IT products or services. However, social networks started taking a novel form with the introduction of Web sites such as GeoCities and Friendster, which gave people the opportunity to express their thoughts in text online. Present attempts at the advancement of social networks have led to the mushrooming of many online social networks; Orkut, Facebook, Hi5, MySpace, Flickr®, and YouTube are best-known and most publicized among networks of this type.

Moving from Traditional to Social

Consumers have started to distrust traditional advertising and the information that is pushed at them with the motive of influencing buying outcomes. People are abandoning not only traditional advertising but also mass media. Internet and gaming activities have replaced television to a great extent, which had itself replaced afternoon newspapers. Even if an advertiser or television network is fortunate enough to catch the attention of the viewer, the viewer usually surfs to an alternative channel or fast-forwards if viewing via TiVo or similar time-shifting technology—just to keep away from viewing the advertisements.

Since people aren't watching traditional ads through traditional media, it's important to give them new ads through a new medium. This is the primary rationalization for media acquisitions of social networks, such as MySpace's acquisition by News Corporation. Products are recommended among friends, for a fee, or products can be directly recommended by MySpace to the users, who can be targeted when they are in a shopping mood, resulting in viral marketing at warp speed. In essence, the users are trading their "attention" to ads in exchange for the services they use. This decision was obviously made with the intention of generating revenues that News Corporation was losing because of attrition of readership in its newspaper domain.

Social networks provide the ability to geo-target any member with advertisements that would meet that person's needs based on his or her profile information. Thus, social networks provide any advertiser the ability to target a very specific audience.

Second Life, with millions of registered users, must be the first to be included on the list. Some companies have even set up virtual shops here, as shown in Figure 13.1.

Figure 13.1 A virtual store in Second Life.

Another social network, Flickr, allows its users to upload thousands of photos to be viewed and commented on by other registered users. Social networking Web sites allow users to post their impressions and respond to the postings of others, on topics as varied as their attitudes toward the IT industry, or a discussion on the latest in technology and IT products or services.

These Web sites resonate with the actual interests of their users. Whether the interest group is all newly admitted freshman of a local technical university, serious users of IT products or services, those interested in learning how to deal with new business problems with the use of IT, those interested in learning how to cope with a newly invented technology, or those interested in learning how an IT product functions, these Web sites provide meaning for their users.

Relevance is increased when these Web sites offer participation. Some social networks even offer the possibility of a transition to physical meetings. This is relevant because meeting with the client is an important sales tactic.

Marketing has changed over time, and advertising alone is not a solution anymore. Marketing managers should learn the importance of communities, engagement with them, and being part of the discussion.

Conclusion

The online world has changed the marketing–sales dynamic. These are no longer separate functions. The Internet provides an almost limitless potential to increase the customer base using a variety of techniques employing immersive technologies such as Second Life and social networking sites such as MySpace.

Chapter 14

E-Commerce as a Sales Medium

Electronic commerce (e-commerce) can be defined as business activities conducted using the Internet and the World Wide Web. Generally, people think exclusively of consumer (business-to-consumer or B2C) shopping on the Web as e-commerce, but in fact, business-to-business (B2B) transactions account for a much larger portion of revenue generated directly by e-commerce. In addition, business processes that are not directly involved in the selling and purchasing of goods and materials account for the majority of business activities on the Internet.

Examples of B2C transactions, such as purchases from Amazon.com, are easy to identify. In these examples, an individual consumer selects and purchases a product or service over the Internet. B2B transactions are similar, except that they occur between two businesses. For example, a publisher might buy paper from a source over the Internet, or a bookstore might order books from the publisher.

Business is not just about buying and selling, and the Internet provides a medium for businesses to exchange information about other processes as well. Product designs and specifications, for example, need to be disseminated to suppliers by a manufacturer. All businesses need to recruit, hire, and manage employees, and all of these processes can be supported by the Internet and related technologies.

Advantages of E-Commerce

E-commerce can help increase profits by decreasing costs and increasing sales. To increase sales, the Internet provides a medium for reaching a global marketplace

165

affordably. Although it would be expensive to run an ad on every television channel in the United States, a Web site could potentially reach an audience of the same size for much less. In addition, most products are of interest to only a small subsection of the general population, which is known as a market segment. The Internet provides a way of targeting just the desired market segment, and potentially even building a virtual community from that group. Costs can be reduced not just by reducing the expense of direct advertising but also by reducing the costs associated with exchanging information between vendors and customers. Businesses also benefit from purchasing over the Internet. They can benefit from reduced information exchange costs, and they can find new and cheaper suppliers for what they purchase.

Disadvantages of E-Commerce

However, e-commerce is limited because it does not allow a customer to inspect the product firsthand. For expensive and unique items such as fashion and antiques, this limitation can be significant. In addition, a better price of a perishable item, such as food, is of little value if the seller is not physically close to the buyer. Because e-commerce is so new, the costs and benefits for a company might be hard to quantify. Companies looking to do business internationally might encounter other problems, such as language and cultural barriers, import and trade restrictions, and currency conversion.

Value Chains in E-Commerce

The concept of a value chain involves the way in which a business unit organizes the primary activities of identifying customers, designing products, purchasing materials and supplies, marketing and selling products, delivering the products to the customer, and providing ongoing support to the customer. In addition to these primary activities, all business units also undertake supporting activities, such as human resources and purchasing. Collectively, the value chain reflects how the business takes raw materials and labor and creates a product of value to a customer. A business unit can function within an industry value chain. For example, a car dealer sells cars to customers. The car dealer buys those cars from automobile manufacturers, who in turn purchase the component parts of cars from parts suppliers.

Value chains can be of use in e-commerce as a technique for analyzing a business or industry to identify opportunities for leveraging e-commerce. One approach is to break up the value chain of a specific business. As discussed earlier, it might be possible to reduce transaction costs by outsourcing components of the value chain. For example, a business strong in design but weak in manufacturing might contract with another company to do manufacturing for them. The other approach is to look at ways of changing the industry value chain. Amazon.com provides an excellent example of this approach. Amazon claims to be the world's biggest bookstore, but in fact, it has no books. Instead, it enters into a relationship with book distributors and orders books as customers order them. This reduces the expense of maintaining an inventory and allows Amazon to have a large product offering. The essential idea is that an e-commerce project should be driven by a business need or opportunity, not by technology.

A marketplace has three main functions: (1) matching buyers and sellers; (2) facilitating the exchange of information, goods, services, and payments associated with market transactions; and (3) providing an institutional infrastructure, such as a legal and regulatory environment. A marketspace is an electronic marketplace. In a marketspace, several of the processes used in trading and supply chains are changed. These changes lead to increased efficiency and lower transaction costs, enabling "friction-free" markets.

There are four main participants in the syndication supply chain: (1) content creators, (2) syndicators, (3) distributors, and (4) consumers. Each participant benefits from syndication. Content creators make money by selling their content to syndicators. Syndication provides them with a ready market and potentially greater reach. Syndicators benefit by acting as intermediaries. The distributor purchases the content from the syndicator and provides it to consumers. Distributors may charge for the content or use it as a loss leader to other services. Consumers benefit from having more content readily available at a potentially lower cost.

The E-Commerce Model

In the middle-to-late 1990s, corporations began to replace their computer-to-computer electronic data interchange (EDI) systems connecting them to their suppliers and distributors with Web-based systems. Many companies transferred their customer service knowledge bases onto "self-service" Web sites. Similarly, companies are managing their sales forces more flexibly and effectively over the Web.

There are also many examples in which Web servers obviate traditional business designs. For example, Quicken Loans, originally a subsidiary of Intuit, Inc. (the developer of Quicken and QuickBooks), received the U.S. Federal Housing Administration's (FHA) approval to be the first mortgage lender to provide FHA loans nationally via the Internet. Before this, mortgage lenders were required to have a brick-and-mortar office in the vicinity where they wanted to originate and close FHA loans. With the Quicken Loans Web site, the business design has been transformed with respect to its expense dimensions. With Web-based loan origination systems, consumers can apply, track, and close a loan directly from the Web site. This is a potential discontinuity that threatens brick-and-mortar-only businesses.

In Table 14.1, Meyer, Friar, and Lax (2000) identify four categories in which the Internet can pose a serious threat to a company's business model. Try to identify

Table 14.1   Business Model Threats

Category	Description	The Threat	Winning Strategies
E-commerce B2C	Online retailers	You are a traditional high-cost retail chain that is challenged by a Web-only retailer having a strategic partnership with a major Internet portal.	Amazon.com offered "any book you want" versus shelf-bound book retailers. Its market capitalization soared relative to traditional retailers such as Barnes & Noble, and forced them to create their own Web stores.
			E*TRADE competes with established industry leaders such as Merrill Lynch through low transaction fees, provision of real-time information, and great analysis tools. Traditional brokerages have been forced to go online and change their own business models.
E-commerce B2B	Web-based brokers of products and services	You are a traditional distributor of industrial goods whose customers are leaving for Web-based auctions and brokers.	ChemConnect, with $180 million (as of 2007) in investment capital, serves as a middleman between buyers and sellers of industrial chemicals.
Digital media	Web portal and content provider	You are a traditional publisher with dozens of hard-copy magazines whose target readership starts turning to Yahoo! and AOL on a daily basis for content related to yours, and many other, services.	AOL merged with Time Warner to gain access to diverse multimedia content and created a supernetwork. AOL also partnered with PALM to provide wireless access to its content. In 2006, AOL became a free portal service.
			Yahoo! continues to be a leading Web search engine. Yahoo!'s growth in electronic retailing and personal finance is accelerating.

Table 14.1   Business Model Threats (*Continued*)

Category	Description	The Threat	Winning Strategies
Enabling technologies	Technologies facilitate access and use of the Web.	You are a manufacturer of computers, computer components, computer peripherals, or computer software that has not kept up with current technology trends.	PALM spins off from 3Com to directly challenge the Windows CE personal digital assistant (PDA) vendors with a new generation of handheld devices and Web-based information services.
			VA Linux Systems achieves a market capitalization of almost $10 billion on sales of $18 million for 1999. Compare this to traditional UNIX workstation leader Silicon Graphics, who had sales of $2.7 billion in 1999 but whose market capitalization was only about $2 billion.

the type of threat facing your company, and then consider the apparent success factors for new-economy leaders in various industries.

The common thread running across all these different industries and periods of time is that next-generation innovations are often introduced by industry outsiders (e.g., Apple and their iPhone). Also, established firms tend to show a reluctance to adopt and integrate these innovations into their own products and business models. However, those that do adapt are amply rewarded. As Table 14.1 shows, the valuations for attacking companies are often much higher than those for the traditional companies, even when sales are much less.

Apart from B2B and B2C, the two most prevalent models, there are a variety of other e-commerce models that companies pursue: software, e-marketers, infrastructure, exchanges, reverse auctions, etc.

Infrastructure. Infrastructure is a category of software that helps Web designers build and run all those millions of e-businesses. The hottest and most ubiquitous of these companies are the Internet service providers (ISPs). ISPs sell end users access to the Web and host business Web sites for rates that are sometimes as low as $9.95 per month.

e-Marketers. Quite a few companies have come to prominence precisely because their forte is marketing on the Web. DoubleClick is one of these. Essentially, publishers and agencies utilize DoubleClick's expertise in ad serving, rich media, video, search, and affiliate marketing to help them make the most of the digital medium.

Exchanges. Exchanges are industry-specific marketplaces where buyers can efficiently meet sellers. This model, in fact, might be the most lucrative opportunity of all. A study by the National Association of Purchasing Management estimated that the average corporate purchase order costs $79 to process. Of that amount, $38 is for meeting internal processing costs such as product selection, requisition, and approval. If you can provide a way to streamline this process, you can save companies a bundle.

Auctions. There is probably no other e-business that captures the unique capabilities of the Web as well as auction sites. Without the Web, the auction would not be possible; and without auctions, the Web would be much duller. While there are now dozens of auction sites, eBay was the great inventor of this exciting concept. It is really a natural for the capabilities of the technology, and it is a true moneymaker, given the volume of transactions and the fees that can be charged.

Reverse auctions. A reverse auction permits companies that need services such as accounting and computer programmers to post requests for those services. Those interested in offering the services then bid for the work.

Services. The services e-business model is what the majority of existing businesses move into. If you are a Merrill Lynch, then it does not make sense to start an auction site or an online furniture store. It does make sense, however, to duplicate online what you do offline. Hence, there will be a proliferation of Merrill Lynch onlines. Not all will be based on a clicks-and-mortar model.

E*TRADE is a good example of this type of business. By jumping in where the bricks-and-mortars failed to tread, it made a lot of money and got a good, long lead. Services types of businesses are just that—they provide a wealth of services. A good service site is a hybrid of service plus portal plus community rather than a pure service business. E*TRADE offers a variety of services, including research reports, quotes, trading, discussion groups, chat, financial services such as retirement planning, etc. Essentially, it is a financial supermarket.

Application service provider (ASP or software as a service [SaaS]). An alternative to the traditional service-business model is the application service provider (ASP). The ASP company offers the use of software, but instead of selling one copy at a time, the company offers the use of it through the Internet for a fee. Nowadays, the tech industry refers to this as **SaaS**. Some ASPs charge a subscription fee. McAfee (www.mcafee.com) uses this revenue model. Geared for both consumers and businesses, McAfee charges a yearly fee per PC for a host of services such as virus scanning and PC tune-up. McAfee has long been a brand name for computer users. Up until 1999, all of McAfee's products were sold in the traditional off-the-shelf manner. With the advent of the Web, McAfee was able to add a new sales channel to its mix, with enormous revenue-enhancing possibilities. There are variations to the ASP model, as shown in Table 14.2.

Content. A plethora of content-oriented sites abound, such as CNET (www.cnet.com) and TheStreet.com (www.thestreet.com). However, Web surfers have been notoriously resistant to spending for any content whatsoever. Slate

Table 14.2   The Application Service Provider (ASP) Model

ASP	Application service providers rent, license, host, and maintain third-party software.
BSP	Business service providers rent suites of typically industry-specific services.
CASP	Consumer application service providers offer software geared toward a corporation's customers.
CSP	Computer service providers oversee server farms that host ASP, BSP, and business hardware.
ESP	E-commerce service providers package customized e-commerce applications.
FSP	Full-service providers offer packaged and customized software.
ISP	Internet service providers connect customers online.
NISP	Network Internet service providers integrate software suites accessible from a single, user-controlled site.

(www.slate.com) is a good example of this phenomenon. Owned by Microsoft, Slate achieved notoriety by bringing in at its helm the ephemeral Michael Kinsley. It also stirred up controversy by announcing that it was going to start charging a subscription fee. This model failed miserably, and today Slate is totally free.

James Cramer, a cofounder of TheStreet.com, admitted that he made a big mistake. He thought he could get the visitors to his financial news service to pay $9.95 for his advice. He now says that Internet users will not pay for news; they are adamant about it, and they are angry.

So, how does one make money when one's site publishes pure content? In Slate's case, it takes advertising. Many content companies are making money by selling their user data demographic information. Since the Web offers highly targeted audiences, these data have proved to be a gold mine.

CNET is also a good example of a content site that manages to make money. CNET touts itself as the place on the Internet for all things technology. While it doesn't sell anything, it does provide users with excellent information on the technology they want to buy, and then links them to one or more affiliate stores where users can purchase the product.

Niche Models

There are several niche models:

Brokerage model: A Web site brings buyers and sellers together and facilitates transactions. Examples: eBay, PayPal, etc.

Advertising model: A Web site provides content (usually, but not necessarily, for free) and services (such as e-mail, chat, forums, etc.) mixed with advertising messages in the form of banner ads. Example: Yahoo!

Merchant model: This model is used by wholesalers and retailers of goods and services. Sales may be made based on list prices or through auction. Example: Amazon.com.

Manufacturer (direct) model: Manufacturer reaches buyers directly and thereby compresses the distribution channel. Example: Dell Computers.

Affiliate model: The affiliate model provides purchase opportunities wherever people may be surfing. It offers financial incentives (in the form of a percentage of revenue) to affiliated partner sites. The affiliates provide purchase-point click-through to the merchant. Example: Amazon.com.

Subscription model: Users are charged a periodic—daily, monthly, or annual—fee to subscribe to a service. Frequently, free content is combined with premium content. Examples: ASPToday.com, America Online, eMarketer, etc.

Utility model: This model is based on metering usage—"pay as you go." Example: Slashdot.com.

Community model: This model is based on user loyalty. Revenue can be based on the sale of ancillary products and services or voluntary contributions. Not-for-profit organizations, "Expert" CSP means different things in different industries. Example: AllExperts.com.

Portals: Portals are gateways to the Web. They are directories, phone books, and indexes. They are the first place people go to when they need to find something. Example: Google.

Chief Selling Propositions

The chief selling proposition **CSP** is not what you sell, but how you sell a product. For example, the radio ads used by Cyberian Outpost, a now defunct reseller of electronic goods, promised free overnight delivery—even if you ordered your DVD player at 23:55 hours. In a world that must have its instant gratification, guaranteed overnight is an excellent ploy—making it free is even better.

What Cyberian Outpost offered was no different from what literally hundreds of other online retailers offer. However, Cyberian Outpost was practicing its form of one-upmanship—the CSP.

Because you are not dealing face-to-face but electron-to-face, there are limited options when it comes to online CSPs. The most popular CSPs are the following:

1. Deliver it faster
2. Provide excellent customer service

3. Give them something free
4. Give them a sense of community
5. Personalize it
6. Be unique
7. Be contrarian
8. Give it an aura with celebrity endorsements

The best time of the year to see competing CSPs at work is just before the holidays. Macys.com has offered purchasers of Joe Boxer 5-packs a $99 companion ticket on Virgin Atlantic, and eve.com (now Sephora.com) tried to lure Web customers with a one-year subscription to beauty products for $199. Even Amazon.com upped the ante by adding a wish list to its amazing array of products and services.

Perhaps, the most interesting CSP is that offered by Lands' End, which is unique, original, and highly profitable. Lands' End, once an old-fashioned catalog seller of down-home sports clothing such as fleece, has not only expanded its catalog but has also created a Web store that simulates the in-store experience.

The site's "My Virtual Model" (http://levdr.mvm.com/pages/leus/layout.html) permits users to create an electronic dress form in their size. This electronic avatar has your measurements, hair coloring, hairstyle, and skin tone.

Internet Failures

Some firms stumble badly on their way to Web-enabling their business. A good example of this is Toys "R" Us (www.toysrus.com). In the traditional toy retailing business, Toys "R" Us had been losing market share to Wal-Mart during the mid-1990s, and it spent hundreds of millions of dollars on revamping its stores and retraining staff. Still, market share continued to decline. On another front, the online-only retailer eToys quickly assembled a broad product mix and secured heavy venture money to build its online brand through deals with AOL and others. Kbkids.com was another successful online competitor during this period. These successes forced Toys "R" Us to come up with its own online retailing solution.

Toys "R" Us created a separate venture. However, most of the energy and resources of the company still went into opening more stores or upgrading existing ones, and building the traditional retail brand. The CEO of the Toys "R" Us Web spin-off resigned, and a new CEO started during the summer of 1999 (he was fired in 2000 over differences with his board). During the 1999 Christmas season, Toys "R" Us could not deliver purchases to 5% of its customers by Christmas Day, because a separate warehousing facility (from those of its stores) could not meet customer demand.

Toys "R" Us's troubles show that the company has to get a number of things right to transition successfully: adequate resource allocation, online branding and marketing to generate volume, and back-end logistics. All this requires a management team with rich experience in online business. We believe that Toys "R" Us will eventually succeed because it has no alternative. It is sufficiently large and has the brand power to go the distance. At the same time, one suspects that the entire process could have been so much easier if the correct integrative strategy had been established and properly executed years before it attempted to go online.

Just what does an e-business do to distinguish itself from the pack and set itself apart from both its online and offline competitors? This differentiation strategy is sometimes referred to as the "chief selling proposition."

Few companies offer a product or service so totally unique that there is no match for it in the market. Even if they did, it wouldn't be long before their competitors start massing at the borders. To take an example from the offline world, not too long ago Procter & Gamble offered one of those rare, unique products. It was called Febreze®. Just a spray or two freshened odoriferous fabrics such as clothing and upholstered furniture. But seemingly seconds after its product launch, P&G's competitors introduced odor-quenching products of their own. Today, there are no fewer than three competitive products on the market—more if you include generic brands.

In this particular product category, P&G can be labeled a "first mover" (i.e., the company was the first one to move into a particular competitive position). Often, being a first mover provides a definite competitive advantage. An e-business example of first-mover competitive advantage is Amazon.com. In spite of the introduction of many more electronic bookstores, including the mammoth Barnes & Noble, Amazon.com has retained its number-one position in this e-business category. But on closer examination, we find that Amazon.com works hard at staying number one. Over the few years it has been in business, Amazon.com has expanded its portfolio of offerings. It can now be considered an e-business superstore rather than just a bookstore, something that Barnes & Noble either does not wish to or cannot emulate.

First-mover status can be short-lived unless the company works hard at staying number one. But, of course, there's only room for one number one. Those e-businesses that aspire to be successful also aspire to the number-one position, understanding full well that in any e-business category, only a handful of the top-tier e-businesses will actually generate any substantial revenue. The importance of first-mover status, then, leads us back to the all-important CSP.

Web Site Legal Issues

The legal issues to be confronted by an organization for creating an e-commerce Web site include (1) construction of a viable privacy policy, (2) ensuring that visitors are aware of the terms and conditions of use, and (3) protection of intellectual property.

Privacy Policy

Web site visitors have every right to be concerned that their private information will be protected. The posting of a privacy policy and the knowledge that you will be adhering to its strict regulations serve to reassure the user and, more importantly, protect the organization from lawsuits. They know you are up to date on all global laws and regulations. They know you are aware that if you plan to resell this data, these transactions will be under the scrutiny of governmental and consumer watchdogs. The main points to be addressed in such a policy are as follows:

1. What information is being collected?
2. Who is doing the collecting?
3. How will the information be used?
4. With whom may the information be shared?
5. What choices do the consumers have in the collection, use, and distribution of the information? Can they opt out? How?
6. What type of security procedures has been put in place to protect the loss, misuse, or alteration of information?
7. How can the consumer correct any inaccuracies?

It should be noted that a number of organizations have developed oversight programs to certify that a specific Web site bearing their certification seal has policies in place that make it trustworthy and reliable with regard to consumer information (e.g., TRUSTe, the AICPA, and the Better Business Bureau "BBBOnline").

Terms and Conditions

Written in clear, easy-to-understand language, the Web site terms and conditions will detail to the visitor his or her rights and responsibilities in relation to interaction with the Web site and any executables downloaded from that Web site. When considering these terms and conditions, prime importance should be given to the precise nature of the goods and services to be offered. For example, if the Web site contains bulletin boards or chat rooms, it must be clearly stipulated who owns what rights to the posted material. The terms and conditions should also provide an indemnification of the organization in case the posted material infringes a third party's rights.

Standard provisions of Web site terms and conditions should include the following:

1. A limitation of liability statement: This limits organization's responsibility for any damages in case of a legal challenge. This is particularly important in cases where executables are going to be downloaded. Since executables are software, the typical "shrink wrap" licensing agreement will usually be the

method of choice. These End User License Agreements, commonly referred to as EULAs, serve both as contract and liability disclaimer.

2. A statement of the applicable governing law and jurisdiction: In other words, the Web site should indicate which state or country will govern a dispute and where such disputes will be resolved, which is usually the country, state, and municipality in which the organization is located.

3. A statement of the organization's proprietary rights for content: This includes a list of all copyrights and trademarks and should specify ownership of the text and imagery as well. A disclaimer that notifies users that the organization does not make any express or implied warranties regarding the currency of content on the site and does not guarantee "uptime" of the site.

False Advertising and Unfair Competition

Organizations need to be cautious about how they laud the benefits of using their products. Statements made on Web sites about software are usually subject to regulations and the common laws concerning false advertising and unfair competition. In the United States, the Federal Trade Commission (FTC) has the authority to require that an organization provide the "reasonable basis" under which it makes advertising statements. For example, the FTC might find fault with a company for making the claim that it provides the fastest possible connection at the lowest cost.

A legal dispute might also arise in situations in which a Web site has linked to a third-party site in such a way as to disguise the fact that information is actually coming from this third-party site. Organizations should also be aware that they may need to defend against an action brought under foreign laws or by foreign regulatory agencies.

Defamation

Chat rooms and bulletin boards provide ample opportunity for defamation (i.e., harming the reputation of another by making a false statement to a third person). Interestingly, the more passive an organization is in monitoring these end-user-oriented facilities, the less likely it is that a court will hold the organization liable.

Use of Domain Names

After selecting a domain name, the organization should use the preemptive approach of registering similarly worded names, including misspellings. Google evidently did not do this, as typing Goggle.com will get you lots of annoying pop-ups completely unrelated to Google.

Domain names are controlled by registrars. Registrars follow the Uniform Domain-Name Dispute-Resolution Policy (often referred to as the "UDRP").

Under this policy, most types of trademark-based domain-name disputes must be resolved by agreement, court action, or arbitration before a registrar will cancel, suspend, or transfer a domain name (http://www.icann.org/udrp/udrp.htm).

A dispute proceeding can only be initiated under certain circumstances: (1) The domain name at issue is identical or confusingly similar to a trademark or service mark in which the party has rights, or (2) the domain name registrant has no rights or legitimate interests in the domain name, and the registrant registered the domain name in "bad faith."

Trademarks

Trademark or service mark notices should be prominently displayed wherever the marks appear. If a mark has been registered with the U.S. Patent and Trademark Office (http://www.uspto.gov/), the ® symbol should be displayed; otherwise, the TM or SM symbols should be displayed in connection with trademarks or service marks, respectively. Organizations should be vigilant in protecting their trademarks and service marks. They should be equally vigilant that they do not infringe on the marks of others. Content within an executable as well as content residing on the organization's Web site needs to be audited to rule out trademark infringement.

Trademark infringement focuses on the question of whether two marks are likely to cause confusion with each other. Marks are considered confusing if the buying public would think that the products or services covered by one mark come from the same source or are affiliated with the goods or services covered by the previously used mark. Courts use the following factors to assess the likelihood of confusion:

1. The defendant's intent in adopting the mark
2. The relative strength of the plaintiffs mark
3. The similarity of the marks at issue
4. The similarity of the products or services covered by the mark
5. The types of purchasers or consumers and whether any actual confusion occurred
6. The advertising media used

Copyrights

A copyright is a form of protection provided to the authors of "original works of authorship" including literary, dramatic, musical, artistic, and certain other intellectual works, such as software, both published and unpublished. Copyright generally gives the owner of the copyright the exclusive right to reproduce the copyrighted work, to prepare derivative works, to distribute copies or audio recordings of the copyrighted work, to perform the copyrighted work publicly, or to display the copyrighted work publicly.

A copyright protects the form of expression rather than the subject matter. For example, a description of a machine could be copyrighted, but this would only prevent others from copying the description; it would not prevent others from writing a description of their own or from making and using the machine.

A work receives copyright protection the moment it is created and fixed in a tangible form so that it is perceptible either directly or with the aid of a machine or device. All text and imagery on a Web site and any associated executables are copyrighted to the organization the moment they are placed on the Web site and inserted into an executable. However, it is important to specify that the Web site, executable, and its works are copyrighted. This is customarily done at the bottom of each Web site page using the copyright symbol—©. In an executable, the copyright is customarily inserted in the About splash screen, usually accessed through the Help menu.

It is also important that the organization audit its Web site and associated executables to ensure that any content, data, or information is not violating anyone else's copyright. For example, an executable dynamically accesses Google and downloads research results to a client PC. Google's content is copyrighted to Google; as a result, you would need permission to use these materials.

Patents

A patent for an invention is the grant of a property right to the inventor, issued by the applicable patent office. Generally, the term of a new patent is 20 years from the date on which the application for the patent was filed in the United States or, in special cases, from the date an earlier related application was filed, subject to the payment of maintenance fees. U.S. patent grants are effective only within the United States, U.S. territories, and U.S. possessions. Under certain circumstances, patent term extensions or adjustments may be available.

The right conferred by the patent grant is, in the language of the statute and of the grant itself, "the right to exclude others from making, using, offering for sale, or selling" the invention in the United States or "importing" the invention into the United States. What is granted is not the right to make, use, offer for sale, sell, or import, but the right to exclude others from making, using, offering for sale, selling, or importing the invention.

In 1993, U.S. Patent 5,193,056, entitled "Data Processing System for Hub and Spoke Financial Services Configuration," was granted by the Patent and Trademark Office (PTO). The PTO held that the transformation of data, representing discrete dollar amounts, by a machine through a series of mathematical calculations into a final share price constitutes a practical application of a mathematical algorithm, formula, or calculation, because it produces a useful, concrete, and tangible result.

In 1998, in the State Street Bank Decision, the Court of Appeals affirmed this decision. This was significant because previously "methods of doing business" had not been widely considered patentable. According to many, this is a major reason that led to a boom in software and business method patents. One example of this is Amazon.com's "one-click" patent, in which a shopper's profile information (including credit card details and shipping address) is stored by a business and then automatically retrieved and utilized when that user wishes to "check out" and purchase an item.

As a result of this ruling, there has been a spate of lawsuits over the use of business processes that probably should never have been patented.

Conclusion

Levy (2001) talks about the following hacker ethics: (1) Access to computers—and anything that might teach you something about the way the world works—should be unlimited and total, and (2) all information should be free. The second hacker ethic has become a guiding principle of the Internet, often repeated by tech mouthpieces such as Esther Dyson. Many believe that anything stored on the Internet should be free for the taking.

Modern technology permits anyone with a PC to download and consume various forms of protected creative works, such as music, video, and graphic and written arts (i.e., "works"), without payment. Of course, storing copyrighted works on a server and allowing free downloads would get the owner of that server into legal trouble. Shawn Fanning and Napster found a way around this. Of course, Fanning did not actually invent peer-to-peer (P2P) networks. These have long been used in academic and research settings. What Fanning did was popularize the idea for the masses by creating a file-sharing service for copyrighted music. Because Napster's form of P2P stored only the index to its collection on its server, with the music being stored on its end users' PCs, the company felt that it would win any copyright violation lawsuits that came its way. This perception was proved wrong and the company had to shut down in order to comply with a court-ordered injunction that required it to stop the trading of copyrighted music, although it has since been resurrected as a pay-for-service company.

What is astonishing is that so many people feel that it is permissible to download works without payment. They seem to "tune out" when you ask whether they'd go into a store and steal a CD. Their response is that the record companies, publishers, artists, etc., overcharge for their products, so downloading for free is a "statement" against this sort of unfairness. One should question whether these people were ever required to take ethics training (civics) in school or whether they had a moral upbringing.

Pegasus Originals, based in South Carolina, provides a good example of the dangers of allowing P2P to run rampant in our society. The company sells patterns for needlework on its Web site. The company's owner found that another Web site was allowing people to download his artists' copyrighted works for free. While Pegasus itself found a way to survive, some of its artists have withdrawn altogether.

It should also be noted that Pegasus's survival is dependent on keeping ahead of those that would break encryption algorithms and find a way to sell Pegasus's designs. All algorithms are ultimately crackable.

The Pegasus case is a bit shocking because the original target of P2P networks was only music. However, today, all manner of intellectual property is being targeted, including software. Thus, if you decide to sell your software over the Internet, it's important to ensure that it's well protected.

References

Levy, S. (2001). *Hackers: Heroes of the Computer Revolution*. New York: Penguin.

Meyer, M. H., Friar, J. H., and Lax, C. R. (2000). Rising to the challenge of the Web. In Keyes, J. (Ed.), *Handbook of E-Business*. New York: Warren Gorham & Lamont.

Appendix A: Sample Marketing Plan for Computer Hardware

"Project YourSelf"

Version	Date	Author	Change Description

1. Executive Summary

Information Systems Machines (ISM) is the world's largest computer vendor, with innovative accessories that improve business performance. It has built a reputation for delivering quality PCs at competitive prices. One of the latest innovations is "Project YourSelf" Professional.

"Project YourSelf" Professional is the first solar laptop with a built-in, detachable, color, lightweight, battery-operated projector having the dimensions of a mouse. The new feature makes it possible to project presentations and slide shows onto any surface for small group business environments or for personal home use. The computer comes with a swivel bracket that holds the projector and a wireless (Bluetooth) connection that can be extended to 10 m.

The primary marketing objective is to achieve more than twice the sales achieved in 2008, which saw unit sales of 10 million units, with revenues exceeding $20 billion (average laptop sale of $1,000).

2. Mission Statement

ISM's mission statement is to be among the top three computer companies in the world to deliver the finest customer experience with the highest quality, leading technology, competitive pricing, and top-class service and support.

3. Market Description

The market consists of consumers and business users traveling or on the road who prefer to use a single device for their presentations, with lower use of their battery for longer performances.

"Project YourSelf" has divided the new innovative laptop series into three lines for targeted customers: students and home users, sales executives, and faculty and doctors. Historically, sales in 2003 have been almost evenly split between customers (45%) and corporate (55%) buyers.

Student and Home User Segment

Students and home users (SHU) require entry-level laptops that incorporate the latest technology at affordable prices. The SHU series offers the user colorful covers with character and style. This targets female and male students as well as home users with a performance that corresponds to what the customer needs in a laptop. The SHU series was developed to replace desktop PCs with high-end speakers (for music and video quality) with built-in wireless modem, equipped with a solar battery that maximizes the computer performance and output. The computer comes with the latest processor, either AMD or Intel Core i7-920, 2.66 GHz, and is customizable for future expansion.

With laptop prices that are closer to those of desktops, the European and American markets should increase by 50% compared to the same period of 2008. The biggest slice of the pie comes from the entry-level and mid-range laptops. This is the volume space in notebooks, which all the vendors target.

Consumers are split between low-end and midrange laptops. Of the 20 most popular laptops on PriceGrabber.com, 45% are low-end laptops (under $1,000), with an average price point of $576 (PriceGrabber.com, 2008).

What customers want: Wireless or Bluetooth connection for cell phones, with low power and a range of 15 m with a high data speed of 723 kbps.

How customers will use the product: "Project YourSelf" laptops will provide its customers with a replacement new notebook every three years, provided they purchase three years' extended warranty. The returned computer must be in good condition with a 50% payment for the new one.

Support requirements: Based on statistics, the company should be able to support the user need, as 58% have a portable-style laptop with a 15″ screen or less, weighing less than 6 lb (PriceGrabber.com, 2008).

How to reach them: Marketing strategies in retail chains; newspapers; road shows in universities, colleges, and schools; and most-visited Web sites.

Price sensitivity: The SHU series—$1,300 with Intel Core i7-920, 2.66 GHz, and solar charger.

Customers should be made aware of what new technology costs.

Processor	Clock Speed (GHz)	Price	QPI Speed (GT/s)	Cache
Intel® Core™ i7-920	2.66	$284	4.8	8 MB

Sales Executives Segment

Sales executives (SEs) require standardized laptops at lower and competitive costs. The series "SE" come with a range of wireless networking options. The processor comes with the latest Intel Core i7-940, 2.93 GHz mobile technology including Pentium M processors, specifically designed for mobile environments saving battery power. The computer is equipped with a built-in projector and a solar battery, which maximizes the computer performance and output.

Expected percentage of sales: Another 45% are mid-range laptops ($1,000–$2,000), with an average price point of $1,424.

What customers want: Combination of Turbo Boost technology and Hyper-Threading technology; faster, smarter, cheaper, and better. Server and Web-based applications that can be accessed from anywhere.

Users will use the new product in their day-to-day work, whether at home, class, or in the office; the product should be user-friendly with provision of restoration for additional backup files and reinstallation in case of crashes and corrupted files.

How to reach them: Marketing strategies in retail chains, newspapers, most-visited Web sites, PC magazines, exhibition fairs, TV commercials, and movie theaters.

Price sensitivity: The SE series—$1,650 with Intel Core i7-940, 2.93 GHz, solar and projector—45% of global market share.

Processor	Clock Speed (GHz)	Price	QPI Speed (GT/s)	Cache
Intel® Core™ i7-940	2.93	$562	4.8	8 MB

Senior Faculty and Doctors Segment

Senior faculty and doctors have a dedicated laptop under series "FAD" designed for professionals who require exceptional performance for applications such as CAD, GIS, or financial analysis and software development that requires high-end performance. The computer has an Intel Core i7-965 (3.20 GHz) with faster, intelligent, multicore technology that applies processing power and delivers an unprecedented breakthrough in PC performance. The user will multitask applications faster and be able to unleash incredible digital media creation capabilities.

Expected sales: Only 10% of the top 20 laptops fall within the high-end price range (more than $2,000), with an average price point of $2,274 (PriceGrabber.com, 2008).

Customers will want the best desktop on the planet, as well as server and Web-based applications that can be accessed from anywhere.

To reach customers, the product should be promoted in combination with support by having FAQs covering servicing manuals, technical specifications, repair, etc.

Users can reach suppliers by customer sales service centers with contact numbers, e-mails, and Web links that allows users and potential customers to quickly and easily obtain accurate and up-to-date information, including installation and spare parts ordering information. Such a service will enhance customer satisfaction and loyalty to the brand.

Marketing strategy: Corporate invitations to seminars, PC magazines, computer exhibitions, most-visited Web sites, and mass e-mails.

Price sensitivity: The FAD series—$2,050 with Intel Core i7-965, 3.20 GHz, solar and projector—10% of global market share.

Processor	Clock Speed (GHz)	Price	QPI Speed (GT/s)	Cache
Intel® Core™ i7-965 Extreme Edition	3.20	$999	6.4	8 MB

Product Review

Employing smaller, quieter, and stylish laptop designs, "Project YourSelf" will use this new mobile technology for a variety of smaller, quieter, and high-performing consumer segments. These computers will enable crystal-clear audio, better graphics, and sharper video playback with a built-in (mobile) projector and solar battery for longer battery life and turbo performance.

Competitive Review

- Fast service, service efficiency, and personal attention make a crucial difference in gaining leverage in the marketplace.
- Recognize and define strengths and weaknesses.
- Keep pace with technological improvements.
- Vendors should target entry-level and mid-range laptops.

Distribution Review

The following review would be an indicator of what the market share should be to be number three; that is, target to reach 17% of the market for the year 2009–2010.

Top Five Notebook Vendors by Marketshare (%) 2005–2006

HP	39
Lenovo	20
Acer	14
Dell	7
Toshiba	7

Support Requirements

In the event customers or users experience any technical difficulties, they are requested to take the following steps for fast and reliable service.

Laptop Support and Repair

For hard drive failure, contact the laptop service manager by e-mail (support@ projectyourself.com) with contact information to receive a new hard drive. We will send the new hard drive, return shipping information, and installation instructions.

Other Hardware Issues

For LCD, system board, battery, etc., please e-mail or call at xxx-xxx-xxxx and provide us with the computer's serial number.

Power Adapter Requirements Worldwide

Use an AC plug adapter and a power cable that are compatible with the local AC power source. The laptop has the appropriate adapters that will accommodate all types of power outlets specific to your travel destinations. The computers are auto-switch enabled between 115 and 220 V.

4. Strengths, Weaknesses, Opportunities, and Threat Analysis

Strengths

- An advantage the company has is its product uniqueness, which reduces competition. "Project YourSelf" is a PC with additional built-in accessories that improve the hardware, user performance, and battery life. The projector gives students and professionals the ability to share their work with small teams with high-resolution outcomes.
- What makes the product better than others is the fact that it also offers a variety of latest processors in addition to its enhanced specifications. Customers would understand the need for buying this product, which is based on continuous research and development, thinking originality, and innovation.
- Price bracket is so tempting when customers become aware of the hidden costs before knowing the profit margin to be an advantage to the customer.
- Students are after gadgets that would make the product appealing, especially when the price is 10% over the norm.
- Users will receive a new computer every three years.

Weaknesses

- As with any new product, users will require marketing awareness as well as campaigns that will affect sales at the start. It will be the beginning of the growth stage in the NPD life cycle.
- Sales could be affected by the sales executive's attitude toward the product; if enthusiasm is lost, then the product will be affected. This requires additional incentives for salespeople to work and improve their skills.
- Launching the new product when the market is in recession can affect sales heavily.
- The company is unaware of its global partners' service centers; technical "train the trainer" programs should be implemented.

Opportunities

- Demand for broadband Internet access is universal.

- Instant Wi-Fi communication as wireless access points multiply; users will be able to test the PC on the spot.
- Greater demand for accessories, peripherals, and software.
- New business opportunities for customers with computer phobia as the computer will be easier to use and direct projection of self even while having fun, that is, while playing games.
- Being the first product with built-in accessories, the buzz will generate word of mouth (WoM) marketing. This will create a change in technology and markets on both a global and local scale.

Threats

Since the product stands third (rank), both competition brands are a threat.

If the company's sales, marketing, and distribution departments lose their aggressive market edge due to long breaks and internal problems, then the effect on growth will be threatening.

The economy could be part of the threat if or when tuitions increase at educational institutions, and if gas prices rise, customers will think twice before their purchase.

Recession can affect sales.

Competition will imitate or improve on the product weakness.

If the company has a bad debt or cash flow problem, this will create a negative effect.

5. Objectives and Issues

First-Year Objectives

- Keep a close eye on competition and create a framework of competition practices and innovations. Competitive intelligence analysis must be conducted on a periodical basis, including recent and latest studies on how major corporations have achieved worldwide leadership in their high-tech markets.
- Analyze the company's new product line strategy as well as the technology used for future improvement (or immediate improvement, if necessary).
- Continuity of the strategic vision for "Project YourSelf" that is translated into the launch of the new product and technological strategies.
- Be proactive and improve on weaknesses, and analyze threats to minimize its impact on the product.
- Use just-in-time inventory to minimize losses and expenses.
- Achieve 25% growth from the previous year's sales.
- Look for aggressive and best marketing firms with international partners to prepare perfect promotional branding for the new product.
- Invest in gift items with product logo and name for new customers.

- Invest heavily in customer care centers for positive feedback.
- Start developing a new design with value-added improvements.

Second-Year Objectives

- Break even and attain 50% growth as per executive summary strategic plan.
- Repackage the laptop carry bag for students (backbag), sales executives, and faculty and doctors as an additional gift with every purchase, with a distinctive style for each type of user.
- Price reductions if possible to attract customers to buy.
- Carry out an aggressive campaign to market the product, and inform customers of any new accessories developed or improved using mass e-mails and Web sites.
- Launch the new design that was developed and tested in year one objectives.
- Improve on investment in customer care centers for positive feedback.

Issues

- Run quick fixes as the product will have some defects that require immediate attention.
- Look at service history as well as hardware and software problems to learn from mistakes and take positive actions for the future.
- Keep an eye open on public blogs as users tend to share their frustrations and complain.
- Resolve any internal management issues or external sources, that is, suppliers that might affect the product growth.
- Any faulty laptop would require immediate replacement (1 year warranty).
- Create a troubleshooting site for hardware and software issues that will add value to the customer seeking additional help.

6. Product Strategy

Product strategy would signify that the product becomes ready to launch. It is critical to have an experienced marketing team and coordination between internal and external teams (engineering, sales, customer service, complaints, etc.) beyond the internal business boundaries. They would grow to become key components of the product itself, driving innovation to valued customers.

Positioning

"Project YourSelf" laptop should be positioned with a simplified message focusing on the perceptions of the customer rather than the product itself. Since the product is the first in its kind, it becomes easier for the customer to remember.

The product should relate itself to the number one processor, that is, the Intel processor. One important aspect of product positioning is market share, which is measured by the product's ability to capture as many customers as possible. This can be accomplished by higher volumes, which can reduce cost, thus making the product more competitive in the market. Reputation can also be used to the firm's advantage, which can increase bargaining power during negotiations with suppliers.

To gain market share and customers, the advertising campaigns should reinforce the fact that the product is selling itself not as the number one product but as a genuine, reliable, and easy-to-use product like "Think practical" that will attract customer attention (Ries and Trout, 2007).

Additionally, the firm should look at positioning its product by age (students), color (for him and her), and profession (faculty and doctors).

Product Strategy

With rapidly changing technology, new developments and upgrades must occur periodically to make product strategy work. This process is known as time to market, and will optimize product performance, cost, and reliability.

The objective will always focus on ensuring high levels of "quality, reliability, and robustness" to avoid the significant costs of correcting problems before and after sale. Then, service responsiveness should kick off, which requires additional resources and their related costs (Crow, 2001).

The company must recognize that it cannot do all things at all times and that it must focus on what will distinguish it in the marketplace, with the use of central repository intelligent software that will transform data into usable, accurate information. There are several types of market input that require immediate attention for a product to survive, that is, customer feedback, call centers, win or loss reports, enhancement requests, incident and analyst reports, and competitive analysis. For example, it should be simple for the company's biggest customers to send product enhancement ideas to the management, and simple for the management to get these ideas integrated with the rest of the market inputs.

This process will save time and money by collecting more accurate generalizations about what customers need, enable a more proactive approach in the trade-offs to sales and management, and permit running what-if analysis scenarios (FeaturePlan, 2006).

Pricing Strategy

It's difficult to calculate accurately unless we have plenty of historical price and volume data. In this example, the price would require to follow market skimming as applied to technology products. In this business, the old unsold models sell at a low price, while new, innovative products will sell at a higher price.

Since the market is distributed as 10% for the high-end price range at an average price of $2274, 45% as midrange laptops at an average price of $1424, and the remaining 45% for low-end laptops at an average price of $576, the organization should employ market skimming. This usually involves a high premium for new or latest versions to generate the maximum possible margin from the customers with the greatest demand. Once the sales volume begins to decrease at the original price, the marketing manager should incrementally lower the price to increase sales again; this is repeated until a stable price with an acceptable margin is determined (Bovay, 2008).

There is no single way to determine pricing strategy. We should look at how to position the new laptop in the market when competing with top players. The price should reflect consumer needs and requirements as buyers want to get the best possible configuration for the price they seek.

According to Scott Allen, an organization should have a continuous contract with a market research firm to run an analysis on how the price of the new product will affect demand. Then comes the cost of goods and how to cover fixed overheads to turn into profits. Another strategy should be to aim at long-term profit and short-term revenue maximization, that is, by increasing market share considering economies of scale (Allen, n.d.).

In summary, price ought to be based on the value it creates for the customer, that is, pay for performance method—with the new computer equipped with a solar charge, the value it gives the consumer by saving x euros or dollars per year would give the impression of a bargain, while of course, the price strategy should be never lower than cost or higher than most competition pricing.

7. Marketing Strategy

Marketing Communications

Marketing communications include customer materials such as brochures, press releases, Web sites, and PR trade show presentations. The advantage of a thoughtfully written communication plan is to keep the company message unified as one coherent voice across the vast number of products' agents and markets by creating integrated and open communications. This serves as a foundation of the company's marketing business plan, where all departments and personnel communicate the same message to the same targeted audience.

Partnerships, as well as association of specialized groups with common aims, would be encouraged. That is, "Project YourSelf" could announce the signing of a Memorandum of Understanding (MoU) in a strategic marketing alliance to develop a small database for the health care industry with the company information systems group.

The relationship will create joint marketing opportunities for the company, with health care hospitals and clinics being the preferred PC vendor for all clients. The alliance will be published in both the company and the health care Web site to increase sales.

This alliance is a key component of a marketing strategy that presents turnkey solutions addressing a physician's need to access patient information anytime, anywhere. It will help change the way medical clinics operate, by realizing greater efficiencies.

The marketing communication for faculty and students will focus on mobile technology as an integral part of an academic institute's daily routine. Whether in a class, the library, or the cafeteria, real-time access to Internet, portal, intranet, online course, and library access enhances the ability to provide superior data access requirements with ease and simplicity.

The marketing effort is all about creating awareness and interest among the current and potential customers identified by previous market research and input from target audience. The company's marketer can spread the word and get the message out in a variety of ways such as newspaper and Internet advertising, yellow pages, e-mails, direct mail, etc.

Advertising

Use a dynamic Web site that permits and encourages customers to build their own PC configuration with an approximate price indication.

Update the Web site on a regular basis to keep and communicate important and relevant messages to current and new customers.

As after-sales service, contact customers who purchased PCs and offer helpful tips, and set the stage for future business and run a check on their e-mail addresses for future products and accessories.

Strong, ongoing customer engagement in events, cocktails, and news releases are the key to long-term business growth and success.

Advertise ease of accessibility when customers need assistance by creating a help desk service.

Create a monthly newsletter to keep customers informed about new products, upcoming events, or discounts.

Work with specialized marketing and advertising agencies to cover the whole area in sales, including channel members.

Promotions

Use eye-catching exterior signage, newspapers, in-store displays, window banners, and other visual elements to draw customers' attention to the PC facility, emphasizing the built-in projector and solar battery recharge.

Promote the PC from a professional and educational perspective, that is, as the first PC for health practitioners.

Promote the product with the latest technology, using Intel and AMD logos and displaying the Intel channel program membership certificate.

Offer a discount on a future purchase, a special prize, or a 3-month service extension for completing a questionnaire.

8. Distribution Strategy

One of the company's channel strategies is to double the number of authorized distributors, each focusing on a specific segment of the market.

Partner with Intel as it recommends that allies invest in evaluating and testing product offerings from different original design manufacturers.

A good and transparent relationship with distributors will be an essential key to the PC business' success. The company must choose a distributor that is easy to work with and demonstrates a high level of commitment to business follow-ups and feedback.

Fully evaluate and understand your distributors' return policies and warranty terms and conditions.

Follow Dell's distribution strategy by replacing traditional distribution with telephone-based sales and ordering.

9. Action Programs

The demand for mobility products and wireless infrastructure is growing day by day. And in order to excel, the business program action plan should evaluate the market before launching the PC in the market; this starts with a survey while conducting an "information audit" of clients, using methods such as questionnaires, telephone surveys, one-on-one interviews, and group interviews (Hammond, n.d.).

To help improve sales and ROI, the company should rely and select marketing tools such as the following:

- Brochures, by covering product lines and services
- Promotional presentations and PR
- Project follow-ups, that is, health care clinics and faculty feedback
- Annual reports, an opportunity to let the management see sales and revenues
- Internet and Web pages, a tool to link customers to latest events, FAQs, backups, and recovery software

Month 1

- According to Intel, the first thing required is to evaluate profitability of the new PC business by determining profit margins. The company should perform calculations based on business or item costs and the final bill of materials for the systems you offer your customers.

- Create a list all of your current and potential customers and start calling or e-mailing them and market your new mobile product offerings.
- Have evaluation units on hand, and give customers a 15-day free trial period that will allow customers to experience the advantages of owning it.
- Evaluate efficiency at the distributor level and partner with those promoting Intel, Dell, and other top brands, either to follow suit or improve on weaknesses.

Month 2

- Evaluate the local and international market by identifying potential customers and goals.
- Hire a business consultant to help in business strategy implementation.
- Evaluate your product offering, and choose a distributor for sourcing.

Month 3

- Start marketing campaigns and road shows, research customer needs, and evaluate what kind of PCs will be right for them. Offer customized specifications to meet their needs, explain to them what features will meet their requirements, and start selling the new product.
- Work with your Intel representative to make use of the marketing resources available to you as an active-status Intel channel program member.

Month 4

- Targeting clients should be linked to evaluation units. Point out specifics of the PC's specifications, such as graphics capabilities for students, wireless capabilities for faculty, etc. The business should focus on the three PCs to market with their various hardware configurations while keeping price in mind.
- Market these three products heavily, and evaluate what people are seeking; have items modified for future product offerings.

Month 5

- Evaluate critical components to include battery, LCD, projector, and processor. Some manufacturers offer larger-capacity battery replacements or even a secondary battery. For LCDs, determine the manufacturer's overall replacement policy. For the new projector, determine durability, color with autofocus, and fixing time or replacements policy. On processors, Intel can provide a wealth of information about the heart of its mobility platform.

- Select the company's distributors; pay careful attention to the mobile-focused authorized Intel distributors, who will provide the latest products. Choose a distributor that is easy to work with and demonstrates commitment to your business success.
- Fully evaluate and understand your distributors' return policies and warranty terms and conditions.

Month 6

- Evaluate feedback from customers and follow up. To be a winner with the new PC, the business should have outstanding customer service.
- Be the customers' technology authority; educating customers is an essential key to success. Consider offering beginner or intermediate "getting started with your PC" classes to help customers feel more comfortable and productive using their laptops.
- Turn the business to do-it-yourself, by offering customers the option of building their own laptops by personalizing the purchase, which helps customers look beyond pricing and understand the importance of having the latest and fastest components and improved performance.

References

Allen, S. Pricing Strategy [Internet]. Available at http://entrepreneurs.about.com/od/salesmarketing/a/pricingstrategy.htm (Accessed December 17, 2008).

Bovay, K. (2008). When to Use Price Skimming or Market Skimming as a Pricing Strategy [Internet]. Available at http://ezinearticles.com/?When-to-Use-Price-Skimming-Or-Market-Skimming-As-a-Pricing-Strategy&id=1341511 (Accessed December 17, 2008).

Crow, K. (2001). Product Development Strategic Orientation [Internet]. Available at http://www.npd-solutions.com/strategy.html (Accessed December 16, 2008).

FeaturePlan. (2006). Product Management—Next Generation End-to-End Solution [Internet]. Available at http://www.featureplan.com/product-management-software/product_management_overview.htm (Accessed December 16, 2008).

Hammond, J. Marketing Program [Internet]. Available at http://www.libsci.sc.edu/bob/class/clis724/SpecialLibrariesHandbook/marketing.htm (Accessed December 30, 2008).

Intel Corporation. (2008). Intel® Core™ i7 Processor Provides Performance on Demand, Adds "Turbo Boost" and "Hyper-Threading" Technologies [Internet]. Available at http://www.intc.com/releasedetail.cfm?ReleaseID=348090 (Accessed December 1, 2008).

Intel, Implementing a Build-to-Order Notebook Business Strategy [Internet]. Available at http://cache-www.intel.com/cd/00/00/23/00/230024_230024.pdf (Accessed December 31, 2008).

PriceGrabber.com. (2008). Consumer Behavior Report [Internet]. Available at https://mr.pricegrabber.com/March_CBR_Portable_Laptop_Trends_v9_FINAL.pdf (Accessed December 3, 2008).

Ries, A., and Trout, J. (2007). Positioning [Internet]. Available at http://www.quickmba.com/marketing/ries-trout/positioning/ (Accessed December 15, 2008).

Shrikanth, G. (2006). Laptop Special: Notable Performance [Internet]. Available at http://dqindia.ciol.com/content/wifi/2006/106101403.asp (Accessed December 2, 2008).

Waldock, L. (2008). Intel Core i7 "Nehalem" processor and X58 chipset [Internet]. Available at http://www.reghardware.co.uk/2008/11/03/review_cpu_intel_core_i7/ (Accessed December 1, 2008).

Appendix B: Sample Marketing Plan for Computer Software

Marketing Plan: Version 0.05

Contents

0. Document Control

Document Location

[List the location details of where this document can be found on the network]

Version History

Version	Change (in Detail)	Author	Date
0.01			
0.02			
0.03			
0.04			
0.05			

Document Review

Version	Reviewed by	Title/Department	Date

Project Document References

Document Title	Version	Location

1. Executive Summary

Since its inception in 1998, Virtual IT has been a leading-edge provider of virtualization technology for virtualization of servers as well as desktop computers running a wide range of operating systems (OSs). The product line so far has consisted of the Virtual IT Business Suite for professional IT service providers and the Virtual IT Personal Suite for private customers. Virtual IT serves a growing worldwide customer base and is present in more than 25 countries with its sales and support operations. Virtual IT's headquarters are in Zurich, Switzerland.

Management has recently decided to respond to the increasing number of customers expressing a need for a tool to deliver and manage cross-platform virtualization technologies. The Virtual IT product management department has designed the specification for a new tool that can manage all virtual resources of a data center from a central management console, offering sophisticated load-balancing features with dynamic deployment and retirement of server capacity on demand without service interruptions. The management tool does support seamless integration of all solutions from major virtualization technology vendors.

The new tool will be incorporated in a new product line targeted at a global customer base managing data center and IT infrastructure operations. The product will be launched under the name **Virtual IT Control Center 1**. Management of Virtual IT expects to further increase its market share with what it believes is the next-generation tool for managing and providing on-demand IT infrastructure by leveraging virtualization technologies. The primary marketing objective is to increase Virtual IT's market share in the global data center virtualization management tool market by 8% to 43% in the first year by licensing Virtual IT Control Center 1 to 30,000 data centers worldwide, with an overall annual licensing revenue target of $300 million. Breakeven is expected to be reached by the end of the first year.

The product launch is planned to take place at the annual trade show CeBIT, in Hannover, Germany, with a special launch event to kick off a global marketing campaign to introduce the Virtual IT Control Center product line to a worldwide business audience. The overall marketing budget is confirmed by management to be $30 million.

The present marketing plan defines the marketing strategy and its implementation over the next two years. The strategy is based on a thorough analysis of markets and customers' needs, and describes the positioning of the product in the global market relative to its competitors. Furthermore, the plan outlines the actions to be taken in order to create the demand required to achieve the sales targets set by management.

2. Current Marketing Situation

A. Market Description

Virtual IT's market for the Virtual IT Control Center consists mainly of businesses that have already adopted a strategy of using virtualization technology for IT service provisioning. For businesses not yet into virtualization technologies, other entry-level products may be placed in the market. Essentially, there are two fundamental categories of services that businesses can support by virtualization:

■ Combined n-tier system and application stacks (server) for diverse user groups and needs
■ Virtual desktop and workstation provisioning (clients)

User needs can further be differentiated on the level of usage characteristics. Three main usage types can be differentiated:

- Data center operations
- Software development and testing environments
- Training and education

From past experience and analysis of existing customer information, we can conclude that differentiation into client- and server-side virtualization is rarely applied, as customers adopting the technology typically provide both as a service. For Virtual IT Control Center, we can therefore assume that a separation of the market segments on this level is not required. The segmentation approach will thus fully concentrate on the usage types identified.

I. Segment 1: Data Center

1. Description

Data center operations provide infrastructure services to various kinds of business solutions, and today, they generally have to consider the provisioning of n-tier OS and application stacks on the server side as well as offering workspaces or client access for users. Data center services are provided either by an enterprise's internal IT services department or through an external outsourcing partner.

2. Expected Percentage of Sales

The data center segment is the biggest market segment among the three segments in question. Virtualization technologies are already generally accepted and used, fostering sales for the Virtual IT Control Center. It is expected that the data center segment can generate 70% of the total revenue of $300 million for Virtual IT Control Center.

3. What Consumers Want

Customers are looking for solutions to support the administration, configuration, and management of growing, heterogeneous IT system landscapes that are characterized by rapid changes and dynamic demand. While the flexibility so far could be gained by introducing virtualization technologies, this exposes a new issue in that one single physical server hosts multiple virtual servers or desktops of different configurations, usage patterns, and software stacks. The tasks of managing and administrating both the physical and virtual machines have increased in complexity and effort. Data center administrators, therefore, want support in managing their physical and virtual resources in an effective and efficient way.

4. How Consumers Will Use the Product

Data centers will be able to decouple physical resources from virtual machines. By providing physical resource pools consisting of various types of hardware, OSs, and configurations, Virtual IT Control Center will manage virtual appliances' deployment onto such physical resource pools. Performance and capacity management will be controlled by setting out policies. Load balancing, deployment, and retirement of virtual servers and desktops will be managed from a central location. Virtual machines will be automatically moved around physical resources within the allocated physical resource pool as required. Based on defined policy, Virtual IT Control Center will automatically adjust and deploy the necessary number of virtual servers to ensure sufficient capacity on each tier layer, such as Web servers.

5. Support Requirements

Data center operations are driving applications at all levels of criticalities to business. A professional service at the highest level is required, since issues with the management software will usually affect a larger part of the operations. Downtime should by all means be avoided. Data center customers are expected to carefully assess supporting services. Service response times are critical, and support times need to cover 24/7.

6. How to Reach Them

The staff and responsible persons for data center operations can be reached by consulting partners, trade and technology shows, direct marketing, and publications in professional journals, either online or in print.

7. Price Sensitivity

Investigation shows that the value of our offering for the customer will by far outweigh the cost incurred. Furthermore, for small data centers, the cost for Virtual IT Control Center is a negligible fraction of the total cost of operation. Thus, the leverage of the investment for the client is very high and will strongly decrease price sensitivity.

II. Segment 2: Software Development and Testing

1. Description

Software development operations can either be integrated as units in the IT departments of enterprises or remain separate businesses producing bespoke or commercial off-the-shelf (COTS) software. Software development and testing require simulation environments, and hence, provisioning of IT services infrastructure of diverse complexity. In software development and testing, regardless of the size of operations, virtualization technologies have been widely adopted due to the flexibility offered by the technology in provisioning various OS and application platform architectures, basically at one's fingertips.

2. Expected Percentage of Sales

Software development and testing customers are increasingly adopting virtualization as a means of simulating their target platforms in their working environments. Increased pressure on both cost and time to market for software applications will increase opportunities in this segment. Management expects to be able to realize 20% of the total sales of $300 million in this segment for the first year.

3. What Consumers Want

Software developers and test engineers need platforms on which they can develop, debug, and test their software in environments mirroring the targeted system architectures and technologies. While software development often takes place on multiple generations of the software, for example, maintenance and new developments, several identical platforms need to be provided in parallel. In addition, software developed for sale will need to be tested for various OS and hardware environments, thereby increasing the number of platforms and testing environments needed. Developers and software testers effectively want complex working platforms in multiple instances on demand, without needing to consider system purchasing and low-level integration issues.

4. How Consumers Will Use the Product

Consumers will use Virtual IT Control Center to configure and define their technology landscape and machine types in whatever outline required for their tasks. They will also take snapshots of live servers and components of environments to transform them into virtual machine templates for introducing downstream systems into their library of system configurations. On demand, they will then trigger through the management console deploy system the landscapes used for developing, debugging, and testing their software. If an environment switch is necessary, users will be able to store a copy of the live systems in their current state, store this as system images, and redeploy it at a later time. Systems are deployed from a central image library. Deployment of even complex system environments can be done within less than an hour; previously, this took days to accomplish, if it was at all possible.

5. Support Requirements

Development and testing teams have somewhat more relaxed requirements regarding service levels with respect to response times, as they are not driving mission-critical operations. Service times during normal office hours should be sufficient. The client base operates globally; hence, support needs to be provided for all relevant time zones.

6. How to Reach Them

Both software development and testing staff are frequent users of online resources, and thus, they can be reached by appropriate presence and promotion on the Internet. Decision makers and professionals can also be reached through direct marketing, professional publications, and at trade or technology shows.

7. Price Sensitivity

Price sensitivity is not a real issue with software development operations because, with this segment, the overall benefit and leverage on investment far outweighs the cost. Productivity and quality gains achieved are major contributions to a customer's competitive advantage.

III. Segment 3: Training and Education Services

1. Description

The training and education operations can be organized as independent businesses, but they do also exist as service units internal to enterprises. Training and education providers do offer their services on various levels as on-site or off-site classrooms, and in groups of diverse sizes ranging from one-to-one courses up to large classes. Today, many training and education businesses either offer their services in the context of business applications or use software as a framework for their courseware. Product demonstration for sales or other purposes are considered part of the training and education segment, mainly because requirements are almost identical.

2. Expected Percentage of Sales

It is expected to be more difficult to place the product in the training and education domain, since cost considerations and adoption of new technologies are more carefully considered. Management therefore expects a share of only 10% of total sales of $300 million for the first year for this segment.

3. What Consumers Want

Consumers in the training and education segment are faced with the challenge that classroom, training facilities, or sales demonstration environments need to be configured for scheduled use. Because content and topic of training, education, or demonstration change frequently, reconfiguration and setup times are becoming critically important. For the various purposes and different subjects, a variety of different technical environments need to be provided. Today, consumers want support that allows them to easily deploy, administrate, and manage their training, education, or demonstration environments according to their schedules. Clients also want a significant reduction of setup times, because this always implies longer lead times, when training facilities cannot be used. While most training centers already use virtualization technologies on the level of providing servers or desktops, managing deployments and administrating virtual component configurations for various classrooms is complex and time consuming. A clear requirement has been identified to support IT services with functionality to reduce configuration efforts and deployment procedures.

4. How Consumers Will Use the Product

The consumer will be the IT services center in charge of providing the necessary infrastructure in terms of networking, hardware, system, and application software stacks required to operate a training facility. To gain maximum flexibility, components of such environments are already mostly virtualized today. Site administrators will use Virtual IT Control Center to store templates of their environment components and define their relationships to each other in the configuration database of the product. These components, jointly forming a complete training or education environment, can be flexibly sized according to differing sizes of classes. Provisioning environments is a matter of initializing the deployment of all virtual machines and their software stacks onto physical hardware. Virtual machines will be directly set up and booted from templates available in the configuration database of Virtual IT Control Center; thus, it can be made available with negligible setup times.

5. Support Requirements

Our customers operate facilities according to fixed course schedules. It is essential that issues be resolved or solutions provided with very short response times to allow the customer to maintain his or her schedule. The client base operates globally; hence, support needs to be provided during office hours for all relevant time zones.

6. How to Reach Them

Education and training service providers can be reached through direct marketing, their IT service departments, professional journals, and online marketing.

7. Price Sensitivity

With the training and education services segment, price sensitivity is more of an issue. While productivity gains are significant, it is assumed that operations are normally relatively small, and thus the investment required is more carefully considered by management.

B. Product Review

Virtual IT Control Center comprises the following key features and functionalities:

- A central management console for all administration, configuration, monitoring, and management functions required to drive a heterogeneous virtual and physical IT environment
- A policy-driven automation of performance and capacity management as well as load balancing
- Automated starting of hot and cold standby hardware to expand capacity when required
- Virtual environment definition method, allowing the definition of not only the single components but also their dependencies and structure to form complex system landscapes as one entity
- Seamless integration of all major virtualization technologies and vendors

C. Competitive Review, Including Discussion of Market Position, Strengths, Weaknesses, and Market Share

Competitors target the same markets and segments with offerings in the same domain as Virtual IT Control Center. They are discussed in the following subsections.

VMware

VMware is the market leader for virtualization tools on the level of stand-alone virtualized servers and client machines. They do offer capabilities for certain functional aspects of managing virtual data centers that are also relevant for cross-platform administration in their ESX product line. VMotion technology, for example, supports the seamless migration of live servers from one physical machine to another without service interruption. With Lab Manager, VMware offers a tool for software development and testing teams that allows managing and deploying development and testing systems based on templates and image libraries. VMware's Stage Manager allows support's system administrators to manage configurations along the staging process of software projects.

Both the management software suites from VMware, Stage Manager and Lab Manager, are priced at $2,120 per processor and have a three-year support contract.

Strength: VMware has a strong position in the market attributable to its leadership in offerings for virtualization technologies for single machines. Their brand is well known and accepted. They have a directly competing offering with Lab Manager, targeting software engineering solutions.

Weakness: Their offering for managing and administrating virtual system platforms does not support Sparc processors and SUN Zoning virtualization. There is no support for handling components of a complex system platform as a single entity and for driving dynamic load balancing and capacity management automatically based on predefined policies. Virtualization cores from other vendors do not seamlessly integrate into their management tool suite.

Market share: Market share information on the level of virtualization management tools is not publicly available, but VMware's share is estimated to be around 35% as of 2007.

Surgient

Surgient extends the VMware base platform with a value-adding management layer, supporting the same three usage types as Virtual IT Control Center. Pricing information is unfortunately not available for Surgient products.

Strengths: Surgient provides a strong offering for all three usage types suggested by Virtual IT. Surgient has a partnership with HP Mercury for the integration of the quality management software into their test laboratory virtualization tool.

Weaknesses: Surgient is not strongly positioned as a brand in the market. Their solution is not known in wide areas of the market, especially not in Europe and Asia. Surgient bases its platform on the foundation of VMware's virtualization tools and thus inherits the technology limitations of VMware. One such limitation is the lack of Sparx processor support and the support for other vendors' virtualization technologies, such as SUN Zoning virtualization.

Market share: Market share information on the level of virtualization management tools is not publicly available, but Surgient's share is estimated to be around 3% as of 2007.

Sun Microsystems

Sun is quickly ramping up to address the virtualization market. However, their offering is not yet clear and defined. While Sun entered the market consolidating Xen-based platforms apart from its zoning and Logical Domain server concepts for virtualization, their offering announced for the management of virtual data centers is not yet as mature and feature rich as customers would expect. Their virtualization management tool Sun xVM Ops Manager is also offered as an open source solution. Pricing information for the product is unfortunately not publicly available.

Strengths: Sun has a strong position in the server market and has the financial and operational resources at hand to make a strong entry into the virtualization market. Sun as a brand in the IT world is highly respected and trusted. The Sun open source approach and its power to drive new developments, however, require us to carefully watch their steps, as they can, and will, accelerate quickly.

Weakness: At this point in time, they do not have a convincing offering in the market providing support at the integration level of virtualization technology.

Market share: Market share information on the level of virtualization management tools is not publicly available, but Sun's share is estimated to be below 1% as of 2007.

Microsoft

Microsoft has also been lagging behind market developments for quite a while. In the meantime, however, they have developed an extensive range of single client and server virtualization tools as well as a set of system administration and management tools. Its virtualization management tool suite has only been available in the market since 2006. From the documentation available, it appears that the complete suite is strongly oriented toward a Microsoft proprietary integration. Further competitor intelligence, however, would be required to get a better picture of the offering, its capabilities, and pricing.

Strength: Microsoft is a dominating vendor in the marketplace for OSs and is building the foundation of many data centers and IT infrastructure services. Therefore, they have the best knowledge and expertise on integration of Microsoft OS system and application stacks. Furthermore, Microsoft has sufficient resources and power to accelerate its entry into the virtualization market.

Weakness: The offering is very new and does not yet have enough recognition in the market. It appears from the available documentation that advanced virtualization management features have not yet been developed at a level comparable with VMware or Surgient.

Market share: Market share information on the level of virtualization management tools is not publicly available, but Microsoft's share is estimated to be below 3% as of 2007.

D. Distribution Review

Virtual IT Control Center will be distributed through the standard Virtual IT distribution channels:

- The Virtual IT Sales and Support Centers in the 20 major markets worldwide
- The Virtual IT Online Internet Shop
- The Business Partnership Network consisting of premium partnerships with leading consultancy businesses all around the globe, currently consisting of 3,400 accredited consultancy enterprises

3. Strengths, Weaknesses, Opportunities, and Threats (SWOT) Analysis

The marketing department has conducted a SWOT analysis to get a comprehensive view of the business context of Virtual IT with respect to the virtualization market and the department's plans to launch Virtual IT Control Center.

A. Strengths

Virtual IT already holds a strong position in the market with representation in more than 25 important markets worldwide. Today, Virtual IT has a market share in virtualization technology management tools of 35%, and is headed for further growth. The competitive positioning of Virtual IT Control Center will allow it to soon take leadership in the virtualization management software domain. Furthermore, Virtual IT has a solid stake in the underlying existing business with virtualization solutions. Being the only provider of a solution that seamlessly integrates virtualization technologies from all major vendors puts the product well ahead of competition for now.

B. Weaknesses

One of the major weaknesses is the lack of protection of intellectual property. Investigations have revealed that there are no patents or other measures that can be taken to protect the advanced features of Virtual IT Control Center. Competitors may simply copy the features or come up with different implementations for the same solutions.

While Virtual IT is financially in a healthy state, capital reserves are not at high enough levels that would allow the company to enter a price war should, for example, Microsoft or Sun try to rapidly grow their market share based on a low-price or even free-offering strategy. There is evidence to suggest that the odds of this happening are quite high, since Sun is strongly engaged in open source initiatives and Microsoft has just entered the market with its aggressively priced Hyper-V server virtualization software.

C. Opportunities

The virtualization market in general and the integration and management tools area specifically enjoy strong growth. According to IDC (2007), the volume of the virtualization services market will grow by more than 100% until 2011 to a total value of $11.7 billion.

The strategy of integrating technology from all major vendors ensures independence from the success of a single technology, product line, or solution. Hence, Virutal IT is less exposed to demand for single vendors, and as other vendors successfully sell the base virtualization technology, demand for Virtual IT's managed solutions will increase.

By introducing a convincing solution for the virtualization management market, additional up-selling opportunities can arise for the existing product portfolio.

D. Threats

Both Microsoft and SUN are strong and powerful competitors that have entered the arena; both do have the capacity to ramp up quickly and aggressively turn to the market. As it is currently unclear what strategy and, hence, product roadmap these competitors will come up with, it is not possible to outline how to counter their approach and defend the company's position. Management will have to ensure that our competitive intelligence department closely observes the development of their strategy and gives early warning should they come up with an approach to aggressively target our markets or directly attack Virtual IT.

The overall attractiveness of the market will most likely spur more suppliers to enter the arena. We need to carefully observe any movements in the competitive environment.

4. Objectives and Issues

A. First-Year Objectives

The management of Virtual IT is very positive about the future development of the virtualization services market, especially the launching of Virtual IT Control Center. The primary marketing objective is to increase Virtual IT's market share in the global data center virtualization management tool market by 8% to 43% in the first year by licensing Virtual IT Control Center to 30,000 customers worldwide with an overall annual licensing revenue target of $300 million. Breakeven is expected to be reached by the end of the first year.

Management has set out specific targets for the three segments chosen, as follows:

Data center: The data center segment is expected to contribute 70%, or a turnover of $210 million during the first year.

Software development and testing: This segment has a target for the first year of 20% of revenues, accounting for $60 million.

Training and education services: A contribution of 10% of sales, or $30 million, is the objective for year one for the training and education segment.

In addition, management expects that an increase of professional services revenue can be achieved in the context of introducing new solutions with Virtual IT Control Center, which will total $23 million, corresponding to a 10% increase in existing sales.

B. Second-Year Objectives

Year two after the launch of Virtual IT Control Center should see another overall improvement of sales results because the awareness of the product in the market will have greatly increased due to strong promotion and presence in the market. In addition, further global growth of the virtualization services market is expected, according to our market research.

Management of Virtual IT has therefore set the primary marketing objective for the second year as licensing Virtual IT Control Center to 74,000 customers worldwide, with an overall annual licensing revenue target of $740 million.

Management has set out specific targets for the three segments chosen, as follows:

Data center: Because an increase in revenue is expected for the other two segments, the percentage target for the data center segment is seen to contribute 60%, or a turnover of $444 million for the second year.

Software development and testing: An improvement of sales revenue for this segment is expected due to an increased trust in virtualization technologies and a greater awareness of the benefits of Virtual IT Control Center. Revenue target is set at 25% of total revenue, or $185 million.

Training and education services: By year two, the smaller segment of training and education services should also be able to further build on the good reputation of Virtual IT Control Center and raise its sales results to contribute 15%, or $111 million.

In addition, management also expects for year two a significant increase in professional services supporting our customers in tailoring their virtualization solutions with Virtual IT Control Center. Thus, a sales target of $47 million is set out for year two.

C. Issues

We need to carefully monitor our competitors because there is a clear issue with their either copying our approach or aggressively attacking us on the basis of price potentially combined with functionality. Our competitive intelligence department is already aware of its tasks and is currently developing a strategy on how to deal with this challenge. It is essential that the department not only monitor our known competitors but also watch for new players entering the scene.

5. Product Strategy

A. Positioning

Using a differentiation strategy, the product shall be positioned as the only virtualization management tool seamlessly integrating all virtualization technologies from top-tier vendors. Virtual IT Control Center supports customers in all their management and administration tasks in their virtual IT environments, regardless of the underlying technology mix.

The positioning will be further refined by a tuned approach for all major virtualization appliances, which consist of data centers, software development, and training. Virtual IT Control Center allows customers to focus on their real businesses, providing the necessary environment and resources at their fingertips.

Virtual IT Control Center is a product designed for use in professional environments.

B. Product Strategy

Architecture

The core product will initially be the same for all three different offerings. Its architecture is service oriented, which allows one to orchestrate the services from the client. The alignment of the products for the different applications is implemented in the client and its graphical user interface (GUI), which is adjusted to serve the different needs, types, and sequences of tasks that need to be performed for the respective business applications. This strategy has the additional advantage that during the introduction phase of the product, adjustments and version upgrades to tune the product for different uses can be more easily rolled out.

The base product platform will allow a further differentiation for the three products with ease, should this become necessary at any point in the future.

Appearance and Branding

The brand will be shaped under the company's existing branding concept and guidelines, which foresee a combination of the company name and a product descriptor. For Virtual IT Control Center, a distinct descriptor for the three main product versions will be applied, which will be DC for the data center, ST for software and testing, and TE for the training and education edition.

Each product version will feature its own brand color, which will be applied to all visual representations of the product name and packaging. Green will be used for data centers, red for development and testing, and blue for training and education.

Delivery Components and Packaging

The product will be delivered in a box including DVDs containing the software, an installation guide, a user manual, a quick reference guide, and the license terms and conditions.

The package will be the same globally; however, the included manuals and guides will be shipped in translated versions according to the main regional languages.

License and Policy

Products are sold under a one-year license that needs to be renewed annually. Along with the product's license, the upgrades and patches for minor versions are included during the license period.

C. Pricing Strategy

Product Licenses

Products will be priced using a value-based pricing model that shall further account for the scale of usage. Hence, the pricing model shall be built around a base setting and scaled with the number of physical processors, which is controlled by Virtual IT Control Center.

The base package will include a license for use with 50 physical processors, and any additional processors will be further licensed in steps of 20 physical processors. With multicore processor technology, each core counts as a single processor.

The base package as well as the supplemental licenses for additional processors shall be priced equally for all three product versions. Furthermore, there is no differentiated pricing for geographic regions.

The base package price is set at $10,000/year. The supplemental licenses for 20 additional processors is set at $3,000/year. For large accounts with IT operations bigger than 1,000 processors, special discounts are available, but they need to be authorized by senior management. This special discount policy will not be published.

To support the market introduction phase, a discount will be offered to customers already using other products from Virtual IT, accounting for an annual licensing revenue of more than $20,000. A discount of 20% shall be offered on the license fee for the first two years.

Professional Services

Professional services will be charged per day and cost $2500. There will be no special rate agreements below 90 person dates. For larger mandates, discounts are available, but they need to be authorized by senior management.

Commission for Our Business Partnership Network

Sales and revenues directly attributable to placement by one of our consultancy partners fall under our business partnership agreement and are thus eligible for 15% commission.

6. Marketing Strategy

The marketing strategy is based on the concept of product differentiation. Virtual IT exclusively targets business customers from a size of 25 employees, with no upper limit. The primary market, however, is defined in the segment of mid- and large-sized enterprises. Because the product builds on existing operations leveraging virtualization technologies, the main focus needs to be on customers already using virtualization technologies. A tight integration with our departments selling base virtualization technologies needs to be established to exchange business intelligence and market information.

In terms of business applications segments, the primary segment is defined as data centers, the secondary target is the software development and testing segments, and the third segment is training and education.

To promote sales by giving examples of business solutions and customer references, existing customers using our base virtualization technologies should be focused on with higher priority. Customers have to be actively encouraged to participate in our reference program, and they must allow us to use their solution scenario for further promotion.

We expect that the sales cycles will be longer for large accounts because product integration and adoption will be more complex. Our marketing team is therefore prepared to further its efforts in supporting the presales phases in the initial period.

To prepare the professional community in the market, preannouncements of the product launch will already be made at early stages, with, however, only limited information on the product design and features.

To quickly make Virtual IT Control Center a known brand, an official launch event is planned in at the CeBIT in Hannover, a worldwide, renowned trade fair for the professional IT business.

A. Marketing Communications

Marketing communications will be aligned to facilitate product launch by focusing on creation of awareness for the new product and supporting the process of turning awareness into interest. The product launch will be staged on a worldwide basis from the very beginning; hence, marketing communications has to address the market globally.

Communication will take place through different channels; thus, an integrated communication strategy needs to be ensured by the marketing department. The objective is to create a unified brand experience and deliver a consistent message throughout all channels used.

To measure and monitor the effectiveness of our marketing communications, we will partner with a marketing service provider to gather relevant intelligence. The marketing team will, in cooperation with the service provider, establish quantifiable objectives and thresholds to track the campaign and take corrective actions where necessary. Key factors to be monitored include awareness, response, perception of brand image, and interest created for the product.

B. Advertising

We are aiming to reach 80% of our market segments within the first six months of product launch. The frequency will be adjusted dynamically to the coverage achieved, and it will be more intensive during the initial period until awareness levels reach targeted levels.

Advertising should focus on media reaching the business community and, specifically, decision makers on the management level. The objective of the advertising campaign is to generate the required awareness for the new product and create leads for our sales department to follow up on.

Advertising in the print media should focus on professional and management magazines as well as newspapers for the business audience. Online ads will be placed with IT communities and online magazines, targeting IT professionals.

As a preparatory step, product launch communication can be integrated in product ads for our existing product lines. Dedicated product campaigns will be started on the official launch date and event.

C. Promotions

The key factor in the promotion and launch of Virtual IT Control Center is the corresponding section on our Web site describing the business and technical aspects of the products. A special announcement during the first three months should be placed on the front page, inviting people to visit the product-specific information pages. In addition, the products will be presented at various international business and IT trade shows.

A press kit will be prepared for the product launch, including product details and technical information. The press kits should be delivered to the following:

■ Professional magazines
■ Business TV channels and editorial departments of normal TV stations featuring technical formats suitable for our products
■ Leading international newspapers having technical sections
■ Press and news agencies

In addition, product documentation for business partners, clients, and prospects should be prepared and delivered to the following:

■ All our consultancy business partners for their own reference and also for further distribution; hence, our marketing team will add a form to allow reordering of additional copies.

- Existing key accounts.
- Customers visiting our booth at trade shows.

As mentioned in the marketing strategy, we will build reference solution scenarios with some of our key customers for further promotion on our Web site and as handouts for prospects. The scenarios should be well documented and should define the business case and customer value delivered.

An important cornerstone in the promotion of the product launch is the event planned during CeBIT in Hannover. CeBIT is the world's largest professional IT trade show, and it builds an excellent platform to spread information to a global audience. Apart from a multimedia presentation of the product and its capabilities and applications, which is open to the public, the event will feature a gala dinner for our key customers, consultancy business partners, and selected media contacts.

For prospects and customers who register for the service, a regular e-mail newsletter will be made available, informing about product updates and real-life use cases. For the subscribers of the existing newsletters of our base virtualization technology, a special should be featured to announce the release of the new product.

7. Distribution Strategy

The distribution strategy is based on two main marketing channels. The primary channel is built as a direct sales channel supported by our local subsidiaries in the major markets or directly through the headquarters in Switzerland. The primary marketing channel is in full control of Virtual IT and is complemented by our shop on the company's Web site.

The second distribution channel is built by treating our business consultancy partners as intermediaries. The business consultancy partners receive a commission for every sale mediated.

8. Action Programs

The following sections give a detailed overview of the activities planned for the initial six months around the product launch.

A. Month 1

- Communication and preparation of the official launch event at CeBIT in Hannover. News should be spread with incremental levels of details as the launch date approaches.

- Our Web site will feature the launch event at CeBIT and give an initial overview of the product's capabilities.
- The advertisement campaign starts with the launch announcements included in the ads published for our base virtualization technologies.
- Relevant media contacts with a higher lead time should have already received the full press kit.

B. Month 2

- Presentation and official launch event at the CeBIT in Hannover. Furthermore, selected persons from business and media shall be invited to a gala dinner held after the official launch event.
- Introduction of the product and launch information on our Web site.
- The dedicated advertisement campaign starts for the Virtual IT Control Center.
- All press kits are delivered.
- Advertisements are published in all major media.

C. Month 3

- Advertisements are iterated.
- Ad campaign on TV channels is started.
- Additional trade shows in all major countries are used as presentation platforms.
- Leads and prospects from the CeBIT presence and promotion are followed up.
- Interviews with major business media are organized.

D. Month 4

- Advertising campaign is now shifting the design and message from pure brand and new product awareness to an emphasis on business value and creating interest for the solution.
- First-solution scenarios can be presented, enhancing the documentation set.
- The first big deals with global players should now be in the stage of agreement of purchase, which can be promoted through news agents and professional media.
- Additional trade shows in all major countries are used as presentation platforms.

E. Month 5

- A first iteration of the adjusted ad campaign is now launched.
- Updated sales documentation with reference customers and solution cases should now be made available to the business consultancy partner network as well as key accounts.
- Additional trade shows in all major countries are used as presentation platforms.

F. Month 6

- The advertisement campaign is reduced to ads in print and online media.
- Promotion and public relations (PR) activities should now focus on solutions for customers in the segments of software development and testing as well as training and education, profiting from the reputation already built for the brand and the product in the primary segment.
- Additional contracts with large customers shall be promoted.

Sources

IDC. (2007). Virtualization Services Market to Reach $11.7 Billion by 2011 [Internet]. Available at http://www.idc.com/getdoc.jsp?containerId=prUS20778407 (Accessed December 11, 2008).

Appendix C: Business Plan for an Established Business

This business plan consists of a narrative and several financial spreadsheets. The narrative template is the body of the business plan. It contains more than 150 questions divided into several sections. Work through the sections in any order you like, except for the section titled "Executive Summary," which should be done last. Skip any questions that do not apply to your business. When you have finished writing your first draft, you will have a collection of small essays on the various topics of the business plan. Then you will want to edit them into a flowing narrative.

The real value of creating a business plan does not lie in having the finished product in hand; rather, the value lies in the process of research and thinking about your business in a systematic way. The act of planning helps you to think things through thoroughly, study and research when you are not sure of the facts, and look at your ideas critically. It takes time but avoids costly, perhaps disastrous, mistakes later.

The business plan narrative is a generic model suitable for all types of businesses. However, you should modify it to suit your particular circumstances. Before you begin, review the section titled "Refining the Plan," found at the end of the business plan. It suggests emphasizing certain areas, depending on your type of business (manufacturing, retail, service, etc.). It also has tips for fine-tuning your plan to make an effective presentation to investors or bankers. If this is why you are writing your plan, pay particular attention to your writing style. You will be judged by the quality and appearance of your work as well as your ideas.

It typically takes several weeks to complete a good plan. Most of that time is spent in research and rethinking your ideas and assumptions. But then, that is the value of the process. So, make time to do the job properly. Those who do never regret the effort. Finally, be sure to keep detailed notes on your sources of information and on the assumptions underlying your financial data.

Business Plan
Owners

Business name: Your business name
Address: Address line 1
Address line 2
City, ST ZIP Code
Telephone: (555) 555-0100
Fax: (555) 555-0101
E-mail: someone@example.com

Contents

Executive Summary

Write this section last.

We suggest that you make it two pages or less.

Include everything that you would cover in a five-minute interview.

Explain the fundamentals of the business: What is your product, who are your customers, who are the owners, and what do you think the future holds for your business and your industry?

Make it enthusiastic, professional, complete, and concise.

If you are applying for a loan, state clearly how much you want, precisely how you are going to use it, and how the money will make your business more profitable, thereby ensuring repayment.

General Company Description

Mission statement: Many companies have a brief mission statement, usually 30 words or fewer, explaining their reason for being and their guiding principles. If you have a mission statement, this is a good place to put it in the plan, followed by company goals and objectives, and business philosophy.

What business are you in? What do you do?

What is your target market? (Explain briefly here, because you will give a more thorough explanation in the section titled "Marketing Plan.")

Describe your industry. Is it a growth industry? What changes do you foresee in your industry, and how is your company poised to take advantage of them?

Now, give a detailed description of the business.

Form of ownership: Sole proprietor, partnership, corporation, or limited liability corporation (LLC)?

Company history: Years in business, previous owners, successes, failures, lessons learned, reputation in community, sales and profit history, number of employees, and events that affected success. Discuss significant past problems and how you solved and survived them.

Most important strengths and core competencies: What factors will make the company succeed? What are your major competitive strengths? What strengths do you personally bring to the business?

Significant challenges the company faces now and will face in the near future: If you are asking for funding, go on to explain how the new capital will help you meet these challenges.

Long term: What are your plans for the future of the business? Growth? If so, at what rate and how will you achieve it?

Are you developing strategies for continued growth, increased production, diversification, or eventual sale of the business? What are your time frames for these?

Products and Services

Describe your products and services in depth (technical specifications, drawings, photos, sales brochures, and other bulky items belong in the section titled "Appendices").

What factors give you competitive advantages or disadvantages (e.g., the level of quality, or unique or proprietary features)?

What is the pricing, fee, or leasing structure of your products and services?

Marketing Plan

Notes on Preparation

Market Research: Why?

You spend so much time on marketing-related matters—customers, competitors, pricing, promotion, and advertising—that it is natural to assume that you have little to learn. However, every small business can benefit from doing market research to make sure it is on track. Use the business-planning process as your opportunity to uncover data and to question your marketing efforts. It will be time well spent.

Market Research: How?

There are two kinds of market research: primary and secondary. Both will be discussed here.

Secondary research means using published information such as industry profiles, trade journals, newspapers, magazines, census data, and demographic profiles. This type of information is available from public libraries, industry associations, chambers of commerce, vendors who sell to your industry, and government agencies.

Start with your local library. Most librarians are pleased to guide you through their business data collection. You will be amazed at what is there. There are more online sources than you could possibly use. Your chamber of commerce has good information on the local area. Trade associations and trade publications often have excellent industry-specific data.

Primary market research means gathering your own data. For example, you could do your own traffic count at a proposed location, use the yellow pages to identify competitors, and do surveys or focus group interviews to learn about consumer preferences. Professional market research can be very costly, but there are many books that show small business owners how to research effectively.

In your marketing plan, be as specific as possible: give statistics, numbers, and sources. The marketing plan will be the basis, later on, of the all-important sales projection.

Economics

- Facts about your industry
- Total size of your market
- Percentage share of the market you have (important only if you are a major player in the market)
- Current demand in target market
- Growth history
- Trends in target market—growth trends, trends in consumer preferences, and trends in product development
- Growth potential and opportunity for a business of your size

■ What barriers to entry keep potential new competitors from flooding into your market?
  – High capital costs
  – High production costs
  – High marketing costs
  – Consumer acceptance/brand recognition
  – Training/skills
  – Unique technology/patents
  – Unions
  – Shipping costs
  – Tariff barriers/quotas
■ How can the following affect your company?
  – Change in technology
  – Government regulations
  – Changing economy
■ Change in your industry

Products

In the section titled "Products and Services," you described your products and services as you see them. Now, describe them from your customers' point of view.

Features and Benefits

List all your major products or services.

For each product or service, describe the most important features. That is, what does the product do? What is special about it?

Now, for each product or service, describe its benefits. That is, what does the product do for the customer?

Note the differences between features and benefits, and think about them. For example, a house gives shelter and lasts a long time; those are its features. Its benefits include pride of ownership, financial security, providing for the family, and inclusion in a neighborhood. You build features into your product so you can sell the benefits.

What after-sales services are supplied? Delivery, warranty, service contracts, support, follow-up, and refund policy are examples.

Customers

Identify your customers, their characteristics, and their geographic locations, that is, demographics.

The description will be completely different depending on whether you sell to other businesses or directly to consumers. If you sell a consumer product but sell it through a channel of distributors, wholesalers, and retailers, you must carefully analyze both the end user and the intermediary businesses to which you sell.

You may have more than one customer group. Identify the most important groups. Then, for each consumer group, construct a demographic profile:

- Age
- Gender
- Location
- Income level
- Social class and occupation
- Education
- Other

For business customers, the demographic factors might be the following:

- Industry (or portion of an industry)
- Location
- Size of firm
- Quality, technology, and price preferences
- Other

Competition

What products and companies compete with you? List your major competitors, including their names and addresses.

Do they compete with you across the board, or just for certain products, certain customers, or in certain locations?

Use Table C.1 to compare your company with your three most important competitors.

The first column lists the key competitive factors. Because these vary with each market, you may want to customize the list of factors.

In the cell labeled "Me," state honestly how you think you stack up in customers' minds. Then decide whether you think this factor is a strength or a weakness for you. If you find it hard to analyze yourself this way, enlist some disinterested party to assess you. This can be a real eye-opener.

Now, analyze each major competitor. In a few words, state how you think they stack up.

In the last column, estimate how important each competitive factor is to the customer: 1 = critical; 5 = not very important.

After you finish filling up the competitive matrix, write a short paragraph stating your competitive advantages and disadvantages.

Table C.1 Competitive Analysis

Factor	Me	Strength	Weakness	Competitor A	Competitor B	Competitor C	Importance to Customer
Products							
Price							
Quality							
Selection							
Service							
Reliability							
Stability							
Expertise							
Company reputation							
Location							
Appearance							
Sales method							
Credit policies							
Advertising							
Image							

Niche

Now that you have systematically analyzed your industry, product, customers, and the competition, you should have a clear picture of where your company fits in the market.

In one short paragraph, define your niche—your unique corner of the market.

Marketing Strategy

Outline a marketing strategy that is consistent with your niche.

Promotion

How do you get the word out to customers?

Regarding advertising, what media do you use, why, and how often? Has your advertising been effective? How can you tell?

Do you use other methods, such as trade shows, catalogs, dealer incentives, word of mouth, and networks of friends or professionals?

If you have identifiable repeat customers, do you have a systematic contact plan?

Why this mix, and not some other?

Promotional Budget

How much will you spend on the items listed in the previous section?

Should you consider spending less on some promotional activities and more on others?

Pricing

What is your pricing strategy? For most small businesses, having the lowest prices is not a good strategy. Usually, you will do better to have average prices and compete on quality and service. Does your pricing strategy fit with what was revealed in your competitive analysis?

Compare your prices with those of your competitors. Are they higher, lower, or the same? Why?

How important is price as a competitive factor?

What are your payment and customer credit policies?

Location

You will describe your physical location in the section titled "Operational Plan" of your business plan. Here, in the section titled "Marketing Plan," analyze your location as it affects your customers.

If customers come to your place of business:

- Is it convenient? Parking? Interior spaces? Not out of the way?
- Is it consistent with your image?
- Is it what customers want and expect?

Where is the competition located? Is it better for you to be near them (e.g., car dealers or fast-food restaurants) or distant from them (e.g., convenience food stores)?

Distribution Channels

How do you sell your products or services?

- Retail
- Direct (via mail order, World Wide Web, or catalog)
- Wholesale
- Your own sales force
- Agents
- Independent reps

Has your marketing strategy proved effective?
Do you need to make any changes or additions to current strategies?

Sales Forecast

Now that you have described your products, services, customers, markets, and marketing plans in detail, it is time to attach some numbers to your plan. Use a forecast spreadsheet to prepare a month-by-month projection. Base the forecast on your historical sales, the marketing strategies that you have just described, your market research, and industry data, if available.

You may want to do two forecasts: (1) a "best guess," which is what you really expect, and (2) a "worst case" low estimate that you are confident you can reach no matter what happens.

Remember to keep notes on your research and your assumptions as you build this sales forecast and all subsequent spreadsheets in the plan. Relate the forecast to your sales history, explaining the major differences between past and projected sales. This is critical if you are going to present it to funding sources.

Operational Plan

Explain the daily operation of the business, its location, equipment, people, processes, and surrounding environment.

Production

How and where do you produce your products or services?
Explain your methods for the following:

- Production techniques and costs
- Quality control
- Customer service
- Inventory control
- Product development

Location

Describe the locations of production, sales, storage areas, and buildings.
Do you lease or own your premises?
Describe access to your buildings (walk-in, parking, freeway, airport, railroad, and shipping).
What are your business hours?
If you are trying to get an expansion loan, include a drawing or layout of your proposed facility.

Legal Environment

Describe the following:

- Licensing and bonding requirements
- Permits
- Health, workplace, or environmental regulations
- Special regulations covering your industry or profession
- Zoning or building code requirements
- Insurance coverage
- Trademarks, copyrights, or patents (pending, existing, or purchased)

Personnel

- Number of employees.
- Type of labor (skilled, unskilled, or professional).
- Where do you find new employees?
- Quality of existing staff.
- Pay structure.
- Training methods and requirements.
- New hiring in the coming year?
- Who does which tasks?

■ Are schedules and procedures in place?
■ Do you have written job descriptions for employees? If not, take time to write some. Written job descriptions really help internal communications with employees.
■ Do you use contract workers as well as employees?

Inventory

■ What kind of inventory do you keep: raw materials, supplies, or finished goods?
■ Average value in stock; that is, what is your inventory investment?
■ Rate of turnover; how does it compare with industry averages?
■ Seasonal buildups?
■ Lead time for ordering?

Suppliers

Note the following information about your suppliers:

■ Their names and addresses
■ Type and amount of inventory furnished
■ Credit and delivery policies
■ History and reliability

Do you expect shortages or short-term delivery problems?

Are supply costs steady or fluctuating? If fluctuating, how do you deal with changing costs?

Should you be searching out new sources of supply, or are you satisfied with present suppliers?

Credit Policies

Do you sell on credit? If so, do you really need to? Is it customary in your industry and expected by your clientele?

Do you carefully monitor your payables (what you owe to vendors) to take advantage of discounts and to keep your credit rating good?

You need to carefully manage both the credit you extend and the credit you receive.

Managing Your Accounts Receivable

If you do extend credit, what are your policies about who gets credit and how much? How do you check the creditworthiness of new applicants?

Table C.2 Accounts Receivable Aging

	Total	Current	30 Days	60 Days	90 Days	Over 90 Days
Accounts receivable aging						

What terms will you offer your customers; that is, how much credit and when will payment fall due?

Do you offer prompt payment discounts? (It is best to do this only if it is usual and customary in your industry.)

Do you know what it costs you to extend credit? This includes both the cost of capital tied up in receivables and the cost of bad debts.

Have you built the costs into your prices?

You should do a receivables aging at least once a month to track how much of your money is tied up in credit given to customers and to alert you to slow-payment problems. A receivables aging looks like Table C.2.

Collecting from delinquent customers is no fun. You need a set policy, and you need to follow it.

- When do you make a phone call?
- When do you send a letter?
- When do you get your attorney to threaten the delinquent customer?

Managing Your Accounts Payable

You should also age your accounts payable (what you owe to your suppliers). Use the format given in Table C.3.

This helps you plan whom to pay and when. Paying too early depletes your cash, but paying late can cost you valuable discounts and damage your credit. (Hint: If you know you will be late making a payment, call the creditor before the due date. It tends to reassure them.)

Are prompt payment discounts offered by your proposed vendors? Do you always take them?

Table C.3 Accounts Payable Aging

	Total	Current	30 Days	60 Days	90 Days	Over 90 Days
Accounts payable aging						

Management and Organization

Who manages the business on a day-to-day basis?

What experience does that person bring to the business; what special or distinctive competencies?

Is there a plan for continuation of the business if this person is lost or incapacitated?

If you have more than 10 employees, prepare an organizational chart showing the management hierarchy and the persons responsible for key functions. Include position descriptions for key employees.

Professional and Advisory Support

List the following:

- Board of directors and management advisory board
- Attorney
- Accountant
- Insurance agent
- Banker
- Consultants
- Mentors and key advisors

Personal Financial Statement

Owners often have to draw on personal assets to finance a business. This statement will show you what is available. Bankers and investors usually want this information as well. They will ask owners to cosign or personally guarantee any business loans.

Document your assumptions, notes, definitions, and any special financial situation. Include details of notes, securities, contracts, etc., on the bottom of a personal financial spreadsheet. Include one such spreadsheet for each principal.

Financial History and Analysis

A solid analysis of the past must precede any serious attempt to forecast the future. A financial history and ratios spreadsheet will allow you to put a great deal of financial information from other statements on a single page for ease of comprehension and analysis. You may also enter industry average ratios for comparison.

In the section titled "Appendices," put year-end balance sheets, operating statements, and business income tax returns for the past three years, plus your most current balance sheet and operating statement.

Debt Schedule

Table C.4 gives in-depth information that the financial statements themselves do not usually provide. Include a debt schedule in the format given in the table for each note payable on your most recent balance sheet.

Financial Plan

The financial plan consists of a 12-month profit and loss projection, a 4-year profit and loss projection (optional), a cash-flow projection, a projected balance sheet, and a breakeven calculation.

Together, these spreadsheets constitute a reasonable estimate of your company's financial future. More important, however, the process of thinking through the financial plan will improve your insight into the inner financial workings of your company.

12-Month Profit and Loss Projection

Explain the major assumptions used to estimate company income and expenses. Your sales projection should come from an annual sales forecast. Pay special attention to areas in which historical performance varies markedly from your projections.

4-Year Profit Projection (Optional)

The 12-month projection is the heart of your financial plan. However, this worksheet is for those who want to carry their forecasts beyond the first year. It is expected of those seeking venture capital. Bankers pay more attention to the 12-month projection.

Of course, keep notes of your key assumptions, especially about things you expect to change dramatically over the years.

Projected Cash Flow

The cash-flow projection is just a forward look at your checking account.

For each item, determine when you actually expect to receive cash (for sales) or when you will actually have to write a check (for expense items).

Your cash flow will show you whether your working capital is adequate. Clearly, if your cash on hand goes negative, you will need more. It will also show when and how much you need to borrow.

Explain your major assumptions, especially those that make the cash flow differ from a profit and loss statement, such as the following:

- If you make a sale in month one, when do you actually collect the cash?
- When you buy inventory or materials, do you pay in advance, upon delivery, or much later?

Table C.4 Debt Schedule

To Whom Payable	Original Amount	Original Date	Present Balance	Rate of Interest	Maturity Date	Monthly Payment	Security	Current/ Past Due

- How will this affect cash flow?
- Are some expenses payable in advance?
- Are there irregular expenses, equipment purchase, or inventory buildup that should be budgeted?

And, of course, depreciation does not appear at all, because you never write a check for it.

Projected Balance Sheet

This is an estimate of what the balance sheet will look like at the end of the 12-month period covered in your projections.

In the business plan section related to your projected balance sheet, state the assumptions that you used for all major changes between your last historical balance sheet and the projection.

Breakeven Analysis

A breakeven analysis determines the sales volume, at a given price, that is required to recover total costs.

Expressed as a formula, breakeven is measured as follows:

$$\text{Breakeven sales} = \frac{\text{Fixed costs}}{1 - \text{Variable costs}}$$

where fixed costs are expressed in dollars, but variable costs are expressed as a percentage of total sales.

Appendices

Include details and studies used in your business plan, for example,

- Brochures and advertising materials
- Industry studies
- Blueprints and plans
- Maps and photographs of locations
- Magazines or other articles
- Detailed lists of equipment owned or to be purchased
- Copies of leases and contracts
- Letters of support from future customers
- Any other material needed to support the assumptions in this plan
- Market research studies

Refining the Plan

The generic business plan presented here should be modified to suit your specific type of business and the audience for which the plan is written.

For Raising Capital

For Bankers

Bankers want assurance of orderly repayment. If you intend to use this plan to present to lenders, include the following details:

- Amount of loan.
- How you will use the funds.
- What this will accomplish (how it will make the business stronger).
- Requested repayment terms (number of years to repay). You will probably not have much negotiating room on interest rate, but you may be able to negotiate a longer repayment term, which will help cash flow.
- Collateral offered, and a list of all existing liens against the collateral.

For Investors

Investors have a different perspective from bankers. They look for dramatic growth and expect to share in the rewards. Include the following in the plan that you present to potential investors:

- Short-term funds needed
- Funds needed in two to five years
- How the company will use the funds, and what this will accomplish for growth
- Estimated return on investment
- Exit strategy for investors (buyback, sale, or IPO)
- Percentage of ownership that you will give up to investors
- Milestones or conditions that you will accept
- Financial reporting that you will provide
- Involvement of investors on the board or in management

For the Type of Business

Manufacturing

- Present production levels
- Present levels of direct production costs and indirect (overhead) costs
- Gross profit margin, overall and for each product line

- Possible production efficiency increases
- Production-capacity limits of existing physical plant
- Production capacity of expanded plant (if expansion is planned)
- Production-capacity limits of existing equipment
- Production capacity of new equipment (if new equipment is planned)
- Prices per product line
- Purchasing and inventory management procedures
- Anticipated modifications or improvements to existing products
- New products under development or anticipated

Service Businesses

Service businesses sell intangible products. They are usually more flexible than other types of businesses, but they also have higher labor costs and generally very little in fixed assets.

- Prices
- Methods used to set prices
- System of production management
- Quality control procedures
- Standard or accepted industry quality standards
- How do you measure labor productivity?
- What percentage of total available hours do you bill to customers?
- Breakeven billable hours
- Percentage of work subcontracted to other firms
- Profit on subcontracting?
- Credit, payment, and collections policies and procedures
- Strategy for keeping client base
- Strategy for attracting new clients

High-Tech Companies

- Economic outlook for the industry
- Does your company have information systems in place to manage rapidly changing prices, costs, and markets?
- Is your company on the cutting edge with its products and services?
- What is the status of research and development (R&D)? And what is required to bring the product or service to market and to keep the company competitive?
- How does the company accomplish the following?
  - Protect intellectual property
  - Avoid technological obsolescence
  - Supply necessary capital
- Retain key personnel

If your company is not yet profitable or perhaps does not even have sales yet, you must do longer-term financial forecasts to show when profit takeoff will occur. And your assumptions must be well documented and well argued.

Retail Business

- Company image.
- Pricing: Explain markup policies. Prices should be profitable, competitive, and should match the company image.
- Inventory:
  - Selection and price should be consistent with company image.
  - Calculate your annual inventory turnover rate. Compare this to the industry average for your type of business.
- Customer service policies: These should be competitive and should match the company image.
- Location: Does it give the exposure you need? Is it convenient for customers? Is it consistent with the company image?
- Promotion: What methods do you use and how much do they cost? Do they project a consistent company image?
- Credit: Do you extend credit to customers? If yes, do you really need to, and do you factor the cost into prices?

Note

An electronic copy of this plan can be found at www.score.org.

Appendix D: Strategic Plan—Sample

Various formats can be used for a strategic plan template. Ideally, you will be able to take advantage of strategic planning work that is already occurring in your organization—using the same template and the same terminology so as to be consistent with the vision and plans prepared in other departments and by the executive team. Remember that strategic planning begins at the highest, macro level and works down toward more specific detail.

If you are not working with an internal template, the plan can be structured in four parts:

- Description of the business or a situational analysis
- Mission statement
- Goals, objectives, and strategies
- Timelines and performance indicators

The strategic plan does not need to be a lengthy document; it can contain as few as three to four pages. (The operating plan is usually built from goals and objectives of the strategic plan; it lists specific activities, resources to be allocated, and timelines for advancing achievement of the strategic plan.)

I. Description of the Business

This section should be a clearly articulated analysis of the business of the information center as it currently exists. It should include the following:

- The information center's key activities that support the business of the larger organization, such as acquiring and managing external information, fulfilling research requests, and providing current awareness services

239

- Customers of the information center and their level of satisfaction with the products and services they are receiving today
- Weaknesses and threats to the existing business of the information center, based on an understanding and analysis of information flow

II. Mission Statement

A mission statement provides the opportunity to create a compelling vision of the value of the information center. A sample reads:

> The information center will collaborate with other departments, using their expertise in evaluating, selecting, distributing, categorizing, and indexing information to promote the corporate objectives of increased knowledge sharing among departments, reduction of development redundancies through more ready access to information, and improved access to information on key customers and competitors.

III. Goals, Objectives, and Strategies

This section of the plan should include short-range plans that can be integrated into a concrete, unified plan of action. You need to establish timelines, determining specific dates for completion of action items and allocating available resources to carry out those actions. The names of individuals or teams who will be responsible for completing these items should be included.

This section is where you have the opportunity to position the information center for the future—highlighting new directions and specifying what will be abandoned and replaced by new initiatives.

If two of the corporate strategic initiatives were to leverage existing technology to enhance knowledge management capabilities and to improve customer responsiveness and retain more top customers, this section might be as follows:

Goal 1	Enhance tools for sharing organizational experience and knowledge to reduce cycle time and to make more informed business decisions.
Objective 1	Define which internal information has highest value, and assess how information is used to prioritize core content for the knowledge-sharing system.
Strategy 1	Conduct needs assessment with statistically relevant number of users in each department who will be accessing the system by end of fiscal Q2.

Objective 2	Determine internal document selection criteria for KM system based on results of analysis in collaboration with Marketing, Communications, R&D, and Engineering departments.
Strategy 1	Analyze sample documents from departments contributing content, and work with IS to propose database structure by end of Q2 fiscal year.
Strategy 2	Propose high-level controlled vocabulary scheme by end of fiscal Q3.
Strategy 3	Evaluate indexing software programs simultaneously with Strategy 3.
Strategy 4	Create process map and tutorial to help users change information-seeking patterns and maximize benefit from new system—for beta release.
Strategy 5	Take leadership role in documenting content selection standards.
Goal 2	Improve corporate customer responsiveness and retain more customers.
Objective 1	Make customer database more robust by adding current, significant news items to internal information about top customers.
Strategy 1	Scan Web for relevant free content about top 15 customers; add content or create links to those services. Begin immediately. Update weekly.
Strategy 2	Set up clipping services in appropriate external databases to complement Web and internal data; obtain copyright permission for adding to internal databases by end of fiscal Q1, and implement once permission is secured. Stop paper-clipping service upon contract renewal.

IV. Performance Indicators

This section of the plan is where quantifiable indicators of success for the plan are outlined. The indicators need to reflect the goals as established in Section III of the plan. Samples might look as follows:

Sample performance indicators for Goal 1
- Less time spent searching for internal documents
- Less duplication of effort as a result of ready access to previous efforts

- Start of document selection and retention policy
- Development of internal standard vocabulary scheme
- Increased visibility for information center participants

Sample performance indicators for Goal 2
- Positive feedback from external customers
- Fewer urgent requests for customer information coming to information center
- Common knowledge of customer activities throughout the organization
- More effective enterprisewide dissemination and sharing of external information
- Increased sales to top customers
- Higher retention of top customers

Successful strategic planning is characterized by honest, objective examination of the status quo, followed by flexible adjustments to emerging organizational priorities and practical, realistic, short-term goal setting to extend the ongoing business. Finally, it requires an open mind, a vision of future possibilities, a desire to improve, and an increasing comfort level with risk taking.

Appendix E: Business Plan Executive Summary

Plan Components

1. The Executive Summary
2. The Management Team
3. Company History
4. Business Opportunities
5. The Competition
6. Research and Development
7. Pricing
8. Marketing Plan
9. The Financials

1. The Executive Summary

Executive summaries can take many forms. The two most popular terms are as follows:

1. The multiparagraph free-form description, which informally summarizes, in less than two pages, the entire business plan
2. The more structured, formal executive summary

Describe the different plan components under their appropriate headings, as shown in the following:

COMPANY: B Software—application development, software engineering/ reengineering. The firm was founded in 1997, with headquarters in New York

City, and is a leader in the development of intelligent software systems for the applications development and reengineering markets. The company is highly innovative and has developed a series of programming tools that use proprietary, intelligent, and document/text analytical and parsing techniques, resulting in exceptional programmer productivity gains. The company is profitable, even after development costs association with the introduction of new toolsets. It intends to accelerate the introduction of new intelligent software engineering products, including Web-based products, which will be sold via the company's Web site (www.b.com), its direct sales force, and through VARs and resellers.

MARKET: The market for the company's core business is the millions of software developers in national and international corporate business arena. Dataquest has estimated this market to exceed $238 billion and growing. Management has identified reengineering, as evidenced by the highly publicized Year 2000, Euro-Money, and Dow 10000 problems, to be a segment of the market that is underserved and suffers from a lack of innovation. Ovum has estimated the size of this market to be over $12 billion annually and growing.

SENIOR MANAGEMENT: Person 1 (40), CEO, is the past managing director of R&D for Z Company, and was a prior officer of several large financial institutions. She was awarded a PhD from X university and is the author of several books and over 200 articles. Person 2 (42), VP Marketing & Sales, has broad experience in both marketing and sales, with solid experience in high tech. Person 3 (46), VP Technology, has over 20 years of valuable experience in the development and management of high-tech systems.

FINANCE: Company B seeks $2 million of growth capital to accelerate the rollout of new, or refinement of existing, XXX tools and for working capital. Revenue is expected to be $25 million in Year 3 and over $100 million in Year 5. The company is free of debt. The exit strategy is initial public offering, sale, or buyout.

Financial Goals in 000

	Year 1	Year 2	Year 3	Year 4	Year 5
Sales (000)	1,500	8,500	25,000	83,000	106,000
Net income	531	3,490	10,944	40,072	50,873

Note: All figures are estimated.

2. The Management Team

The team is as important as the product. The management team is more than just window dressing for public relations. Not only should it have a firm grasp of the technology but it should also be savvy in the management aspects of running a business.

The Mix (eBay Example)

The management team eBay describes on its Web site encompasses the full range of management capabilities:

- Founder/Chairman
- President/CEO
- Chief Financial Officer
- Senior Vice President of Marketing
- Vice President of International Operations
- Chief Scientist
- General Counsel
- Vice President of Strategic Planning

3. Company History

It is necessary to provide sufficient information to the reader that he or she understands how the company got to the point of being able to make its presence felt in this particular market segment. This includes information on (1) the expertise the company possesses that permits it to navigate unknown waters, (2) any marketing expertise it might have that will enable the new venture to successfully enter the market, and (3) how the idea for the business originated.

Answer the following questions:

1. Is it a new company?
    1.1 When was it founded?
    1.2 How was it funded?
    1.3 Who were the founders?
    1.4 Why was it founded? Mission and goals.
2. Is it an existing company?
    2.1 Is this a division, subsidiary, or spin-off of the company?
    2.2 If it is a spin-off, then go to section 1 of this list.
    2.3 What are the missions and goals?
    2.4 What is the budget?
3. How was the business idea arrived at?
    3.1 It was derived out of an existing product or service.
        3.1.1 What's the market share for the existing product or service?
        3.1.2 If it is a service, how do you propose to turn it into a business?
    3.2 It is a new idea.
        3.2.1 Provide market data to demonstrate validity of the new idea.

4. Make the case for the business.
   4.1 In one paragraph, summarize your business concept.
   4.2 Your mission and goals.

The mission or vision example:

> *The vision of this company, simply put, is to help other enterprises succeed. We will do this by unleashing the full potential of an exciting new product—Precise. This product will be a valuable, cost-effective tool that can be delivered to customers in a variety of ways, thus enabling it to be of value to organizations of all sizes, from the largest companies in the world to midsize and smaller organizations as well.*

Now itemize your specific goals.

4. Product Description

4.1 How to Describe What It Is You Are Trying to Sell

In this section, you will provide more details about the product or service you are offering. For the most part, this section can be split into two subsections:

4.1.1 Features
4.1.2 Benefits

4.1.1 Features

For example, an e-business offers employee testing over the Internet.
   An example of the way you might describe its features follows:

- Can test any number of (prospective) employees at one time, utilizing any number of tests at one time.
- Tests can consist of 1 to 1,000 questions, each with an image and unlimited hyperlinks.

4.1.2 Benefits

Whereas the features section describes the nitty-gritty of what the product or service does, the benefits section is used to make a case for actually paying or using the product or service. An example of the way you might describe its benefits follows:

- Utilizes a neutral, impartial source to assess prospective and current employee skills
- Saves administrative costs associated with skills assessment

4.2 The Importance of the Prototype

Computer systems are by their very nature very graphical. If the product Web site has already been built, even in prototype form, it would be worthwhile to add some color to the business plan by adding screenshots to the plan.

5. Business Opportunities

5.1 Pinpointing Your Markets

For any business to survive, it must be adaptable and continually look for new opportunities. For example, a company develops a software product but realizes that there are more opportunities to deploy it as a service across the Web than as a stand-alone software product.

5.2 Estimating Expected Sales

Estimating customer sales will require you to perform some competitive research:

1. Make a list of potential competitors that are already public companies.
2. Go to www.hoovers.com to look up each competitor.
3. Go to www.sec.gov to review 10Q and 10K (you can also get this from Hoover's).
4. Extrapolate your potential sales figures from analysis of your competitors.

6. The Competition

6.1 Performing Competitive Analysis

1. Use services already mentioned (i.e., www.hoovers.com and www.sec.gov) to review public company financials.
2. Surf competitor sites.
    - Download all competitor sales brochures.
    - Read all press releases.
    - Sign up for any free trials or free offers.
    - Collect information from the About Us page.
    - Find out who is advertising on their site.
    - Find out who is linking to their site (use AltaVista's link: www. yourcompetitor.com).
3. Use a search engine to see who is writing about each competitor and what they are saying.

6.2 Describing Your Competitive Advantage

In this section, list all known competitors and then explain how they pose a threat to you. It would be an excellent idea to also explain how you intend to minimize that threat (i.e., via a massive marketing campaign, through public relations, etc.).

For phantom competitors, you will need to include one or more paragraphs that explain the potential of the introduction of competition from unknown sources.

7. Research and Development (R&D)

7.1   Next 6 months
7.2   Next 12 months
7.3   Next 3 years
7.4   Next 5 years
    1. Discuss what you will spend your money on
    2. Discuss either dollar amounts or percentage of revenue that you will spend

8. Pricing

8.1 What Are You Going to Charge?

1. Sell items
2. Sell services
3. Sell advertising
4. Be a Web portal
5. Other items

In this section, you will need to spell out exactly how you intend to make money: What will be the fees for your products or services, and how much do you expect to gross during the coming year and the next five years?

8.2 How Are You Going to Get Paid?

1. Credit cards
2. Cybercash
3. Billing
4. Via sponsors or partners

9. Marketing Plan

The marketing plan brief consists of sections on the following:

1. Public relations
2. Marketing efforts such as direct mail, telemarketing, and trade shows
3. Advertising
4. Reseller and affiliate agreements
5. Partnerships

9.1 Your Advertising Strategies

1. Where are you going to advertise?
2. How much is it going to cost?

9.2 Listing Your Public Relations Strategy

1. The average PR firm costs $6,000/month (for a small business).
2. PR costs rise dramatically with company size.

10. Financials

The Pro Forma

Starting a business will require you to estimate both your expenses and revenues.

10.1 Estimating Revenue

As discussed, estimating customer sales will require you to perform some competitive research:

1. Make a list of potential competitors that are already public companies.
2. Go to www.hoovers.com to look up each competitor.
3. Go to www.sec.gov to review 10Q and 10K (you can also get this from Hoover's).
4. Extrapolate your potential sales figures from analysis of your competitors.

10.1.1 Estimating Revenue

Example

	Company A				
	Year 1	Year 2	Year 3	Year 4	Year 5
Sales	2,500.00	8,500.00	25,000.00	83,000.00	106,000.00
Profit	1,548.50	6,497.00	16,457.00	60,258.00	76,501.00

If you are going to use the business plan to raise money, then be extra careful to ensure that you offer a substantially high return on investment. Venture firms usually want at least 40% back on their investment—anything lower is a definite "red flag." On the other hand, unrealistic projections can be just as damaging to your funding well-being.

10.1.2 What VCs and Banks Want

1. Part of a large market
2. Profitability
3. A market leader
4. A properly valued company
5. Realistic projections
6. A good analysis of the competition
7. A high return on investment
8. A three- to five-year return

10.2 Estimating Selling, Marketing, and Other Promotional Expenses

Company A					
	Year 1	Year 2	Year 3	Year 4	Year 5
Selling expenses	300	1,050	3,000	5,500	7,500
Advertising/Marketing/PR	150	850	2,500	6,300	10,600
Commissions	12	47	69	160	320
T&E	462	1,947	5,580	13,960	18,420

10.3 Estimating Administrative Costs

Company A					
	Year 1	Year 2	Year 3	Year 4	Year 5
Administrative					
Salaries	135	765	2,250	7,470	9,540
Insurance	14	77	225	747	954
Total	149	842	2,475	8,217	10,494

10.4 Estimating Facilities Costs

	Company A				
	Year 1	Year 2	Year 3	Year 4	Year 5
General					
Rent	18	120	120	120	120
Utilities	5	18	20	20	20
Telephone	12	50	44	60	70
Office expenses	10	45	45	45	45
Supplies	5	15	20	25	35
Postage	.50	15	30	45	45
Research	10	100	100	100	100
Hardware and software	30	100	100	150	150
Total	90.50	463	479	565	585

10.5 Describing Effects of Investment

Outlays are described in the Pro Forma Financial Statement in the previous text. These outlays will enable us to operate at a level that will allow us to meet our conservation sales goals for the first three years. Descriptive notes follow:

1. Salaries refer to professional employees. We expect to hire three to five (or use consultants) programmers in year one. We also expect to hire three telemarketers in year one. An office administrator will also be hired.
2. Advertising covers advertising on the Web, computer trades, and trade shows.
3. Public relations covers the cost of an outside PR agency.
4. Although computer equipment is already available, it is necessary to maintain a state-of-the art presence in terms of hardware and software.

10.6 Describing the Investment Exit Strategy

It is expected that the investors will receive shares of the company's stock, which may be disposed of in the following manner:

1. If our plan is successful, we would like to start the process of going public within 18 months of funding. Investors can recoup their investment and profit from the proceeds.

2. Investors may recoup their investments and profits from revenue if the revenue exceeds projected profits as expected in this business plan.
3. Percentage ownership for capital invested is negotiable.

Appendix F: Business Plan for a Start-Up Business

The business plan consists of a narrative and several financial worksheets. The narrative template is the body of the business plan. It contains more than 150 questions divided into several sections. Work through the sections in any order you like, except for the section titled "Executive Summary," which should be done last. Skip any questions that do not apply to your type of business. When you have finished writing your first draft, you'll have a collection of small essays on the various topics of the business plan. Then you'll want to edit them into a smooth-flowing narrative.

The real value of creating a business plan does not lie in having the finished product in hand; rather, the value lies in the process of researching and thinking about your business in a systematic way. The act of planning helps you to think things through thoroughly, study and research if you are not sure of the facts, and look at your ideas critically. It takes time now but avoids costly, perhaps disastrous, mistakes later.

This business plan is a generic model suitable for all types of businesses. However, you should modify it to suit your particular circumstances. Before you begin, review the section titled "Refining the Plan," found at the end. It suggests emphasizing certain areas, depending on your type of business (manufacturing, retail, service, etc.). It also has tips for fine-tuning your plan to make an effective presentation to investors or bankers. If this is why you're creating your plan, pay particular attention to your writing style. You will be judged by the quality and appearance of your work as well as by your ideas.

It typically takes several weeks to complete a good plan. Most of that time is spent in research and rethinking your ideas and assumptions. But then, that is the value of the process. So, make time to do the job properly. Those who do never regret the effort. And finally, be sure to keep detailed notes on your sources of information and on the assumptions underlying your financial data.

Business Plan

Owners

Your business name
Address line 1
Address line 2
City, ST ZIP code
Telephone
Fax
E-mail

I. Table of Contents

II. Executive Summary

Write this section last.

We suggest that you make it two pages or fewer.

Include everything that you would cover in a five-minute interview.

Explain the fundamentals of the proposed business: What will your product be? Who will your customers be? Who are the owners? What do you think the future holds for your business and your industry?

Make it enthusiastic, professional, complete, and concise.

If applying for a loan, state clearly how much you want, precisely how you are going to use it, and how the money will make your business more profitable, thereby ensuring repayment.

III. General Company Description

What business will you be in? What will you do?

Mission statement: Many companies have a brief mission statement, usually in 30 words or fewer, explaining their reason for being and their guiding principles. If you want to draft a mission statement, this is a good place to put it in the plan, followed by

Company goals and objectives: Goals are destinations—where you want your business to be. Objectives are progress markers along the way to goal achievement. For example, a goal might be to have a healthy, successful company that is a leader in customer service and has a loyal customer following. Objectives might be annual sales targets and some specific measures of customer satisfaction.

Business philosophy: What is important to you in business?

To whom will you market your products? (State it briefly here; you will give a more thorough explanation in the section titled "Marketing Plan.")

Describe your industry. Is it a growth industry? What changes do you foresee in the industry, short term and long term? How will your company be poised to take advantage of them?

Describe your most important company strengths and core competencies. What factors will make the company succeed? What do you think your major competitive strengths will be? What background experience, skills, and strengths will you personally bring to this new venture?

Legal form of ownership: sole proprietor, partnership, corporation, limited liability corporation (LLC)? Why have you selected this form?

IV. Products and Services

Describe in depth your products or services (technical specifications, drawings, photos, sales brochures, and other bulky items belong in the section titled "Appendices").

What factors will give you competitive advantages or disadvantages? Examples include level of quality, or unique or proprietary features.

What are the pricing, fee, or leasing structures of your products or services?

V. Marketing Plan

Market Research—Why?

No matter how good your product and your service, the venture cannot succeed without effective marketing. And this begins with careful, systematic research. It is very dangerous to assume that you already know about your intended market. You need to do market research to make sure you're on track. Use the business-planning process as your opportunity to uncover data and to question your marketing efforts. Your time will be well spent.

Market Research—How?

There are two kinds of market research: primary and secondary. Both will be discussed here.

Secondary research means using published information such as industry profiles, trade journals, newspapers, magazines, census data, and demographic profiles. This type of information is available from public libraries, industry associations, chambers of commerce, vendors who sell to your industry, and government agencies.

Start with your local library. Most librarians are pleased to guide you through their business data collection. You will be amazed at what is there. There are more online sources than you could possibly use. Your chamber of commerce has good information on the local area. Trade associations and trade publications often have excellent industry-specific data.

Primary research means gathering your own data. For example, you could do your own traffic count at a proposed location, use the yellow pages to identify competitors, and do surveys or focus-group interviews to learn about consumer preferences. Professional market research can be very costly, but there are many books that show small business owners how to do effective research themselves.

In your marketing plan, be as specific as possible: give statistics, numbers, and sources. The marketing plan will be the basis, later on, of the all-important sales projection.

Economics

Facts about your industry:

- What is the total size of your market?
- What percentage share of the market will you have? (This is important only if you think you will be a major player in the market.)
- What is the current demand in the target market?
- What are the trends in the target market—growth trends, trends in consumer preferences, and trends in product development?
- What is the growth potential and opportunity for a business of your size?
- What barriers to entry do you face in entering this market with your new company? Some typical barriers are as follows:
  - High capital costs
  - High production costs
  - High marketing costs
  - Consumer acceptance and brand recognition
  - Training and skills
  - Unique technology and patents
  - Unions
  - Shipping costs
  - Tariff barriers and quotas

- And of course, how will you overcome the barriers?
- How can the following affect your company?
  - Change in technology
  - Change in government regulations
  - Change in the economy
- Change in your industry

Products

In the section titled "Products and Services," you described your products and services as you see them. Now describe them from your customers' point of view.

Features and Benefits

List all your major products and services. For each product or service:

- Describe the most important features. What is special about it?
- Describe the benefits. That is, what will the product do for the customer?

Note the differences between features and benefits, and think about them. For example, a house that gives shelter and lasts a long time is made with certain materials and to a certain design; those are its features. Its benefits include pride of ownership, financial security, providing for the family, and inclusion in a neighborhood. You build features into your product so that you can sell the benefits.

What after-sales services will you give? Some examples are delivery, warranty, service contracts, support, follow-up, and refund policy.

Customers

Identify your targeted customers, their characteristics, and their geographic locations, otherwise known as their demographics.

The description will be completely different depending on whether you plan to sell to other businesses or directly to consumers. If you sell a consumer product but sell it through a channel of distributors, wholesalers, and retailers, you must carefully analyze both the end consumer and the middleman businesses to which you sell.

You may have more than one customer group. Identify the most important groups. Then, for each customer group, construct what is called a demographic profile having the following details:

- Age
- Gender
- Location
- Income level

- Social class and occupation
- Education
- Other (specific to your industry)

For business customers, the demographic factors might be the following:

- Industry (or portion of an industry)
- Location
- Size of firm
- Quality, technology, and price preferences
- Other (specific to your industry)

Competition

What products and companies will compete with you?

List your major competitors, including their names and addresses.

Will they compete with you across the board, or just for certain products, certain customers, or in certain locations?

Will you have important indirect competitors (e.g., video rental stores compete with theaters, although they are different types of businesses)?

How will your products or services compare with those of competitors?

Use Table F.1 to compare your company with your two most important competitors. The first column lists the key competitive factors. Since these vary from one industry to another, you may want to customize the list of factors.

In the column labeled "Me," state how you honestly think you will stack up in customers' minds. Then check whether you think this factor will be a strength or a weakness for you. Sometimes, it is hard to analyze our own weaknesses. Try to be very honest here. Better yet, get some disinterested strangers to assess you. This can be a real eye-opener. And remember that you cannot be all things to all people. In fact, this causes many business failures because efforts become scattered and diluted. You want an honest assessment of your firm's strong and weak points.

Now, analyze each major competitor. In a few words, state how you think they compare with you.

In the final column, estimate the importance of each competitive factor to the customer: 1 = critical; 5 = not very important.

Now, write a short paragraph stating your competitive advantages and disadvantages.

Niche

Now that you have systematically analyzed your industry, product, customers, and the competition, you should have a clear picture of where your company fits in the market.

In one short paragraph, define your niche—your unique corner of the market.

Table F.1 Competitive Analysis

Factor	Me	Strength	Weakness	Competitor A	Competitor B	Importance to Customer
Products						
Price						
Quality						
Selection						
Service						
Reliability						
Stability						
Expertise						
Company reputation						
Location						
Appearance						
Sales method						
Credit policies						
Advertising						
Image						

Marketing Strategy

Outline a marketing strategy that is consistent with your niche.

Promotion

How will you get the word out to customers?

Regarding advertising, what media will you use, why, and how often? Why this mix, and not some other?

Have you identified low-cost methods to get the most out of your promotional budget?

Will you use methods other than paid advertising, such as trade shows, catalogs, dealer incentives, word of mouth (how will you stimulate it?), and networks of friends or professionals?

What image do you want to project? How do you want customers to see you?

In addition to advertising, what plans do you have for graphic image support? This includes logo design, cards and letterheads, brochures, signage, and interior design (if customers come to your place of business).

Should you have a system to identify repeat customers and then systematically contact them?

Promotional Budget

How much will you spend on the items listed in the previous section?

Before start-up? (These figures will go into your start-up budget.)

Ongoing? (These figures will go into your operating plan budget.)

Pricing

Explain your method or methods of setting prices. For most small businesses, having the lowest price is not a good policy. It robs you of needed profit margin, customers may not care as much about price as you think, and large competitors can underprice you anyway. Usually, you will do better to have average prices and compete on quality and service.

Does your pricing strategy fit with what was revealed in your competitive analysis?

Compare your prices with those of your competitors. Are they higher, lower, or the same? Why?

How important is price as a competitive factor? Do your intended customers really make their purchase decisions mostly on price?

What will be your customer service and credit policies?

Proposed Location

Probably, you do not have a precise location picked out yet. This is the time to think about what you want and need in a location. Many start-ups run successfully from home for a while.

You will describe your physical needs later, in the section titled "Operational Plan." Here, analyze your location criteria as they will affect your customers.

Is your location important to your customers? If yes, how?

If customers come to your place of business:

- Is it convenient? Parking? Interior spaces? Not out of the way?
- Is it consistent with your image?
- Is it what customers want and expect?

Where is the competition located? Is it better for you to be near them (e.g., car dealers or fast-food restaurants) or distant (e.g., convenience food stores)?

Distribution Channels

How will you sell your products or services?

- Retail
- Direct (via mail order, Web, or catalog)
- Wholesale
- Your own sales force
- Agents
- Independent representatives
- Bid on contracts

Sales Forecast

Now that you have described your products, services, customers, markets, and marketing plans in detail, it's time to attach some numbers to your plan. Use a sales forecast spreadsheet to prepare a month-by-month projection. The forecast should be based on your historical sales, the marketing strategies that you have just described, your market research, and industry data, if available.

You may want to do two forecasts: (1) a "best guess," which is what you really expect, and (2) a "worst-case" low estimate that you are confident you can reach no matter what happens.

Remember to keep notes on your research and your assumptions as you build this sales forecast and all subsequent spreadsheets in the plan. This is critical if you are going to present it to funding sources.

VI. Operational Plan

Explain the daily operation of the business, its location, equipment, people, processes, and surrounding environment.

Production

How and where are your products or services produced?
Explain your methods for the following:

- Production techniques and costs
- Quality control
- Customer service
- Inventory control
- Product development

Location

What qualities do you need in a location? Describe the type of location you'll have.
Physical requirements:

- Amount of space
- Type of building
- Zoning
- Power and other utilities

Access:

Is it important that your location be convenient to transportation or to suppliers? Do you need easy walk-in access?

What are your requirements for parking and proximity to freeway, airports, railroads, and shipping centers?

Include a drawing or layout of your proposed facility if it is important, as it might be for a manufacturer.

Construction: Most new companies should not sink capital into construction, but if you are planning to build, costs and specifications will be a big part of your plan.

Cost: Estimate your occupation expenses, including rent. Include also maintenance, utilities, insurance, and initial remodeling costs (to make the space suit your needs). These numbers will become part of your financial plan.

What will be your business hours?

Legal Environment

Describe the following:

- Licensing and bonding requirements
- Permits
- Health, workplace, or environmental regulations
- Special regulations covering your industry or profession
- Zoning or building code requirements
- Insurance coverage
- Trademarks, copyrights, or patents (pending, existing, or purchased)

Personnel

- Number of employees.
- Type of labor (skilled, unskilled, or professional).
- Where and how will you find the right employces?
- Quality of existing staff.
- Pay structure.
- Training methods and requirements.
- Who does which tasks?
- Do you have schedules and written procedures prepared?
- Have you drafted job descriptions for employees? If not, take time to write some. They really help internal communications with employees.
- For certain functions, will you use contract workers in addition to employees?

Inventory

- What kind of inventory will you keep: raw materials, supplies, finished goods?
- Average value in stock (i.e., your inventory investment)?
- Rate of turnover and how this compares to the industry averages?
- Seasonal buildups?
- Lead time for ordering?

Suppliers

Identify key suppliers, and note the following information about them:

- Names and addresses
- Type and amount of inventory furnished
- Credit and delivery policies
- History and reliability

Should you have more than one supplier for critical items (as a backup)?

Do you expect shortages or short-term delivery problems?

Are supply costs steady or fluctuating? If fluctuating, how would you deal with changing costs?

Credit Policies

- Do you plan to sell on credit?
- Do you really need to sell on credit? Is it customary in your industry and expected by your clientele?
- If yes, what policies will you have about who gets credit and how much?
- How will you check the creditworthiness of new applicants?
- What terms will you offer your customers; that is, how much credit and when is payment due?
- Will you offer prompt payment discounts? (Hint: Do this only if it is usual and customary in your industry.)
- Do you know what it will cost you to extend credit? Have you built the costs into your prices?

Managing Your Accounts Receivable

If you do extend credit, you should do a receivables aging at least once a month to track how much of your money is tied up in credit given to customers and to alert you to slow-payment problems. A receivables aging looks like the following table:

	Total	Current	30 Days	60 Days	90 Days	Over 90 Days
Accounts receivable aging						

You will need a policy for dealing with slow-paying customers:

- When do you make a phone call?
- When do you send a letter?
- When do you get your attorney to threaten them?

Managing Your Accounts Payable

You should also age your accounts payable (what you owe to your suppliers). This helps you plan whom to pay and when. Paying too early depletes your cash, but paying late can cost you valuable discounts and can damage your credit. (Hint: If you know you will be late making a payment, call the creditor before the due date.)

Do your proposed vendors offer prompt payment discounts?

A payables aging looks like the following table:

	Total	Current	30 Days	60 Days	90 Days	Over 90 Days
Accounts payable aging						

VII. Management and Organization

Who will manage the business on a day-to-day basis? What experience does that person bring to the business; what special or distinctive competencies? Is there a plan for continuation of the business if this person is lost or incapacitated?

If you'll have more than 10 employees, create an organizational chart showing the management hierarchy and who is responsible for key functions.

Include position descriptions for key employees. If you are seeking loans or investors, include resumes of owners and key employees.

Professional and Advisory Support

List the following:

- Board of directors
- Management advisory board
- Attorney
- Accountant
- Insurance agent
- Banker
- Consultants
- Mentors and key advisors

VIII. Personal Financial Statement

Include personal financial statements for each owner and major stockholder, showing assets and liabilities held outside the business and personal net worth. Owners will often have to draw on personal assets to finance the business, and these statements will show what is available. Bankers and investors usually want this information as well.

IX. Start-Up Expenses and Capitalization

You will have many start-up expenses before you even begin operating your business. It's important to estimate these expenses accurately and then to plan where you will get sufficient capital. This is a research project, and the more thorough your research efforts, the less chance that you will leave out important expenses or underestimate them.

Even with the best of research, however, opening a new business has a way of costing more than you anticipate. There are two ways to make allowances for surprise expenses. The first is to add a little "padding" to each item in the budget. The problem with that approach, however, is that it destroys the accuracy of your carefully wrought plan. The second approach is to add a separate line item, called contingencies, to account for the unforeseeable. This is the approach we recommend.

Talk to others who have started similar businesses to get a good idea of how much to allow for contingencies. If you cannot get good information, we recommend a rule of thumb that contingencies should equal at least 20% of the total of all other start-up expenses.

Explain your research and how you arrived at your forecasts of expenses. Give sources, amounts, and terms of proposed loans. Also, explain in detail how much will be contributed by each investor and what percentage of ownership each will have.

X. Financial Plan

The financial plan consists of a 12-month profit and loss projection, a 4-year profit and loss projection (optional), a cash-flow projection, a projected balance sheet, and a breakeven calculation. Together, they constitute a reasonable estimate of your company's financial future. More important, the process of thinking through the financial plan will improve your insight into the inner financial workings of your company.

12-Month Profit and Loss Projection

Many business owners think of the 12-month profit and loss projection as the centerpiece of their plan. This is where you put it all together in numbers and get an idea of what it will take to make a profit and be successful.

Your sales projections will come from a sales forecast in which you forecast sales, cost of goods sold, expenses, and month-by-month profit for one year.

Profit projections should be accompanied by a narrative explaining the major assumptions used to estimate company income and expenses.

Keep careful notes on your research and assumptions so that you can explain them later if necessary, and also so that you can go back to your sources when it's time to revise your plan.

4-Year Profit Projection (Optional)

The 12-month projection is the heart of your financial plan. The 4-year profit projection is for those who want to carry their forecasts beyond the first year.

Of course, keep notes of your key assumptions, especially about factors that you expect will change dramatically after the first year.

Projected Cash Flow

If profit projection is the heart of your business plan, cash flow is the blood. Businesses fail because they cannot pay their bills. Every part of your business plan is important, but none of it means a thing if you run out of cash.

The point of this worksheet is to plan how much you need before start-up, as preliminary expenses, operating expenses, and reserves. You should keep updating this information and use it afterward. It will enable you to foresee cash shortages in time to do something about them—perhaps by cutting expenses or by negotiating a loan. But first and foremost, you shouldn't be taken by surprise.

There is no great trick to preparing it: The cash-flow projection is just a forward look at your checking account.

For each item, determine when you actually expect to receive cash (for sales) or when you will actually have to write a check (for expense items).

You should track essential operating data, which is not necessarily part of cash flow but allows you to track items that have a heavy impact on cash flow, such as sales and inventory purchases.

You should also track cash outlays prior to opening in a pre-start-up column. You should have already researched those for your start-up expenses plan.

Your cash flow will show you whether your working capital is adequate. Clearly, if your projected cash balance ever goes negative, you will need more start-up capital. This plan will also predict just when and how much you will need to borrow.

Explain your major assumptions, especially those that make the cash flow differ from the profit and loss projection. For example, if you make a sale in month one, when do you actually collect the cash? When you buy inventory or materials, do you pay in advance, upon delivery, or much later? How will this affect cash flow?

Are some expenses payable in advance? When?

Are there irregular expenses, such as quarterly tax payments, maintenance and repairs, or seasonal inventory buildup, that should be budgeted?

Loan payments, equipment purchases, and owner's draws usually do not show on profit and loss statements but definitely do take cash out. Be sure to include them. And, of course, depreciation does not appear in the cash flow at all because you never write a check for it.

Opening-Day Balance Sheet

A balance sheet is one of the fundamental financial reports that any business needs for reporting and financial management. A balance sheet shows what items of value are held by the company (assets), and what its debts are (liabilities). When liabilities are subtracted from assets, the remainder is owners' equity.

Use a start-up expenses and capitalization spreadsheet as a guide to preparing a balance sheet as of opening day. Then, detail how you calculated the account balances on your opening-day balance sheet.

Optionally, some people may want to add a projected balance sheet showing the estimated financial position of the company at the end of the first year. This is especially useful when selling your proposal to investors.

Breakeven Analysis

A breakeven analysis predicts the sales volume, at a given price, required to recover total costs. In other words, it's the sales level that is the dividing line between operating at a loss and operating at a profit.

Expressed as a formula, breakeven is as follows:

$$\text{Breakeven Sales} = \frac{\text{Fixed Costs}}{1 - \text{Variable Costs}}$$

where fixed costs are expressed in dollars, but variable costs are expressed as a percentage of total sales.

Include all assumptions on which your breakeven calculation is based.

XI. Appendices

Include details and studies used in your business plan, for example:

- Brochures and advertising materials
- Industry studies
- Blueprints and plans
- Maps and photographs of locations
- Magazines or other articles
- Detailed lists of equipment owned or to be purchased
- Copies of leases and contracts

- Letters of support from future customers
- Any other material needed to support the assumptions in this plan
- Market research studies
- List of assets available as collateral for a loan

XII. Refining the Plan

The generic business plan presented here should be modified to suit your specific type of business and the audience for which the plan is written.

For Raising Capital

For Bankers

Bankers want assurance of orderly repayment. If you intend to use this plan to present to lenders, include the following details:

- Amount of loan.
- How the funds will be used.
- What this will accomplish—how it will make the business stronger.
- Requested repayment terms (number of years to repay). You will probably not have much negotiating room on interest rate, but you may be able to negotiate a longer repayment term, which will help cash flow.
- Collateral offered, and a list of all existing liens against the collateral.

For Investors

Investors have a different perspective from bankers. They are looking for dramatic growth, and they expect to share in the rewards. Include the following details in the plan:

- Short-term funds needed
- Funds needed in two to five years
- How the company will use the funds, and what this will accomplish for growth
- Estimated return on investment
- Exit strategy for investors (buyback, sale, or IPO)
- Percentage of ownership that you will give up to investors
- Milestones or conditions that you will accept
- Financial reporting to be provided
- Involvement of investors on the board or in management

For the Type of Business

Manufacturing

- Planned production levels
- Anticipated levels of direct production costs and indirect (overhead) costs—how do these compare to industry averages (if available)?
- Prices per product line
- Gross profit margin, overall and for each product line
- Production/capacity limits of planned physical plant
- Production/capacity limits of equipment
- Purchasing and inventory management procedures
- New products under development or anticipated to come online after start-up

Service Businesses

Service businesses sell intangible products. They are usually more flexible than other types of businesses, but they also have higher labor costs and generally very little in fixed assets.

- What are the key competitive factors in this industry?
- Your prices
- Methods used to set prices
- System of production management
- Quality control procedures
- Standard or accepted industry quality standards
- How will you measure labor productivity?
- Percentage of work subcontracted to other firms—will you make a profit on subcontracting?
- Credit, payment, and collections policies and procedures
- Strategy for keeping client base

High-Tech Companies

- Economic outlook for the industry
- Will the company have information systems in place to manage rapidly changing prices, costs, and markets?
- Will you be on the cutting edge with your products and services?
- What is the status of research and development? And what is required to do the following?
  - Bring product or service to market
  - Keep the company competitive

- How does the company accomplish the following?
    - Protect intellectual property
    - Avoid technological obsolescence
    - Supply necessary capital
- Retain key personnel

High-tech companies sometimes have to operate for a long time without profits and sometimes even without sales. If this fits your situation, a banker probably will not want to lend to you. Venture capitalists may invest, but your story must be very good. You must do longer-term financial forecasts to show when profit takeoff is expected to occur. And your assumptions must be well documented and well argued.

Retail Business

- Company image.
- Pricing:
    - Explain markup policies.
    - Prices should be profitable, competitive, and should match company image.
- Inventory:
    - Selection and price should be consistent with company image.
    - Inventory level: Find industry average numbers for annual inventory turnover rate (available in RMA book). Multiply your initial inventory investment by the average turnover rate. The result should be at least equal to your projected first year's cost of goods sold. If it is not, you may not have enough budgeted for start-up inventory.
- Customer service policies: These should be competitive and should match company image.
- Location: Does it give the exposure that you need? Is it convenient for customers? Is it consistent with the company image?
- Promotion: Methods used, cost. Do they project a consistent company image?
- Credit: Do you extend credit to customers? If yes, do you really need to, and do you factor the cost into prices?

Note

An electronic copy of this plan can be found at www.score.org.

Appendix G: Marketing Plan Template with Directions

Marketing Plan

The Marketing and Sales section of your plan will make or break the prospects for your venture. A great idea is meaningless if you cannot find customers. Carefully drafted and logical financial projections are irrelevant if nobody buys your product. In this Marketing Strategy section, you must convince first yourself, and then the reader, that there is indeed an eager market for your product. The Marketing Strategy section is where you show how you are going to fit into the market structure you have just finished describing. What are unmet needs in the marketplace and how are you going to fill them? How will you differentiate your product or service from what your competitors offer? What unique features, benefits, or capabilities will you bring to the marketplace? Who are your customers? The research you do for this subsection will be with customers and potential customers. It is imperative that you do sufficient customer research to convince potential investors (and yourself) that customers will indeed come flocking to buy your product or service. Customer research can include simply talking with potential customers to get reactions to your product idea, conducting focus groups, undertaking walk-up or mailed surveys, putting up a mock demonstration of your concept and soliciting customer feedback, etc. Be creative in finding ways to get honest customer input about your product or service. And finally, don't inadvertently cook the books here. You are undoubtedly enthused about your concept. Customers will pick up on your enthusiasm and often reflect it back to you, leading to erroneous conclusions about customer acceptance. So, be neutral and factual as you collect data.

Introduction

Write a one-paragraph description of the critical elements of your marketing plan.

Describe your target customer and explain why he or she would buy from you. What is the compelling need that you are satisfying? How will you position your product or service relative to your competition? Describe the distribution channel and how you will sell the product or service.

Create a seven-sentence marketing strategy statement:

1. The first sentence states the purpose of the marketing strategy.
2. The second tells how you'll achieve this purpose, focusing on your benefits.
3. The third deals with your target market—or markets.
4. The fourth, the longest sentence, names the marketing weapons you'll employ.
5. The fifth discloses your niche.
6. The sixth reveals your identity.
7. The seventh mentions your budget, expressed as a percentage of your projected gross revenues.

Example:

> *The purpose of Prosper Press is to sell the maximum number of books at the lowest possible selling cost per book. This will be accomplished by positioning the books as being so valuable to freelancers that they are guaranteed to be worth more to the reader than their selling price. The target market will be people who can or do engage in freelance earning activities. Marketing tools to be utilized will be a combination of classified advertising in magazines and newspapers, direct mail, sales at seminars, publicity in newspapers and on radio and television, direct sales calls to bookstores, and mail-order display ads in magazines. The niche to be occupied is one that provides valuable information that helps freelancers succeed. We will be the ultimate authority for freelancers. Our identity will be one of expertise, readability, and quick response to customer requests. Thirty percent of sales will be allocated to marketing.*

Adapted from Levinson, *Guerilla Marketing*, 1998

Target Market Strategy

Explain your strategy for defining your target market. Describe the unmet needs of your target customers that your product or service fulfills or the problems that it solves.

- What segment of the market are we targeting?
- What characteristics define our target customers?

- How big is our target market? What share of the market will we capture?
- Who are our customers? End users? OEMs? Distributors? Retailers?
- What needs does our product fulfill with our target market?
- What problems are we solving for these customers?
- What evidence do we have that potential customers want our product?
- How will we position our product or service with our customers?
- What evidence do we have that our target market wants our product?

Product or Service Strategy

Describe how your product has been designed and tailored to meet the needs of your target customer, and how it will compete in your target market:

- What specific product or service design characteristics meet the needs of our customers?
- What differentiates our product in our target market?
- How does it differ from that of our competitors?
- What are the strengths of our product or service?
- What are its weaknesses?
- Why will customers in our target market buy our product rather than the competition's?
- How will we differentiate ourselves from our competitors; that is, how is our product or service positioned?
- Why will customers switch to or select us?
- How quickly and how effectively can our competitors respond to our business?

Pricing Strategy

Explain your pricing strategy and why it will be effective with your target customer in your marketplace:

- What is our pricing strategy?
  - How was it determined?
- How does our pricing strategy compare with our competition's?
- What evidence do we have that our target market will accept our price?

Distribution Strategy

Describe your distribution strategy, and explain why it is the best for your marketplace:

- How will we distribute our product or service?

- What distribution channels will we use?
  - Why?
- How will we gain access to these channels?

Advertising and Promotion Strategy

Explain your advertising and promotion strategy. It is critical that you inform your target market about the availability or your product or service, and that you continue to communicate your benefits to that market.

- How will we advertise and promote our product or service?
- How will we communicate with our customers?
  - Advertising?
  - Public relations?
  - Personal selling?
  - Printed materials?
  - Other means of promotion?
- Why will this strategy be effective in reaching our target customer?

Sales Strategy

Depending on your business, sales may be a critical component of your success. Remember, "Nothing happens until the sale is made." An effective sales strategy is critically important for most manufacturers, publishers, software firms, and many service providers. Don't overlook the importance of formulating an effective sales strategy!

- How will our product or service be sold?
  - Personal selling?
  - TV infomercials?
  - Direct mail?
- Who will do the selling?
  - An internal sales force?
  - Manufacturer's representatives?
  - Telephone solicitors?
- How will we recruit, train, and compensate our sales force?
- How will we support our sales effort (e.g., internal staff, service operations, etc.)?

Marketing and Sales Forecasts

Summarize your marketing expenses and revenue forecasts here. Include enough information to inform, but not so much that the reader is overwhelmed. For example, you might include a table summarizing revenues for a simple business that looks like this:

Revenues	Year 1	Year 2	Year 3	Year 4	Year 5
Units sold	25,000	35,000	50,000	100,000	150,000
Price per unit	$25.00	$23.00	$21.00	$18.00	$17.00
Net revenue	$625,000	$805,000	$1,050,000	$1,800,000	$2,550,000

A table summarizing sales and marketing expenses might look like this:

Sales and Marketing	Year 1	Year 2	Year 3	Year 4	Year 5
Salaries and fringes	0	23,000	29,250	84,000	102,000
Commissions	31,250	40,250	52,500	90,000	127,500
Telephone, fax	5,000	7,000	10,000	15,000	20,000
Travel and entertainment	5,000	6,000	7,000	8,000	10,000
Brochures and literature	15,000	20,000	15,000	25,000	35,000
Recruiting and relocation	10,000				
Total sales and marketing	66,250	96,250	113,750	222,000	314,500
Percentage of revenue	10.6%	12.0%	10.8%	12.3%	12.3%

For each table, explain the principal assumptions used to create the table and describe important results such as revenue growth rates, extraordinary expenses, etc.

Operations Plan

The Operations section outlines how you will run your business and deliver value to your customers. Operations are the processes used to deliver your products and services to the marketplace and can include manufacturing, transportation, logistics, travel, printing, consulting, after-sales service, etc. In all likelihood, about 80% of your expenses will be for operations, 80% of your employees will be working in operations, and 80% of your time will be spent worrying about operating problems and opportunities. Be sure that you carefully link the design of your operations to your marketing plan. For example, if high quality will be one of your comparative advantages in the marketplace, then design your operations to deliver high quality, not low costs.

Remember that you will probably have to make trade-offs with your operations. It is impossible to have the lowest costs, highest quality, best on-time performance, and most flexibility in your industry all at the same time. Often, higher quality means higher costs, and lower costs mean less variety and less flexibility. Be careful how you make these trade-offs so that you can deliver products to the market in accordance with your marketing plan!

Introduction

Write a brief introduction to the Operations section. This can also be a good place to include a more colorful and evocative description of how you will use operations to add value for your customers.

Operations Strategy

In this subsection, describe how you will fulfill your marketing strategy using operations:

- How will you use operations to add value for customers in your target market?
- How will you win in the marketplace on the dimensions of cost, quality, timeliness, and flexibility?
- Which dimensions will you stress and which will you de-emphasize?
- What comparative advantages do you have with your operational design?

Scope of Operations

Describe the scope of your operations. Include details in an appendix, if necessary.

- What will you do in-house and what will you purchase (make versus buy)?
  - Why does this make sense for your business?
- What will be your relationship with vendors, suppliers, partners, and associates?
- What kind of people will you need to hire?

Ongoing Operations

How will your company operate on an ongoing basis? Include details in an appendix, if necessary.

Operational Costs

Include a brief summary of anticipated cost of revenue, which might look like this table:

Cost of Revenue	Year 1	Year 2	Year 3	Year 4	Year 5
Direct costs	275,000	313,250	395,000	725,000	990,000
Salaries and fringes	70,000	95,000	120,000	175,000	215,000
Facilities	50,000	50,000	50,000	100,000	150,000
Depreciation	17,143	25,714	42,143	66,429	107,143
Warehouse and shipping	10,000	12,000	15,000	25,000	40,000
Production supplies	5,000	10,000	10,000	15,000	25,000
Total COGS	$427,143	$505,964	$632,143	$1,106,429	$1,527,143
Percentage of revenue	68.3%	62.9%	60.2%	61.5%	59.9%

Be sure to describe your assumptions and the implications of the forecasts you summarize.

Development Plan

In this section, you will outline how you intend to ramp up your business. This section is often woefully underdeveloped in many business plans. Assuming you have a dynamic marketing plan and customers do indeed come flocking for your product or service, you must be able to deliver it to them. The Development section is a road map of how you are going to get from where you are now to where you want to be in the future. If you are starting a business, what are the steps that you need to accomplish to get the business up and running? If you are expanding a business, what do you need to do to make it grow? These steps can be as routine as securing retail space, or as critical as applying for and getting a patent on a key technology.

Development Strategy

- What work remains to launch your company and your products?
- What factors need to come together to make your concept work?
- What are you doing to bring them together?

Development Timeline

What is your timetable for launching your company and your products? (Add a chart or table here.) Go out as far in the future as you have plans.

Development Expenses

Include a table summarizing anticipated development expenses; also include the assumptions behind your estimates.

Appendix H: Strategic Plan Outline

1. Executive Summary
2. Company Background
3. Vision Statement
4. Mission Statement
5. Values Statement
6. Environmental Analysis
    a. Internal Environment
    b. External Environment
7. Long-Term Objectives
8. Strategic Analysis and Choice
9. Plan Goals and Implementation
10. Financial Projections and Analysis
11. Critical Success Factors
12. Controls and Evaluation

Appendix I: Marketing Glossary

A/B testing: A/B testing, at its simplest, is randomly showing a visitor one version of a page—(A) version or (B) version—and tracking the changes in behavior based on which version he or she saw. (A) version is normally your existing design ("control" in statistics lingo), and (B) version is the "challenger" with one copy or design element changed. In a "50/50 A/B split test," you're flipping a coin to decide which version of a page to show. A classic example would be comparing conversions resulting from serving either version (A) or (B), where the versions display different headlines. A/B tests are commonly applied to clicked-on ad copy and landing page copy or designs to determine which version drives the more desired result.

Ad: An advertisement a searcher sees after submitting a query in a search engine or Web site search box. In Pay Per Click (PPC), these ads are usually text format, with a title, description, and display URL. In some cases, a keyword the searcher used in his or her query appears boldfaced in the displayed ad. Ads can be positioned anywhere on a search results page; commonly, they appear at the top—above the natural or organic listings—and on the right side of the page, also known as "Right Rail."

Ad copy: The main text of a clickable search or context-served ad. It usually makes up the second and third lines of a displayed ad, between the ad title and the display URL.

Ad title: The first line of text displayed in a clickable search or context-served ad. Ad titles serve as ad headlines.

Advertising: The paid promotion of goods, services, companies, or ideas by an identified sponsor. Marketers see advertising as part of an overall promotional strategy.

Advertising campaign: A series of advertisements, commercials, and related promotional materials that share a single idea or theme. Designed to be used simultaneously as part of a coordinated advertising plan.

Advertising managers: Advertising managers oversee advertising and promotion staffs, which usually are small except in the largest firms. In a small firm, managers may serve as liaisons between the firm and the advertising or promotion agency to which many advertising or promotional functions are contracted out. In larger firms, advertising managers oversee in-house account, creative, and media services departments. The account executive manages the account services department, assesses the need for advertising, and, in advertising agencies, maintains the accounts of clients. The creative services department develops the subject matter and presentation of advertising. The creative director oversees the copy chief, art director, and associated staff. The media director oversees planning groups that select the communication media—for example, radio, television, newspapers, magazines, the Internet, or outdoor signs—to disseminate the advertising.

Advertorial: An advertisement in a print publication that has the appearance of a news article.

Affiliate marketing: Affiliate marketing is a process of revenue sharing that allows merchants to duplicate sales efforts by enlisting other Web sites as a type of outside sales force. Successful affiliate marketing programs result in the merchant attracting additional buyers, and the affiliate earning the equivalent of a referral fee, based on click-through referrals to the merchant site.

Affinity marketing: Affinity marketing targets promotional efforts toward one group or category of clients based on established buying patterns. The marketing offer is communicated via e-mail promotions, and online or offline advertising.

Algorithm: A set of rules that a search engine uses to rank listings in response to a query. Search engines guard their algorithms closely, as they are the unique formulas used to determine relevance. Algorithms are sometimes referred to as the "secret sauce."

Angle: The viewpoint from which a story is told. Publicists, reporters, and journalists all use a specific angle, or approach, to communicate their story to a targeted audience. Typically, it is not possible to write about subjects in their entirety. The "angle" narrows the focus of the story to communicate a clear, yet limited, perspective of an issue, event, etc.

Arbitrage: A practice through which Web publishers—second-tier search engines, directories, and vertical search engines—engage in the buying and reselling of Web traffic. Typically, arbitrage occurs when such publishers pool client budgets to engage in PPC campaigns on Tier I search engines (Google, Yahoo!, MSN). If the publishers pay $0.10 per click for traffic, they typically resell those visitors to clients who bid $0.20 or more for the same keywords. Successful arbitrage requires that the arbitrageur must pay less per click than what the traffic sells for. The variation called affiliate arbitrage involves a Web site owner or blogger bidding on keywords from programs such as Yahoo! Search Marketing or Google AdWords, which then link the ads either to their own Web site or directly to a merchant site displaying ads (from programs such as the Yahoo! Publisher Network or Google AdSense).

Arbitron: A radio audience research company that collects data by selecting a random sample of the population. The participants maintain written diaries detailing what radio programs they have listened to within a specified time period. (See also Nielsen Media Research.)

Auction model bidding: The most popular type of Pay Per Click bidding. First, an advertiser determines what maximum amount per click it is willing to spend for a keyword. If there is no competition for that keyword, the advertiser pays its bid, or less, for every click. If there is competition at the auction for that keyword, then the advertiser with the highest bid will pay one penny more than its nearest competitor. For example, advertiser A is willing to bid up to $0.50; advertiser B is willing to bid up to $0.75. If advertiser A's actual bid is $0.23, then advertiser B will only pay $0.24 per click. Also referred to as market or competition-driven bidding.

Automatic optimization: Search engines identify which ad for an individual advertiser demonstrates the highest CTR (click-through rate) as time progresses, and then optimizes the ad serve, showing that ad more often than other ads in the same ad group/ad order.

B2B: Stands for "business to business." A business that markets its services or products to other businesses.

B2C: Stands for "business to consumer." A business that markets its services or products to consumers.

Ban: Also known as *delisting*. Refers to a punitive action imposed by a search engine in response to being spammed. Can be an IP address or a specific URL.

Baseline metrics: Time-lagged calculations (usually averages of one sort or another) that provide a basis for making comparisons of past performance to current performance. Baselines can also be forward looking, such as establishing a goal and seeking to determine whether the trends show the likelihood of meeting that goal. They become an essential piece of a key performance indicator (KPI). (See also KPI.)

Behavioral targeting: The practice of targeting and serving ads to groups of people who exhibit similarities not only in their location, gender, or age, but also in how they act and react in their online environment. Behaviors tracked and targeted include Web site topic areas they frequently visit or subscribe to; subjects or content or shopping categories for which they have registered, profiled themselves, or requested automatic updates and information, etc.

Bid: The maximum amount of money that an advertiser is willing to pay each time a searcher clicks on an ad. Bid prices can vary widely depending on competition from other advertisers and keyword popularity.

Bid boosting: A form of automated bid management that allows you to increase your bids when ads are served to someone whose age or gender matches your target market. This level of demographic focus and the "bid boosting" tool are current Microsoft adCenter offerings.

Bid management software: Software that manages Pay Per Click campaigns automatically, called either rules-based (with triggering rules or conditions set by the advertiser) or intelligent software (enacting real-time adjustments based on tracked conversions and competitor actions). Both types of automatic bid management programs monitor and change bid prices, pause campaigns, manage budget maximums, and adjust multiple keyword bids based on CTR, position ranking, and more.

Billboard: (1) An outdoor sign or poster that is typically displayed on the sides of buildings or alongside highways, or (2) an introductory list of program/sponsor highlights that appears at the beginning or end of a television show or magazine.

Blacklist: A list of Web sites that are considered off limits or dangerous. A Web site can be placed on a blacklist because it is a fraudulent operation or because it exploits browser vulnerabilities to send spyware and other unwanted software to the user.

Blog: A truncated form of "Web log." A blog is a frequently updated journal that is intended for general public consumption. It usually represents the personality of the author or Web site.

Boilerplate: Often found in press releases, a boilerplate is standard verbiage that gives a brief history of the organization and is located at the bottom of all company-issued releases. The term comes from the early 1900s, when steel was issued in steam boilers—the boilerplate text is as "strong as steel."

Brand: Customer or user experience represented by images and ideas, often referring to a symbol (name, logo, symbols, fonts, colors), a slogan, and a design scheme. Brand recognition and other reactions are created by the accumulation of experiences with the specific product or service, both from its use and as influenced by advertising, design, and media commentary. Brand is often developed to represent implicit values, ideas, and even personality.

Brand and branding: A brand is a customer experience represented by a collection of images and ideas; often, it refers to a symbol such as a name, logo, slogan, and design scheme. Brand recognition and other reactions are created by the accumulation of experiences with the specific product or service, both directly relating to its use and through the influence of advertising, design, and media commentary.

Brand identity: The outward expression of the brand, which is the symbolic embodiment of all information connected with a product or service, including its name and visual appearance. The brand's identity is its fundamental means of consumer recognition and differentiates the brand from competitors' brands.

Brand lift: A measurable increase in consumer recall for a specific, branded company, product, or service. For example, brand lift might show an increase in respondents who think of Dell for computers, or Wal-Mart for "every household article."

Brand messaging: Creative messaging that presents and maintains a consistent corporate image across all media channels, including search.

Brand reputation: The position a company brand occupies.

Branding strategy: The attempt to develop a strong brand reputation to increase brand recognition and create a significant volume of impressions.

Broadcast media: Communication outlets that utilize airspace, namely, television and radio. Advertising in broadcast media often targets a specific demographic group, is designed to create buzz, and can also be used as a strategic branding tool.

Broadsheet: Standard-size newspaper (e.g., *New York Times*) characterized by long, vertical pages (typical size: 16 × 24 inches). Another popular newspaper format is the tabloid.

Bucket: An associative grouping for related concepts, keywords, behaviors, and audience characteristics associated with your company's product or service. A "virtual container" of similar concepts used to develop PPC keywords, focus ad campaigns, and target messages.

Buying funnel: Also called the *buying cycle, buyer decision cycle,* and *sales cycle,* "buying funnel" refers to the multistep process of a consumer's path to purchase a product—from awareness to education to preferences and intent to final purchase.

Buzz monitoring services: Services that will e-mail a client regarding his or her status in an industry. Most buzz or publicity monitoring services will e-mail anytime a company's name, executives, products, services, or other keyword-based information on a subscriber are mentioned on the Web. Some services charge a fee; others, such as Yahoo! and Google Alerts, are free.

Buzz opportunities: Topics popular in the media and with specific audiences that receive news coverage or pass along recommendations that help increase exposure for a brand. Ways to uncover potential buzz opportunities include reviewing incoming traffic to a Web site from organic links and developing new keywords to reach those visitors, or scanning special-interest blogs and social media sites to learn what new topics attract rising interest; also, develop new keywords and messages.

Buzzword: Considered hip and trendy, a buzzword is a word or phrase that takes on added significance through repetition or special usage. Although buzzwords are widely used, they rarely have definitive meanings.

Byline: The name, and often the position, of the writer of the article. Bylines are traditionally placed between the headline and the text of the article, or at the bottom of the page to leave more room for graphical elements around the headline.

Campaign integration: Planning and executing a paid search campaign concurrently with other marketing initiatives, online or offline, or both. More than simply launching simultaneous campaigns, true paid search integration takes all marketing initiatives into consideration prior to launch, such as consistent messaging and image, driving offline conversions, supporting brand awareness, increasing response rates, and contributing to ROI business goals.

Channels of distribution: The means (i.e., mail order, wholesalers, retailers) a company uses to distribute products.

Circulation: In the media industry, "circulation" typically refers to the number of copies a print publication sells or distributes.

Click bot: A program generally used to artificially click on paid listings within the engines in order to artificially inflate click amounts.

Click fraud: Clicks on a Pay-Per-Click advertisement that are motivated by something other than a search for the advertised product or service. Click fraud may be the result of malicious or negative competitor/affiliate actions motivated by the desire to increase costs for a competing advertiser or to garner click-through costs for the collaborating affiliate. Also affects search engine results by diluting the quality of clicks.

Click through: When a user clicks on a hypertext link and is taken to the destination of that link.

Click-through rate: The percentage of those clicking on a link out of the total number who see the link. For example, imagine 10 people do a Web search. In response, they see links to a variety of Web pages. Three of the 10 people all choose one particular link. That link then has a 30% click-through rate. Also called CTR.

Client-side tracking: Client-side tracking entails the process of tagging every page that requires tracking on the Web site with a block of JavaScript code. This method is cookie based (available as first- or third-party cookies) and is readily available to companies that do not own or manage their own servers.

Cloaking: The process by which a Web site can display different versions of a Web page under different circumstances. It is primarily used to show an optimized or content-rich page to the search engines and a different page to humans. Most major search engine representatives have publicly stated that they do not approve of this practice.

Collateral materials: A wide range of documents including catalogs, brochures, counter displays, and sell sheets that companies use to promote themselves to their target audience.

Communications audit: The systematic appraisal of all of an organization's communications. A communications audit analyzes all messages sent out by the organization and may also examine messages received by audiences about the organization.

Concept story: Feature story designed to pique the interest of a particular demographic audience.

Consumer-generated media (CGM): Refers to posts made by consumers to support or oppose products, Web sites, or companies, which are very powerful when it comes to company image. They can reach a large audience and, therefore, may change your business overnight.

Content management system (CMS): In computing, a content management system (CMS) is a document-centric collaborative application for managing documents and other content. A CMS is often a Web application and is used as a method of managing Web sites and Web content. The market for content management systems remains fragmented, with many open source and proprietary solutions available.

Content network: Also called *contextual networks*, content networks include Google and Yahoo! Contextual Search networks that serve paid search ads triggered by keywords related to the page content a user is viewing.

Content targeting: An ad-serving process in Google and Yahoo! that displays keyword-triggered ads related to the content or subject (context) of the Web site a user is viewing. Contrast to search network serves, in which an ad is displayed when a user types a keyword into the search box of a search engine or one of its partner sites.

Contextual advertising: Advertising that is automatically served or placed on a Web page based on the page's content, keywords, and phrases. Contrast to a SERP (search engine result page) ad display. For example, contextual ads for digital cameras would be shown on a page with an article about photography, not because the user entered "digital cameras" in a search box.

Contextual distribution: The marketing decision to display search ads on certain publisher sites across the Web instead of, or in addition to, placing Pay Per Click ads on search networks.

Contextual network: Also called *content ads* and *content network*, contextual network ads are served on Web site pages adjacent to content that contains the keywords being bid upon. Contextual ads are somewhat like traditional display ads placed in print media and, like traditional ad buys, are often purchased on the same CPM (cost per thousand) model for purchased keywords, rather than on a CPC basis.

Contextual search: A search that analyzes the page being viewed by a user and gives a list of related search results. Offered by Yahoo! and Google.

Contextual search campaigns: A paid placement search campaign that takes a search ad listing beyond search engine results pages and onto the sites of matched content Web partners.

Conversion action: The desired action you want a visitor to take on your site. Includes purchase, subscription to the company newsletter, request for follow-up or more information (lead generation), download of a company free offer (research results, a video, or a tool), subscription to company updates, and news.

Conversion rate: Conversion rates are measurements that determine how many of your prospects perform the prescribed or desired action step. If your prescribed response is for a visitor to sign up for a newsletter, and you had 100 visitors and one newsletter signup, then your conversion rate would be 1%. Typically, micro-conversions (for instance, reading different pages on your site) lead to your main conversion step (making a purchase or signing up for a service).

Co-op advertising: A joint advertising program by which ad costs are shared between two or more parties. Many national manufacturers offer these programs to their wholesalers or retailers, as a means of encouraging these parties to promote goods. The manufacturer typically reimburses the local advertiser in part or in full for its placement of ads (print and broadcast).

Corporate fact sheet: A document describing a company's principles, services, philosophy, and fees, along with all company contact information: address, telephone, fax, and e-mail.

Corporate identity and positioning: The physical manifestation of the brand, including logo and supporting devices, color palettes, typefaces, page layouts, and other means of maintaining visual continuity and brand recognition. Positioning defines the application of the identity.

Cost per thousand (CPM): This is an industry standard that represents the cost per 1,000 people reached during the course of an advertising campaign. The CPM model refers to advertising purchased on the basis of impression opposed to pay for performance options (price per click, registration). (Note: "M" denotes thousand in Roman numerology).

CPA: Acronym for cost per acquisition. Also referred to as cost per action. This is a metric used to measure the total monetary cost of each sale, lead, or action from start to finish.

CPC: Acronym for cost per click, or the amount search engines charge advertisers for every click that sends a searcher to the advertiser's Web site. For an advertiser, CPC is the total cost for each click-through received when its ad is clicked on.

CPM: Acronym for cost per thousand impressions (ad serves or potential viewers). Compare to CPC pricing (defined earlier). CPM is a standard monetization model for offline display ad space, as well as for some context-based networks serving online search ads to, for example, Web publishers and sites.

CPO: Acronym for cost per order. The dollar amount of advertising or marketing necessary to acquire an order. Calculated by dividing marketing expenses by the number of orders. Also referred to as CPA (cost per acquisition).

Crawler: Automated programs in search engines that gather Web site listings by automatically crawling the Web. A search engine's crawler (also called a spider or robot) "reads" page text content and Web page coding, and also follows links to other hyperlinked pages on the Web pages it crawls. A crawler makes copies of the Web pages found and stores these in the search engine's index, or database.

Creatives: Unique words, design, and display of a paid-space advertisement. In paid search advertising, creative refers to the ad's title (headline), description (text offer), and display URL (clickable link to advertiser's Web site landing page). Unique creative display includes word emphasis (boldfaced, italicized, in quotes), typeface style, and, on some sites, added graphic images, logos, animation, or video clips.

CTR: Acronym for click-through rate: the number of clicks that an ad gets, divided by the total number of times that ad is displayed or served (represented as total clicks/total impressions for a specific ad). For example, if an ad has 100 impressions and 6 clicks, the CTR is 6%. The higher the CTR, the more visitors your site is receiving.

Custom feed: Create custom feeds for each of the shopping engines that allow you to submit XML feeds. Each of the engines has different product categories and feed requirements.

Dayparting: The ability to specify different times of day—or days of the week— for ad displays, as a way to target searchers more specifically. An option that limits serves of specified ads based on day and time factors.

Deep linking: Linking that guides, directs, and links a click-through searcher (or a search engine crawler) to a very specific and relevant product or category Web page from search terms and Pay Per Click ads.

Demographics: Selected characteristics of a population, such as ethnicity, income, and education, that define a particular consumer population.

Direct mail: A form of marketing that attempts to send its messages directly to consumers using "addressable" media, such as mail. Direct mail may include a marketing letter, brochure, or postcard.

Distribution network: A network of Web sites (content publishers, ISPs) or search engines and their partner sites on which paid ads can be distributed. The network receives advertisements from the host search engine, paid for with a cost per click (CPC) or cost per thousand impressions (CPM) model. For example, Google's advertising network includes not only the Google search site but also searchers at AOL, Netscape, and the *New York Post* online edition, among others.

DKI: Acronym for Dynamic Keyword Insertion, the insertion of the exact keywords a searcher included in his or her search request in the returned ad title or description. As an advertiser, you have bid on a table or cluster of these keyword variations, and DKI makes your ad listings more relevant to each searcher.

DMCA: Acronym for Digital Millennium Copyright Act. The Digital Millennium Copyright Act (DMCA) is a United States copyright law which … criminalizes production and dissemination of technology, devices, or services that are used to circumvent measures that control access to copyrighted works (commonly known as DRM), and criminalizes the act of circumventing an access control, even when there is no infringement of copyright itself.

E-commerce: Conducting commercial transactions on the Internet in which goods, information, or services are bought and sold.

eCPM: Acronym for effective cost per thousand, a hybrid cost per click (CPC) auction calculated by multiplying the CPC times the click-through rate (CTR), and multiplying the product by one thousand. (Represented by: (CPC × CTR) × 1000 = eCPM.) This monetization model is used by Google to rank site-targeted CPM ads (in the Google content network) against keyword-targeted CPC ads (Google AdWords Pay Per Click) in their hybrid auction.

E-mail marketing: A form of direct marketing that uses electronic mail as a means of communicating messages to an audience. In its broadest sense, every e-mail sent to a potential or current customer could be considered e-mail marketing.

Eye-tracking studies: Studies by Google, Marketing Sherpa, and Poynter Institute using Eyetools technology to track the eye movements of Web page readers, in order to understand reading and click-through patterns.

FCC: Federal Communications Commission. Established under the U.S. Communications Act of 1934, the FCC is a government agency that regulates broadcast and electronic communications. Its board of commissioners is appointed by the president of the United States.

Free-standing insert (FSI): An advertisement in a print publication that is not bound and separated by any editorial. FSIs are typically distributed with newspapers, magazines, and catalogs.

Frequency: The estimated number of times individuals are exposed to an advertising message.

FTC: Federal Trade Commission. A federal agency whose purpose is to encourage free enterprise and prevent restraint of trade and monopolies. This organization maintains the primary responsibility for regulating national advertising.

Full position ad: An ad bordered by reading matter in a newspaper, increasing the likelihood that consumers will read the ad.

Geo-targeting: The geographic location of the searcher. Geo-targeting allows you to specify where your ads will or won't be shown, based on the searcher's location, enabling more localized and personalized results.

Ghostwriters: As writers with no byline, ghostwriters usually work without the recognition that credited authors receive. They often get flat fees for their work without the benefit of royalties.

Grand opening event: A promotional activity held by newly established businesses to notify the public of their location, and products or services available to the community.

Graphic designer: The person who arranges image and text to communicate a specific message. Graphic design may be applied in any media, such as print, digital media, motion pictures, animation, product decoration, packaging, and signs.

Head terms: Search terms that are short, popular, and straightforward; for example, helicopter skiing. These short terms are called "head terms" based on a bell-curve distribution of keyword usage that displays the high numbers of most-used terms at the "head" end of the bell curve graph.

Hidden text: (Also known as *invisible text*.) Text that is visible to the search engines but not visible to the viewer of the Web.

Hit: The request or retrieval of any item located within a Web page. For example, if a user enters a Web page with five pictures on it, it would be counted as six "hits." One hit is counted for the Web page itself, and another five hits count for the pictures.

Horizontal publications: Business publications intended to appeal to people with similar interests in a variety of companies or industries.

Image advertising: Advertising that is directed at the creation of a specific image or perception of a company, product, or service. The unique personality (e.g., luxury, reliability) is promoted as being different from advertising directed at the specific attributes of the entity. Advertisers believe brand image advertising is effective in leading consumers to select one brand over another.

Impression: One view or display of an ad. Ad reports list total impressions per ad, which tells you the number of times your ad was served by the search engine when searchers entered your keywords (or viewed a content page containing your keywords).

Index: A search engine's "index" refers to the number of documents found by a search engine's crawler on the Web.

Indexability: Also known as *crawlability* and *spiderability*. Indexability refers to the potential of a Web site or its contents to be crawled or "indexed" by a search engine. If a site is not "indexable," or if a site has reduced indexability, it has difficulties getting its URLs included.

Insertion order: A formal authorization to place an ad campaign that identifies the specific print publication, run dates, and associated fees. This serves as a contract between the publisher selling the advertising space and the media buyer.

Key performance indicators (KPIs): KPIs are metrics used to quantify objectives that reflect the strategic performance of your online marketing campaigns. They provide business and marketing intelligence to assess a measurable objective and the direction in which that objective is headed.

Keyword: A single word that relates to a specific subject or topic. For example, "glossary" would be a keyword for this document. See also Keyword phrase.

Keyword/keyword phrase: A specific word or combination of words that a searcher might type into a search field. Includes generic, category keywords; industry-specific terms; product brands; common misspellings and expanded variations (called *keyword stemming*); or multiple words (called *Long Tail* for their lower CTRs but sometimes better conversion rates). All might be entered as a search query. For example, someone looking to buy coffee mugs might use the keyword phrase "ceramic coffee mugs." Also, keywords—which trigger ad network and contextual network ad serves— are the auction components on which Pay Per Click advertisers bid for all ad groups/orders and campaigns.

Keyword density: The number of times a keyword or keyword phrase is used in the body of a page. This is a percentage value determined by the number of words on the page, as opposed to the number of times the specific keyword appears within it. In general, the higher the number of times a keyword appears in a page, the higher its density.

Keyword stemming: To return to the root or stem of a word and build additional words by adding a prefix or suffix, or using pluralization. The word can expand in either direction and even hook up with words, increasing the number of variable options.

Keyword stuffing: Generally refers to the act of adding an inordinate number of keyword terms into the HTML or tags of a Web page.

Keyword tag: Refers to the META keywords tag within a Web page. This tag is meant to hold approximately 8 to 10 keywords or keyword phrases, separated by commas. These phrases should be either misspellings of the main page topic, or terms that directly reflect the content on the page on which they appear. Keyword tags are sometimes used for internal search results; they are also viewed by search engines.

Keyword targeting: Displaying Pay Per Click search ads on publisher sites across the Web that contain the keywords in a context advertiser's ad group.

Landing page/destination page: The Web page at which a searcher arrives after clicking on an ad. When creating a Pay Per Click ad, the advertiser displays a URL (and specifies the exact page URL in the code) on which the searcher will land after clicking on an ad in the SERP. Landing pages are also known as "where the deal is closed," as it is landing page actions that determine an advertiser's conversion rate success.

Latent semantic indexing (LSI): LSI uses word associations to help search engines know more accurately what a page is about.

Lead generation: Web sites that generate leads for products or services offered by another company. On a lead generation site, the visitor is unable to make a purchase but will fill out a contact form in order to get more information about the product or service presented. A submitted contact form is considered a lead. It contains personal information about a visitor who has some degree of interest in a product or service.

Link popularity: Link popularity generally refers to the total number of links pointing to any particular URL. There are typically two types of link popularity: internal and external. Internal link popularity typically refers to the number of links or pages within a Web site that link to a specific URL. External link popularity refers to the number of inbound links from external Web sites that are pointing to a specific URL. If you have more "links" than your competitors, you are typically said to have link cardinality or link superiority.

Linkbait: Also known as *link bait*, this is something on your site that people will notice and link to. By linking to your site, other sites are saying they value the content of your site and that they think other people will be interested in it too.

Linking profile: A profile is a representation of the extent to which something exhibits various characteristics. A linking profile is the result of an analysis of where your links are coming from.

Log file: All server software stores information about Web site incoming and outgoing activities. Web log files function like the "black box" that records everything during an airplane's flight. The log file is usually in the root directory, but it may also be found in a secondary folder. If you do not have permission to access these files, then you will need the help of the server administrator.

Log file analysis: The analysis of records stored in the log file. In its raw format, the data in the log files can be hard to read and overwhelming. There are numerous log file analyzers that convert log file data into user-friendly charts and graphs. A good analyzer is generally considered an essential tool in SEO because it can show search engine statistics such as the number of visitors received from each search engine, the keywords each visitors used to find the site, visits by search engine spiders, etc.

Logo: A logo, or logotype, is the graphic element of a trademark or brand, and is set in a special typeface/font and arranged in a particular way. The shape, color, and typeface should all be distinctly different from others in a similar market.

Marketing: The craft of linking the producers of a product or service with customers, both existing and potential. Marketing creates, communicates, and delivers value to customers in ways that benefit the organization and its stakeholders.

Marketing campaign: A specific, defined series of activities used in marketing a product or service. The future estimated effects of a new marketing campaign must be included in demand and resource planning.

Marketing managers: Marketing managers develop the firm's marketing strategy in detail. With the help of subordinates, including product development managers and market research managers, they estimate the demand for products and services offered by the firm and its competitors. In addition, they identify potential markets—for example, business firms, wholesalers, retailers, government, or the general public. Marketing managers develop pricing strategy to help firms maximize profits and market share while ensuring that the firm's customers are satisfied. In collaboration with sales, product development, and other managers, they monitor trends that indicate the need for new products and services, and they oversee product development. Marketing managers work with advertising and promotion managers to promote the firm's products and services and to attract potential users.

Marketing plan: A strategic plan that details the actions necessary to achieve specified marketing objectives. It can be for a product, service, brand, or a product line. Many marketing plans cover one year (referred to as an annual marketing plan), but may cover up to five years.

Marketing research: The process of systematically gathering, recording, analyzing, and interpreting data pertaining to the company's market, customers, and competitors, with the goal of improving marketing decisions.

Market share: A company's sales, in terms of dollars or units, in relation to total industry sales. It is typically expressed as a percentage and can be represented as brand, line, or company.

Media advisory: A written document sent to local media outlets about an upcoming press conference, briefing, or other event. A media advisory usually includes the basic details about the event and its schedule and location. The goal of a media advisory is not to tell the complete story, but instead to entice media to attend and learn more.

Media interview: A recorded conversation, usually conducted by a reporter, in which an individual provides information and expertise on a certain subject for use in the reporter's article.

Media intranet/extranet: A company's privately maintained computer network that can be used only by authorized personnel.

Media kit: A media kit, sometimes called a press kit, is a set of promotional and informative materials about an organization or event. It includes company information, specifically, a letter of introduction, press releases, news articles, and a company profile.

Media outlet: A publication or broadcast program that provides news and feature stories to the public through various distribution channels. Media outlets include newspapers, magazines, radio, television, and the Internet.

Media plan: A plan designed to target the proper demographics for an advertising campaign through the use of specific media outlets.

Media planning and buying: The role of an advertising agency in finding the most appropriate media products for each client and negotiating/buying "space" based on a predetermined budget.

Media policy: Organizational instructions as to how company representatives will communicate with the media.

Media tour: A series of engagements or a single event to promote a certain organization, product, or service to members of the public press. Common resources for a media tour include a press kit, presentation material, and a representative (internal or external) to interact with the press.

Media training: Providing individuals with guidelines, strategies, and skills to work efficiently and effectively with media for public relations purposes.

Meta feeds: Ad networks that pull advertiser listings from other providers. They may or may not have their own distribution and advertiser networks.

Metrics: A system of measures that helps to quantify particular characteristics. In SEO, the following are some important metrics to measure: overall traffic, search engine traffic, conversions, top traffic-driving keywords, top conversion-driving keywords, keyword rankings, etc.

Minimum bid: The least amount that an advertiser can bid for a keyword or keyword phrase and still be active on the search ad network. This amount can range from $0.01 to $0.50 (or more, for highly competitive keywords), and is set by the search engine.

Multivariate testing: A type of testing that varies and tests more than one or two campaign elements at a time to determine the best-performing elements and combinations. Multivariate testing can gather significant results on many different components of, for example, alternative Pay Per Click ad titles or descriptions in a short period of time. Often, it requires special expertise to analyze complex statistical results. (Compare to A/B testing, which changes only one element at a time, alternately serving an "old" version ad and a changed ad.) In search advertising, you might do A/B split or multivariate testing to learn what parts of a landing page (background color, title, headline, fill-in forms, design, images) produce higher conversions and are more cost effective.

Negative keywords: Filtered-out keywords to prevent ad serves on them in order to avoid irrelevant click-through charges on, for example, products that you do not sell, or to refine and narrow the targeting of your ad group's keywords. Microsoft adCenter calls them "excluded keywords." Formatting negative keywords varies with search engine, but they are usually designated with a minus sign.

New product launch: The introduction of new merchandise to the general public. This can be executed through a special event, ad campaign, or PR push.

News conference: A media event staged by an individual or group wishing to attract media coverage for an item of news value. Television stations and networks especially value news conferences as sources of "news" footage.

Newsletter: A publication sent out at specific intervals in print or via e-mail and generally about one main subject or topic that is of interest to its subscribers.

Newswire: An electronic data stream sent via satellite that delivers the latest news directly to print, broadcast, and online media databases across the world. Many organizations submit press releases to a newswire service to alert the world's media about their latest news.

Nielsen rating: A measurement of the percentage of U.S. television households tuned to a program for a designated time period. Similar to Arbitron, A.C. Nielsen is a marketing/media research company that conducts diary surveys to measure television-viewing habits.

Outdoor advertising: A form of advertising (e.g., billboards, movie kiosks) that promotes a product or service in high-traffic outside locations.

P4P: Acronym for Pay for Performance; also designated as PFP.

PageRank (PR): PR is the Google technology developed at Stanford University for determining the relative importance of pages and Web sites. At one point, PageRank (PR) was a major factor in rankings. Today it is one of hundreds of factors in the algorithm that determines a page's rankings.

Paid inclusion: Refers to the process of paying a fee to a search engine in order to be included in that search engine or directory. Also known as *guaranteed inclusion*. Paid inclusion does not impact rankings of a Web page; it merely guarantees that the Web page itself will be included in the index. These programs were typically used by Web sites that were not being fully crawled or were incapable of being crawled, due to dynamic URL structures, frames, etc.

Partnership marketing: Aligning one's business with other organizations and businesses to equally expose partner brands to one another's customers. Typically, partnerships are formed when two or more companies find value for their customers in each other's products or services.

Pass-along rate: The number of times a received document (article, newsletter, brochure, report, etc.) is shared with other individuals. This number is higher than the circulation numbers because it is an estimate of how many readers view the same copy rather than how many copies are distributed.

Pay Per Call: A model of paid advertising similar to Pay Per Click (PPC), except that advertisers pay for every phone call that comes to them from a search ad, rather than for every click-through to their Web site landing page for the ad. Often higher cost than Pay Per Click advertising, but valued by advertisers for higher conversion rates from consumers who take the action step of telephoning an advertiser.

Personas: These are "people types" or subgroups that encompass several attributes, such as gender, age, location, salary level, leisure activities, lifestyle characteristics, marital or family status, or some kind of definable behavior. Useful profiles for focusing ad messages and offers to targeted segments.

PFP: Acronym for pay for performance; also designated as P4P.

Pitch: A concise verbal (and sometimes visual) presentation of an idea for a story, generally made to a media outlet in the hope of attracting positive coverage for a client.

Podcast: A podcast is a media file that is distributed over the Internet using syndication feeds, for playback on portable media players and personal computers. Like radio, it can refer to both the content and the method of syndication. The latter may also be termed *podcasting*. The host or author of a podcast is often called a *podcaster*.

Point-of-purchase (POP) display: Promotional piece typically placed in an area of a retail store where payment is made.

Position: In Pay Per Click advertising, position is the placement on a search engine results page of your ad relative to other paid ads and to organic search results. Top-ranking paid ads (high-ranking 10 to 15 results, depending on the engine) usually appear at the top of the SERP and on the "right rail" (right-side column of the page). Ads appearing in the top three paid ad or sponsored ad slots are known as premium positions. Paid search ad position is determined by confidential algorithms and quality score measures specific to each search engine. However, factors in the engines' position placement under some advertiser control include bid price, the ad's CTR, relevancy of your ad to searcher requests, relevance of your click-through landing page to the search request, and quality measures search engines calculate to ensure quality user experience.

Position preference: A feature in Google AdWords and in Microsoft adCenter enabling advertisers to specify in which positions they would like their ads to appear on the SERP. Not a position guarantee.

PPC advertising: Acronym for Pay Per Click advertising, a model of online advertising in which advertisers pay only for each click on their ads that directs searchers to a specified landing page on the advertiser's Web site. PPC ads may get thousands of impressions (views or serves of the ad), but unlike more traditional ad models billed on a CPM (cost-per-thousand-impressions) basis, PPC advertisers only pay when their ad is clicked on. Charges per ad click-through are based on advertiser bids in hybrid ad space auctions and are influenced by competitor bids, competition for keywords, and search engines' proprietary quality measures of advertiser ad and landing page content.

PPC management: The monitoring and maintenance of a Pay Per Click campaign or campaigns. This includes changing bid prices, expanding and refining keyword lists, editing ad copy, testing campaign components for cost-effectiveness and successful conversions, and reviewing performance reports for reports to management and clients, as well as results to feed into future PPC campaign operations.

PPCSE: Acronym for Pay Per Click Search Engine.

Press release: A press release or news release is a concise written statement distributed to targeted publications for the purpose of announcing something of news value. Typically, it is mailed, faxed, or e-mailed to assignment editors at newspapers, magazines, radio stations, television stations, and television networks. Commercial newswire services can be hired to distribute news releases.

Print media: A medium consisting of paper and ink, including newspapers, magazines, classifieds, circulars, journals, yellow pages, billboards, posters, brochures, and catalogs.

Product differentiation: Establishing clear distinction between products serving the same market segment. This is typically accomplished through effective positioning, packaging, and pricing strategies.

Promotional mix: Advertising, publicity, public relations, personal selling, and sales promotion used to promote a specific product or service.

Promotions: Communications activities, excluding advertising, that call attention to a product or service by creating incentives. Contests, frequent buyer programs, unique packaging, and coupons are all examples of tools commonly used in promotions.

Promotions managers: Promotions managers supervise staffs of promotions specialists. These managers direct promotions programs that combine advertising with purchase incentives to increase sales. In an effort to establish closer contact with purchasers—dealers, distributors, or consumers—promotions programs may use direct mail, telemarketing, television or radio advertising, catalogs, exhibits, inserts in newspapers, Internet advertisements or Web sites, in-store displays or product endorsements, and special events. Purchasing incentives may include discounts, samples, gifts, rebates, coupons, sweepstakes, and contests.

Proof: A paper rendering for the purpose of checking the quality and accuracy of the material to be printed.

Public relations: Considered both an art and a science, public relations is the management of communications between an organization and its key public to build, manage, and sustain its positive image. It is any activity used to influence media outlets to print stories that promote a favorable image of a company and its products or services.

Public relations managers: Public relations managers supervise public relations specialists. These managers direct publicity programs to a targeted audience. They often specialize in a specific area, such as crisis management, or in a specific industry, such as health care. They use every available communication medium to maintain the support of the specific group upon whom their organization's success depends, such as consumers, stockholders, or the general public. For example, public relations managers may clarify or justify the firm's point of view on health or environmental issues to community or special-interest groups. Public relations managers also evaluate advertising and promotions programs for compatibility with public relations efforts and serve as the eyes and ears of top management. They observe social, economic, and political trends that might ultimately affect the firm, and they make recommendations to enhance the firm's image on the basis of those trends. Public relations managers may confer with labor relations managers to produce internal company communications—such as newsletters about employee-management relations—and with finance managers to produce company reports. They assist company executives in drafting speeches, arranging interviews, and maintaining other forms of public contact; oversee company archives; and respond to requests for information. In addition, some of these managers handle special events, such as the sponsorship of races, parties introducing new products, or other activities that the firm supports in order to gain public attention through the press without advertising directly.

Public relations plan: A document that details precise actions to achieve a public relations result. It can consist of target publications and media lists, planned events, community outreach, etc.

Publicity: A component of the promotional mix, the deliberate attempt to manage the public's perception of a subject; whereas public relations is the management of all communication between the client and selected target audiences, publicity is the management of product- or brand-related communications between the firm and the general public.

Qualitative research: Research that is conducted to determine subjective information about a company, product, or ad campaign. Two methods of securing information include focus groups and in-depth interviews.

Quantitative research: This method of market research utilizes sampling techniques (opinion polls, customer satisfaction surveys) to collect objective data. Numeric relevance of various kinds of consumer behavior, attitudes, or performance is tabulated and statistically analyzed.

Rank: How well positioned a particular Web page or Web site appears in search engine results. For example, if you rank at position #1, you're the first listed paid or sponsored ad. If you're in position #18, it is likely that your ad appears on the second or third page of search results, after 17 competitor-paid ads and organic listings. Rank and position affect your click-through rates and, ultimately, conversion rates for your landing pages.

Raw data feed: Raw data is information that has been collected but not formatted, analyzed, or processed. This raw data can be used to build an optimized XML feed.

Reach: Reach refers to the estimated number of individuals or households exposed to an advertising message during a specified period of time. It can be given as either a percentage or number of individuals.

Readership: The total number of primary and pass-along readers of a publication.

Reciprocal links: Two different sites that link to each other. Also referred to as *cross linking.*

Relevance: In relation to Pay Per Click advertising, relevance is a measure of how closely your ad title, description, and keywords are related to the search query and the searcher's expectations.

Revshare/revenue sharing: A method of allocating per-click revenue to a site publisher, and click-through charges to a search engine that distributes paid ads to its context network partners, for every page viewer who clicks on the content site's sponsored ads. A type of site finder's fee.

Rich media: Media with embedded motion or interactivity. A growing option for PPC advertisers as rates of broadband connectivity increase.

Right rail: The common name for the right-side column of a Web page. On a SERP, right rail is usually where sponsored listings appear.

ROAS: Acronym for return on advertising spending, the profit generated by ad campaign conversions per dollar spent on advertising expenses. Calculated by dividing advertising-driven profit by ad spending.

ROI: Acronym for return on investment, the amount of money you make on your ads compared to the amount of money you spend on them. For example, if you spend $100 on Pay Per Click ads and make $150 from those ads, then your ROI would be 50% (calculated as: ($150 – $100)/100 = $50/100 = 50%). The higher your ROI, the more successful your advertising, although some practitioners in search advertising consider ROAS a more useful metric, as it breaks down cost and expenses by conversions per advertising dollar spent.

RSS: Acronym for Rich Site Summary or Really Simple Syndication, a family of Web feed formats that leverages XML for distributing and sharing headlines and information from other Web content (also known as syndication).

Sales managers: Sales managers direct the firm's sales program. They assign sales territories, set goals, and establish training programs for the sales representatives. Sales managers advise the sales representatives on ways to improve their sales performance. In large, multiproduct firms, they oversee regional and local sales managers and their staffs. Sales managers maintain contact with dealers and distributors. They analyze sales statistics gathered by their staffs to determine sales potential and inventory requirements and to monitor customers' preferences. Such information is vital in the development of products and the maximization of profits.

Saturation (search engine saturation): A term relating to the number of URLs included from a specific Web site in any given search engine. The higher the saturation level or number of pages indexed into a search engine, the higher the potential traffic levels and rankings.

Search directory: Similar to a search engine, in that they both compile databases of Web sites. A directory does not use crawlers in order to obtain entries in its search database. Instead, it relies on user interaction and submissions for the content it contains. Submissions are then categorized by topic and normally alphabetized, so that the results of any search will start with site descriptions that begin with some number or nonletter character, then move from A to Z.

Search engines: A search engine is a database of many Web pages. Most engines display the number of Web pages they hold in their database at any given time. A search engine generally "ranks" or orders the results according to a set of parameters. These parameters (called algorithms) vary among search engines; algorithms are always being improved to identify spam as well as improve relevance. (See also SERP, Algorithm.)

Search funnel: Movement of searchers, who tend to perform several searches before reaching a purchase decision, that works from broad, general keyword search terms to narrower, specific keywords. Advertisers use the search funnel to anticipate customer intent and develop keywords targeted to different stages. Also refers to potential for switches at stages in the funnel when, for example, searchers start with keywords for a desired brand but switch to other brands after gathering information on the category. Microsoft adCenter tested a search funnel keyword tool in 2006 to target keywords to search funnel stages.

Search query: The word or phrase a searcher types into a search field, which initiates search engine results page listings and Pay Per Click (PPC) ad serves. In PPC advertising, the goal is to bid on keywords that closely match the search queries of the advertiser's targets. (See also Query.)

Search Submit Pro (SSP): Search Submit Pro is Yahoo!'s paid inclusion product that uses a "feed" tactic. With Search Submit Pro, Yahoo! crawls your Web site as well as an optimized XML feed that represents the content on your site. Yahoo! applies its algorithm to both the actual Web site pages and the XML feed to determine which listing is most appropriate to appear in the organic search results when a user conducts a search for relevant terms. Yahoo! charges a CPC, determined by category, for each time a listing established through SSP is clicked.

Seasonality: The seasonal fluctuation in sales for services and products throughout the year.

Secondary links: Links that are indirectly acquired links, such as a story in a major newspaper about a new product your company released.

Semantic clustering: A technique for developing relevant keywords for Pay Per Click ad groups, by focusing tightly on keywords and keyword phrases that are associative and closely related, referred to as "semantic clustering." Focused and closely related keyword groups, which would appear in the advertiser's ad text and in the content of the click-through landing page, are more likely to meet searchers' expectations and, therefore, support more effective advertising and conversion rates.

SEO: Acronym for search engine optimization. This is the process of editing a Web site's content and code in order to improve visibility within one or more search engines. When this term is used to describe an individual, it stands for search engine optimizer, or one who performs SEO.

SERP: Acronym for search engine results page, the page delivered to a searcher that displays the results of a search query entered into the search field. Displays both paid ad (sponsored) and organic listings in varying positions or rank.

Server-side tracking: The process of analyzing Web server log files. Server-side analytics tools make sense of raw data to generate meaningful reports and trends analysis.

Share of voice (SOV): A brand's (or group of brands') advertising weight, expressed as a percentage of a defined total market or market segment in a given time period. SOV advertising weight is usually defined in terms of expenditure, ratings, pages, poster sites, etc.

Site-targeted ads: Site targeting lets advertisers display their ads on manually selected sites in the search engine's content network for content or contextual ad serves. Site-targeted ads are billed more like traditional display ads, per 1,000 impressions (CPM), and not on a Pay Per Click basis.

Social media, or social search: Sites where users actively participate to determine what is popular.

Speaking engagements: A planned event in which an individual educates the public on a particular topic. In marketing, speaking engagements are used to increase a client's visibility and strengthen his or her reputation as an expert in the field. In addition, these opportunities give the speaker direct contact with his or her target audience.

Sponsored listing: A term used as a title or column head on SERPs to identify paid advertisers and distinguish between paid and organic listings. Alternate names are *paid listings* or *paid sponsors*. Separating paid listings from organic results enables searchers to make their own purchase and site trust decisions and, in fact, resulted from an FTC complaint filed by Commercial Alert in 2001 alleging that the confusion caused in consumers who saw mixed paid and unpaid results constituted fraud in advertising.

Statistical validity: The degree to which an observed result, such as a difference between two measurements, can be relied upon and not attributed to random error in sampling or in measurement. Statistical validity is important for the reliability of test results, particularly in multivariate testing methods.

Survey: An accumulation of a sample of data or opinions considered to be representative of a whole. Surveys are useful in public relations to support a client's claims. They can be cited from other sources or funded by the client and conducted by a third party.

Syndicated program: A radio or television program that is distributed in various markets by a specialized organization.

Tabloid: A newspaper that measures at 12″ wide by 14″ high and is approximately half the size of a standard newspaper.

Tagline: A meaningful phrase or slogan that sums up the tone and premise of an organization in a way that is memorable to the public. A tagline is often the theme for a larger campaign.

Target audience: Groups in the community selected as the most appropriate for a particular marketing campaign or schedule. The target audience may be defined in demographic or psychographic terms, or a combination of both.

Targeting: Narrowly focusing ads and keywords to attract a specific, marketing-profiled searcher and potential customer. You can target to geographic locations (geotargeting), by day of the week or time of day (dayparting), or by gender and age (demographic targeting). Targeting features vary by search engine. Newer ad techniques and software focus on behavioral targeting, based on Web activity and behaviors that are predictive for potential customers who might be more receptive to particular ads.

Tear sheet: A page sent to the advertiser that serves as proof of the ad insertion.

Telemarketing: The process of using the telephone as a medium to sell goods and services directly to prospective customers.

Trade publication: A trade publication often falls between a magazine and a journal, with articles focusing on information relating to a particular trade or industry. Trade publications typically contain heavy advertising content focused on the specific industry with little, if any, general audience advertising.

Trademarks: Distinctive symbols, pictures, or words that identify a specific product or service. Received through registration with the U.S. Patent and Trademark Office. Tier I search engines prohibit bids on trademarks as keywords if the bidder is not the legal owner, though this keyword bid practice is still allowed by Google.

Traffic: Refers to the number of visitors a Web site receives. It can be determined by examination of Web logs.

Traffic analysis: The process of analyzing traffic to a Web site to understand what visitors are searching for and what is driving traffic to a site.

Unique selling proposition (USP): The distinct features and benefits that differentiate a company's product or service from the competition.

Unique visitor: Identifies an actual Web surfer (as opposed to a crawler) and is tracked by a uniquely identifiable attribute (typically IP address). If a visitor comes to a Web site and clicks on 100 links, it is still only counted as one unique visit.

Value propositions: A customer value proposition is the sum total of benefits a customer is promised to receive in return for his or her custom and the associated payment (or other value transfer).

Vertical: A vertical is a specific business group or category, such as insurance, automotive, or travel. Vertical search offers targeted search options and Pay Per Click opportunities to a specific business category.

Viral marketing: Also called *viral advertising*, viral marketing refers to marketing techniques that use preexisting social networks to produce increases in brand awareness. The awareness increases are the result of self-replicating viral processes, analogous to the spread of pathological and computer viruses. It can often be word-of-mouth delivered and enhanced online; it can also harness the network effect of the Internet and can be very useful in reaching a large number of people rapidly.

Wiki: Software that allows people to contribute knowledge on a particular topic. A wiki is another Web publishing platform that makes use of technologies similar to blogs and also allows for collaboration with multiple people.

XML: Stands for eXtensible Markup Language, a data delivery language.

Index